Britain's Most Prolific Burglar

Britain's Most Prolific Burglar

Flannelfoot and the Scotland Yard Men Who Hunted Him

Martyn Beardsley

PEN & SWORD
HISTORY

First published in Great Britain in 2023 by
Pen & Sword History
An imprint of Pen & Sword Books Limited
Yorkshire – Philadelphia

Copyright © Martyn Beardsley 2023

ISBN 978 1 39905 483 6

The right of Martyn Beardsley to be identified as
Author of this Work has been asserted by him in accordance
with the Copyright, Designs and Patents Act 1988.

A CIP catalogue record for this book is
available from the British Library

Typeset by Mac Style
Printed in the UK by CPI Group (UK) Ltd, Croydon, CR0 4YY.

Pen & Sword Books Limited incorporates the imprints of After
the Battle, Atlas, Archaeology, Aviation, Discovery, Family History,
Fiction, History, Maritime, Military, Military Classics, Politics,
Select, Transport, True Crime, Air World, Frontline Publishing, Leo
Cooper, Remember When, Seaforth Publishing, The Praetorian Press,
Wharncliffe Local History, Wharncliffe Transport, Wharncliffe True
Crime and White Owl.

For a complete list of Pen & Sword titles please contact

PEN & SWORD BOOKS LIMITED
47 Church Street, Barnsley, South Yorkshire, S70 2AS, England
E-mail: enquiries@pen-and-sword.co.uk
Website: www.pen-and-sword.co.uk
or
PEN AND SWORD BOOKS
1950 Lawrence Rd, Havertown, PA 19083, USA
E-mail: Uspen-and-sword@casematepublishers.com
Website: www.penandswordbooks.com

Contents

For Jane

Introduction

I will be acknowledging the help of various people and institutions at the end of this introduction, but I want to start by expressing a debt of gratitude to the Talking Pictures television channel, because without them this book certainly would not have been written or even thought of.

Talking Pictures is a wonderful treasure trove of old films and TV programmes. It has enabled me to find hidden gems I either never knew existed or failed to appreciate when they were first aired, and so to relive my youth (Richard Greene's *Robin Hood*, and my favourite TV detective Frank Marker of *Public Eye*, to name but two). A few precious episodes of *No Hiding Place* have avoided being wiped and made their way back onto our screens, thanks solely to Talking Pictures. That, along with *Gideon's Way* starring the wonderful John Gregson, is one of the very first TV programmes I can recall being hooked on as a child. One programme I'm pretty sure I was never aware of when it was first shown is *Scotland Yard*, which was what we would now call a docudrama, with each episode focusing on a notable case from 'the annals of Scotland Yard'.

It apparently began in 1953, but I suspect most of the episodes I've seen aired were made in the late 1950s or early 1960s, and I was surprised at how well it stood up today as an informative programme with dramatic reconstructions. I have seen all of the *Scotland Yard* episodes Talking Pictures have broadcast (at least twice!) and although there have been many interesting and entertaining ones, it was the one featuring a bicycling burglar called Flannelfoot which, for some reason, captured my imagination. Something prompted me to delve into the man behind the nickname, and within minutes I had decided I would write a book about him if I possibly could.

It's the story of an interesting character and of very different times, a very different England, despite it being still within living memory for some people at the time of writing.

I have been burgled. I know how it feels, what the psychological effects are and how long they linger. There is no romance or glamour in burglary. Flannelfoot was a crook who sneaked into your house while you were asleep in bed, a man probably too lazy and selfish to do a proper day's work. So Flannelfoot was not a hero, and I have not tried to glamorise him in this book.

But the man, his methods and the way he remained elusive for so long are nevertheless fascinating, as are the stories of the Scotland Yard officers who chased him for so long.

This book has been largely researched and written during the lockdowns of one form or another, which has made things that bit harder. But, of course, although primary sources are invaluable, the internet has changed the whole nature of research. I will be listing the primary sites in the bibliography, but apart from the genealogical site Ancestry, through which I have been able to discover so much about the characters who feature in this story, I think Britain from Above deserves a special mention. On it, readers can access high-resolution photographs taken during aerial surveys of Britain. What was especially helpful and insightful for me is that many of them were taken during the Flannelfoot era of the 1930s. As many will know, and as I shall briefly describe later, this was a time of unprecedented levels of housebuilding, with new homes being built on a scale never before known and which will almost certainly never be equalled again. The ever-expanding populations of cities were able to spread out into the suburbs – which latter point is highly relevant because Flannelfoot deliberately targeted such areas. The Britain From Above site enabled me to examine areas – and sometimes specific streets and houses – and compare the modern, densely built-up look of today with the relatively undeveloped, even rural look of such areas in the inter-war years. We shall see that the location of Flannelfoot's eventual capture is a good example of this.

I would like to thank my two true-crime author friends, Jeanette Hensby and Margaret Drinkall. They have both always been very ready to listen to my grumbles when things weren't running smoothly, and to offer useful pointers and a helpful perspective.

I first came into contact with Jeanette years ago because of a local connection with her book *The Rotherham Trunk Murder*. It was only after I'd spent some months researching the Flannelfoot case and keeping Jeanette informed of my progress, that I twigged that the Chief Inspector Thompson (who led the team of detectives hunting Flannelfoot) was one and the same officer who had been sent to Rotherham to help the Yorkshire police on the Trunk Murder case.

I have often swapped notes with Margaret, 'Mags', and it was suggestions from her which gave me the idea for the title.

Thanks are also due to Mark Vickers, a genealogist and descendant of Flannelfoot, who had been independently gathering information about the man and his crimes, and who was very generous with his findings.

And finally a mention to Jonathan Wright and Laura Hirst at Pen and Sword for their support on this and past books, and Michelle Higgs for her editorial support and suggestions.

My main hope is that you will enjoy reading this story as much as I enjoyed the journey of researching and writing it.

Prologue

One night in early September 1921, a shadowy figure crept into the Hounslow home of Mr H. Boulton, a celebrated local singer of the day. For the most part, only a few things of low value were missing. What troubled Mr Boulton more than anything else when he woke to find he had been burgled while he slept, was that among the items taken were his false teeth.

Certain purloined articles were later found discarded in another burgled house not far away and returned to their owner, such as the pair of gloves the intruder had made use of to avoid leaving fingerprints. But not, for some reason, the teeth, 'Which is unfortunate,' commiserated the *Sunday Post*, 'as Mr Boulton had an engagement to sing this weekend'.

Whether the unlucky Mr Boulton cancelled, or decided that the show must go on and put a brave but gummy face on it, we don't know. What we do now know, and what the press of the day worked out, was that this was the work of a burglar who was already prolific. What they would never have expected was that he would go on to drive the greatest minds of Scotland Yard to distraction for a further sixteen years.

The man in question, thanks to his habit of wrapping his shoes in any household textiles he found lying around, such as towels and socks, had earned the sobriquet by which he became famous not just in Britain, but internationally: *Flannelfoot*.

More and more detectives were allocated to the attempts to catch him as time went by, and a map of London devoted only to the locations of Flannelfoot crimes hung on a wall at Scotland Yard, with pins marking the places where he had struck. The Yard probably had to send out for more pins as the years passed, and the embarrassment grew each time Flannelfoot's name adorned the newspapers. The man himself always slipped away into the night unseen and unheard, free to strike once more. The police became more and more frustrated at not being able to nail their man.

In point of fact, unbeknownst to them the police *had* caught Flannelfoot – but they had been ahead of their time. Ten years before absconding with the illustrious Mr Boulton's teeth, he had been arrested, convicted and sentenced to nine months with hard labour. However, not only was that before he had been christened 'Flannelfoot', but he had adopted the cunning strategy of giving the authorities a false name. And apparently no one had ever bothered to corroborate his identity from the moment of his arrest till the day of his release – not the police, not the courts, not the prison service. A man who did not exist served his sentence, emerging in 1911 to embark on an unhindered criminal spree that lasted, with a short break for the Great War (when even he did his bit) until 1937. In that year, finally, Flannelfoot's past would come back to haunt him, thanks in large part to a bizarre combination of one person's amnesia and a soon-to-retire copper's long memory.

Chapter 1

Nicked

The man convicted of burglaries in the Acton and Ealing areas of London in January 1911, known to the authorities as Henry Williams, was in fact Harry Edward Vickers. Vickers was born in 1888, the year of the Jack the Ripper murders, one of at least six children of Jack and Louisa Edwards. Father Jack, a Berkshire man, was a butcher, something Harry would try his hand at for a time when he wasn't burgling. The family originally lived in Reading, where Harry was born, but the birthplaces of his later siblings and evidence from censuses show that the family moved around during the next few years: Windsor, Twyford (father Jack's birthplace), Slough and Strood in Kent. Harry's paternal grandmother was from Ealing, West London, and this was the area to which Harry himself would gravitate in later years.

The crimes known to have been committed by Vickers are many, but there are almost certainly numerous others that we shall never know about. He mostly satisfied himself with swift burglaries involving small amounts of cash and easily portable articles of no major worth. That he was happy to act in this low-key way, in fact, is probably one of the keys to his lengthy, unhindered and prolific career – Vickers was a serial offender, but he never got greedy, never took unnecessary risks. (In fact, quite the opposite, as we shall see.)

We can say with some confidence that he was an active criminal for the whole of his adult life apart from his army service. Vickers was still pretty much a newly-wed when he received that first prison sentence for burglary: he was married in the Fulham Register Office at the age of 22 on 19 August 1910, was arrested in November of the same year, and entered prison in January 1911. When arrested, Vickers was living at 36 Leysfield Road, Shepherd's Bush; he would go on to lead a somewhat nomadic life, but he would be living only around a mile away from that address at the time of his second and final capture. He gave his profession as butcher in the 1911 census, but although it's quite possible that he was trained in that trade by his father, whether he held down a job for any length of time is very doubtful. He much preferred working for himself. At night.

If Harry Vickers *had* chosen to earn his living as described in the census, his marriage would have cemented something of a butchery dynasty because the woman he married was his cousin Alice Maud Vickers – whose father, like

Harry's, was yet another butcher. Alice was three years Harry's senior, and at the time of the union was living in their home town of Reading – specifically, in a house on York Road which was probably owned by her parents, since she would move back and spend most of the rest of her life there when things with Harry turned sour.

The couple initially lived in London after they got married. This may have been to do with the fact that Alice was a domestic servant in London at around the time of the marriage. The 1911 census was undertaken while Harry was serving his prison sentence, and in it Alice appears as a servant of an elderly widow in Notting Hill. She is listed as single, even though she had been married for a few months by then. Alice perhaps kept the marriage a secret rather than have to explain the whereabouts of her new husband, although it's also possible that as a married woman she would have been expected to leave her job (even in this new century, when Victorian ways and values were being rapidly left behind). Harry was described as a shop assistant on the marriage certificate, and presumably it was a butcher's shop.

Their first real home together was in Hampstead. On the evening of 23 November 1910, Harry set out from there to commit his first known burglary. What did he say to Alice when he slipped away that evening? That he was going out for a drink? Did she at this point suspect the truth? And if she did, was she concerned, or did she approve of what he got up to? Much later, she would claim to have no idea of what he was doing when he was away from the house. Perhaps not initially, but the details of Vickers' lifestyle as they subsequently came to light make her protests seem disingenuous.

In many ways, what Harry would get up to on that autumn night became a template for his later activities. He headed west towards Acton in the borough of Ealing, and although he was to strike in different parts of London during the coming years (and sometimes further afield), this western (mostly north-western) side of the capital would draw him back again and again. The place he was aiming for was a street of relatively newly built houses. This is significant – he had specific reasons for targeting such areas which will come to light in due course. And he would employ on this occasion what would become his trademark trick of the trade, earning him his famous nickname.

Harry probably left the house quite late. He may have taken the tube, but if he went by bus his route would have taken him close to Wormwood Scrubs; if so, did it give him even momentary pause for thought regarding the career he was about to embark on?

He made his way on foot to Chatsworth Gardens in Acton, and, probably after a lengthy period of observation, singled out No. 58. He would have 'gone equipped', to use the modern terminology, and one of the items in his kit was a drill. Flannelfoot was no smash and grab man; people didn't always realise they had been burgled for some time after the event. His preferred method of entry was to bore or drill a hole in the window frame near the latch which allowed him to insert a piece of wire, knife or other thin implement, and open the fastener. (In future years, when he discovered that he could work his way through certain types of woodwork with just a thin, sharp instrument like an awl or knife, he would dispense with the drill.) The Chatsworth Gardens house provided him with £10, which would become a pretty typical Flannelfoot haul from a single property.

There are no reports of further break-ins on this trip, but it would become much more common for him to burgle several homes in one night – usually all close together, and often on the same street. Three days later Vickers was out again, around 3 miles further west in Ealing. Kingsley Avenue was another typical leafy suburban, lower middle-class London street, much quieter than the more central part of the capital where he and Alice currently lived. Here he obtained property to the value of £5 6s. Flannelfoot generally preferred cash, and only ever took small, easily-concealed items – probably in part to avoid looking suspicious when heading home in the early hours, and perhaps also to cut down on the need for the services of a 'fence' or having to dispense with stolen goods at pawn shops. (Some pawn shop owners turned a blind eye to suspected stolen goods, but others contacted the police if anything suspicious was offered to them. Vickers would, anyway, have been well aware that at that time pawn shops were among the first places police visited when searching for the proceeds of burglaries.)

Among his pickings in Ealing were a cigar case and a money box. When the police were called to investigate, they found a number of cloths in the scullery which had apparently been used to muffle his footsteps, and it later emerged that these had been taken from a house he had burgled the previous night. This was the defining Flannelfoot trait: ready-to-hand items such as rags, underwear and other textiles to cover his shoes or boots. Another of his notable motifs was to steal a bicycle at some point during his evening's venture and later make the first leg of his getaway on it, completing his journey home by public transport.

In the modern world, such actions would provide the police with clues such as fibres, DNA and so on, but at the turn of the twentieth century the main forensic evidence a criminal might leave behind was fingerprints, and Flannelfoot was known for always (with one possible exception) taking the precaution of wearing gloves.

So Vickers was careful and cautious from the outset – but at this stage he was still a novice, still lacked experience and his beginner's luck was about to run out.

In the early hours of 30 November 1910, PC West was patrolling West Dulwich when his eyes fell on a lone figure trudging through the dark and silent streets; it wasn't so unusual for people like market porters to be making their way to work at odd hours, but there was something about the man that prompted West to investigate anyway. The man, giving his name as Henry Williams, offered no resistance and allowed the constable to search him – which soon revealed both the tools of his trade and the proceeds of a burglary he had just committed on Turney Road. He had, in fact, entered at least two homes, taking £2 from one and £5 from another. Vickers was several miles from his escapades of a few days previously, and, relatively unusually for him, south of the Thames. His change of venue had proved disastrous.

He was escorted by West to Ludgate Hill Police Station, where he was charged with breaking and entering. He was subsequently charged with the Acton and Ealing crimes, though whether he gave this information up voluntarily, or whether the police were able to match the items found on him with those crimes, we don't know. Vickers made no reply when the charges were put to him, but it seems likely that he had at least some conversation with the officers at Ludgate Hill. When, about six weeks later on 14 January 1911, 'Henry Williams' appeared at the Central Criminal Court, the Common Serjeant (presiding judge) gave his own opinion as to what had led to the prisoner's downfall, and must have based his view on information that could only have originally come from Vickers himself. The prisoner had been betting, he declared, and 'it is this betting and gambling which misleads people who were living honestly to go beyond their means and take other people's property'.

The Common Serjeant sentenced the man he believed to be Henry Williams to nine months' imprisonment with hard labour. Doubtless not quite the start to married life Vickers had envisaged.

A significant footnote to this episode is that the detective sergeant who visited the Acton and Ealing homes after the break-ins was a local man – in fact, living at that time about a twenty-minute walk away from the Kingsley Avenue burglary. This enterprising police officer did some digging regarding the criminal in question. 'Williams' had refused to tell either the police or the prison authorities anything about himself other than that he had been born in Reading, but thanks to some old-fashioned police work the sergeant discovered that not only was his name Vickers, not Williams, but that by then he had been living with his wife at an address in Shepherd's Bush. (I mentioned earlier that it was 'Williams' not 'Vickers' who served the sentence, and this was because no one seemed to be interested in correcting the error.)

A Shepherd's Bush address would later come to play a crucial part in the Flannelfoot story, but that was many years off. Meanwhile, the diligent policeman himself would rise through the ranks: first as a regular detective, and eventually as one of the leading lights of the fledgling Flying Squad. Ultimately, he would play his part in Flannelfoot's downfall. His name was Walter Edward Hambrook.

Chapter 2

A Country Boy

Detective Sergeant Walter Hambrook, who, as we have seen, lived just up the road from one of Flannelfoot's recent burglaries and who was sent to investigate the scenes of the crimes, had joined the police almost as soon as he was old enough to sign up. (His only other employment had been as a house boy at 'The Mansion' in his home village of Betteshanger, Kent.)

He pounded the beat as a constable in Paddington, then joined the detective branch in 1901 and by 1904 at the latest, he had been promoted to the rank of sergeant. He married in 1905, and was living in Ladbroke Road, Notting Hill. One of the first issues he had to deal with as a new detective sergeant must almost have been enough to make him regret his career decision – and wonder whether the police force he had joined was all he had expected it to be.

Allegations of corruption have dogged the Metropolitan Police seemingly since it was formed right up to today, and for Hambrook it got a little close for comfort very early in his career. In 1905 he was part of F Division, Paddington, under a Detective Inspector called James McCarthy. There were lots of rumours surrounding McCarthy, and Hambrook himself didn't like him. In fact, not wanting to be tainted by association, Hambrook put in a request for a transfer – which may well be how he later ended up at Scotland Yard.

But in the meantime, stories were in circulation that McCarthy was taking money from bookies and turning a blind eye to their illegal activities (betting at that time being only allowed at the racecourse itself – high street betting shops were not yet legalised). It reached the stage where senior officers in F Division assigned their own detectives to keep an eye on him, and this led to his eventual dismissal. Astonishingly, McCarthy subsequently sued one bookmaker, who had been talking openly about the detective's shady activities, for slander. It was an unwise move to say the least. It was in the court case that Hambrook's grave misgivings about the man were cited as evidence for McCarthy's bad character, and a lot of other damaging and humiliating stories emerged. Needless to say, the ex-detective lost his case. That same year, Hambrook was assigned to his very first murder investigation.

Mrs Ellen Gregory arrived at the Paddington police station one day to make a report that her daughter Beatrice was missing, along with Beatrice's 21-month-old twin sons Laurance and Evelyn. Beatrice's married name was Devereux, and, this being an uncommon name, it rang a bell with Hambrook. As a beat bobby he had in the past become familiar with Beatrice's husband, Arthur – not from any criminal connection, but because the young man managed a chemist's shop in that area where Hambrook had been an occasional customer. The detective had always thought of him as a quiet, pleasant, happily married man.

He learned from Mrs Gregory that a baker's boy had called at the Devereux's flat on two consecutive days with a delivery, but no one had answered. On the third time of trying, their eldest son Stanley, 5, opened the door and took in the bread. On the same day, the milkman visited and was surprised that Arthur Devereux answered the door, not Beatrice as was usual. Arthur explained that his wife had just 'gone up the road with the babies'. But when the same thing happened the following day, the story had changed – his wife had now 'gone away with the babies', and the milk delivery was to be cancelled until further notice. Within a week, he had moved out.

When the removal men arrived to transport the furniture to the new lodging house, among the items to be taken was a large tin trunk. Devereux urged them to take care with it and not tip it up when they hauled it down the stairs, as, he said, it contained books and chemicals.

Whether or not they thought this an odd combination, they certainly noticed that the trunk was very heavy; in fact, they had to carefully slide it down the stairs inch by inch rather than try to carry it. When they all got to the destination on Harrow Road, Devereux ordered everything to be taken in except for the trunk. This was to be taken to Bannisters' warehouse in Kensal Rise, and put in storage.

Unaware of the move, Ellen Gregory, Beatrice's mother, made repeated fruitless trips to the old address, becoming more and more worried each time, resulting in her trip to the Paddington police station. A team led by Detective Inspector Pollard began to make enquiries as to the whereabouts of Beatrice Devereux and her two infant twins, while Walter Hambrook was given the task of finding Arthur Devereux – probably because the two were already acquainted and identification would be straightforward.

It didn't take him long to discover that the chemist had moved and left no forwarding address, and that he had supposedly taken his twin sons with him. Where he was, Hambrook had no idea, but he and his fellow officers already had concerns about the ominous course the investigation was taking. Hambrook's first clue came when the owners of the storage warehouse revealed that they had received a letter from Devereux with a Coventry address: he had sold the trunk and its contents, but it would be some time before the buyer could come and collect it. Would Bannisters mind hanging on to it for a few months?

Bannisters might not have minded waiting, but Hambrook's boss did. He took the young sergeant and a few others to the storage facility, and ordered that the trunk be brought out. It was very securely fastened with straps and padlocks, and the padlock itself bore a red wax seal. The detectives came to the same conclusion that the removal men had – it seemed extremely heavy for something supposedly containing just a few books and some chemicals. Pollard decided they were going to force it open. Devereux had gone to surprising lengths to secure it. It took a lot of sweat and elbow grease to breach the trunk's outer defences, only for the officers to find an inner lid comprising pieces of timber both screwed and heavily glued in place. Like some sort of Russian doll, when this second barrier was removed a *third* layer was revealed. It was just a table cloth and bed quilt, but huge quantities of glue had been poured over it which had hardened into a thick, plastic-like membrane. Devereux *really* did not want anyone to see what was inside his trunk, and as they carefully picked away at the last obstacle, the policemen already had a pretty shrewd idea of what they were going to find beneath. Hambrook later admitted that, this being his first murder case and he being the least experienced man present, he was becoming rather apprehensive about what lay beneath the protective layers.

The sight that finally met their eyes shocked and dismayed all of the officers present, not just him.

'I shall never forget the grim moment of silence that followed,' Hambrook reflected of the opening of the trunk. Even in his memoirs written many years later, he still couldn't bring himself to describe in any detail the tragic sight of the bodies of a once-attractive professional piano teacher and her two 21-month-old boys. The only good thing about the discovery from a professional point of view was that Devereux – for Hambrook was sure that this was the culprit – had, thanks to his professional knowledge, done such a good job of sealing the trunk and making it airtight that he had preserved evidence which would hopefully go some way to bringing him to justice.

The Paddington detectives lost no time in contacting their Coventry colleagues, explaining the situation and requesting that they arrest Devereux. He was probably traced solely from the address on the letter he had sent to Bannisters, since he had assumed the identity of a widower called Taylor. He had even got a new job at a chemist's in Coventry (thanks to a forged reference, it later transpired), which is where the police found and arrested him.

'It's all right,' he assured them confidently. 'I'm quite clear of this – it's ridiculous!'

He would admit to concealing the bodies of his wife and children, but not to their murder. He freely admitted that he had called upon his scientific know-how to overcome the usual giveaway in such cases – the smell. He had used glue mixed with boric acid to create his final seal, 'which prevents fungi from growing, and it would never have allowed any smell to penetrate', he explained with what almost seemed to amount to professional pride.

Despite his denials, he was charged with the murder of Beatrice and the two members of his young family, and it was Hambrook to whom Devereux dictated his statement with 'extraordinary composure'. His story, though, was not nearly as clever as his attempt to conceal the bodies. He claimed that he had returned home to find them all dead in bed, with a smell of chloroform lingering in the air. He said he believed that his wife, with whom he had rowed the previous day, had taken it from his own supplies and used it to kill the two toddlers and then herself.

'Rather than face an inquest', and inspired by a story he had read recently of a murderer who had disposed of a body by putting it in a trunk and filling it with cement and quicklime, Devereux set about entombing Beatrice and the twins in the trunk using his own improved version of the described method – a process which took him a full three days.[1]

Hambrook was in charge of the exhibits at the trial, and noted the horror of the jury when the trunk was hauled into the courtroom – while Devereux himself looked at it 'as if it was just an ordinary piece of luggage'. The jury did not believe his fanciful tale. Devereux was found guilty, and was hanged just a few days later.

This case continued to haunt not only novice detective Hambrook but even the experienced Inspector Pollard, who was a friend as well as being his boss. Pollard fell ill just three years after the Devereux case, having previously been involved in the equally gruesome and harrowing Crossman 'trunk murder' case described in the footnote below. Realising, correctly, that he didn't have long to live, he sent for Walter Hambrook to help him draw up his will. As they talked, Pollard told the younger man that he believed the things he had seen and experienced during those two investigations lay behind his failing health.

---

1. Devereux was referring to the case of George Crossman, who killed one of the many women he had bigamously married. Quicklime hastened the breakdown of a body and the cement was supposed to prevent any smell of decomposition from escaping, but it didn't.

By 1906 Hambrook had moved to Willesden, and here he got a taste of the medicine that Flannelfoot would soon be dishing out to his victims – he himself was burgled. One James Ryan was given three years for stealing a watch, cigarette case and other items. Whether Hambrook was involved in catching the thief isn't recorded, but perhaps it prompted him to move from the area because he was soon living at Bonchurch Road, Ealing – little knowing at the time that he had, in a sense, jumped out of the frying pan into the fire – this *was* Flannelfoot territory (although we don't know whether he was active yet).

A sign of how times have changed is that not long after his move, a conviction Hambrook had been involved in was appealed in the High Court of Justice, no less – a case of a stolen bicycle. A witness to the theft had given a description of the perpetrator to Hambrook, who in turn passed it on to a beat constable. That officer, believing he had come across his man – a known criminal – made his arrest. The court at the original trial was happy with the identification, but not the appeal court, which quashed the conviction.

At around the time of Vickers' first arrest, an idea of the variety of Hambrook's work came in the form of *The Case of The Begging Letter Imposter*, as the press termed it. Hambrook's man on this occasion was 61-year-old William Anderson, a tailor, who was brought for sentence 'as an incorrigible rogue and vagabond'. Adding to the calumny, Hambrook himself described Anderson as 'one of the most notorious begging-letter impostors of the present day, and a pest to society'. The man, he said, made a career out of fraud. Born in Calcutta, Anderson, for some reason, passed himself off as a 'needy Scotsman' whose poor health was such that he must have a 'change of air' but could not afford to get away. He specialised in approaching unwitting Scots, enclosing a forged medical certificate (which he had specially printed at his own expense) signed by a fictitious doctor. Anderson even managed to rope a naive archdeacon into his subterfuge – the clergyman provided him with a letter of support, which Anderson then had copied but with the wording altered to suit the circumstances of whatever current scam he was up to. Thanks to Hambrook, Anderson received a ten-month sentence with hard labour.

Chapter 3

War and Peace

The second decade of the twentieth century was not a great time for Harry Vickers. He served his nine-month sentence in Wandsworth Prison, just south of the Thames and not too far away from the scene of the crime which had led to his arrest. It would have been a bit of a trek for wife Alice, but not so far that she couldn't have visited him regularly. Wandsworth wasn't a particularly old establishment, and it initially had a reputation as one of the Victorian era's more humane prisons, complete with toilets in every cell – most poorer Victorian homes lacked such indoor amenities. But as time went by and the prison population increased, the authorities decided to rip out the toilets in order to accommodate more and more prisoners. This meant that Vickers would have been subject to the notorious 'slopping out' regimen, involving buckets or chamber pots which obviously had to be used in the presence of other cellmates, and which could only be emptied at certain times.[1]

Vickers would have left his civilian clothes behind and been issued with the archetypal convict uniform of white button-up coat and trousers bearing black, upward-facing arrows printed on both. Even the prison-issue boots had the broad arrow on the soles – literally pointing the way for those on the trail of an escaped prisoner, unless, of course, he discarded them. It's also likely that Vickers' hair would have been cropped, and he may well have had to sleep on a bed made of planks for the first two weeks of his sentence.[2]

Only fifteen years earlier, Oscar Wilde had been a Wandsworth inmate for a time, and the programme of 'hard labour, hard fare and a hard bed' had broken his health (even before his better-known spell in Vickers' hometown prison in Reading). Vickers' imprisonment came at a time of gradual change in attitudes concerning things like hard labour in prisons. It was being phased out, and the most common manifestation by Vickers' day involved walking on a treadmill for long periods, although picking oakum and 'turning the crank' had still been in use when Wilde was there and may have persisted into the early twentieth century. Oakum is the term given to old ships' ropes, which

---

1. A practice which continued until the 1990s, and even then lingered in some prisons after it had been officially outlawed.
2. This practice continued until 1945: Rupert Cross, *Punishment, Prison and the Public* (1971).

may or may not have been tarred; prisoners had to tease the fibres apart for re-use. (Strictly speaking, it was the resultant fibres which were called oakum, but the phrase is generally used to refer to the unpicked rope.) Turning the crank is pretty much self-explanatory: the turning of a crank handle similar to the kind used to wind up early gramophones, but larger. It was a pointless exercise – which in fact was the 'point' – and, in many cases, turning the crank could be made either harder or easier by the warder making a simple adjustment.

Wandsworth was then also a place of execution, and a sensational double hanging took place just a few weeks after Flannelfoot arrived. The Stratton brothers, Albert and Alfred, battered an elderly couple to death during the course of robbing their shop in Deptford. The pair were hanged on 5 May 1905, and it would undoubtedly have been the talk of the prison just as much as it had been among the population in general. When he heard the details, it must have been a sobering moment for Vickers. He was never violent in any way during his robberies, but the Stratton brothers emptied the shop cashbox, which was exactly the kind of thing he targeted. Moreover, the criminals made history in becoming the first to be convicted thanks to the relatively new science of fingerprint evidence.

Whatever the effect that case, in addition to his own time in Wandsworth, had on Vickers, it certainly didn't deter him in the long term. In fact, his career was only just beginning …

For now, though, the troubled times continued for Vickers. Two years after his release, he and Alice had their first baby. It was a boy and he was baptised in Bexleyheath in south-east London, but the parish register reveals that the Vickers were living at Whitehall Mansions, an impressive-sounding address which was actually a late-Victorian tenement building on Elderfield Road in Hackney. Elegant, but not quite a mansion. The entry also gives Vickers' occupation as 'clerk'. They named the child Jack after Vickers' father, but sadly the boy died when he was just nine months old. By this time Harry and Alice had for some reason moved back to their home town of Reading. A daughter, Vera, followed in 1915, but by then, of course, Britain was at war. Shortly after Vera's first birthday, Vickers joined the Rifle Brigade. He must have volunteered, since conscription wasn't introduced till the following year. (Though even by this point, an enormous amount of moral and psychological pressure was being exerted on young men to join up, and it was becoming increasingly difficult for able-bodied males in their twenties to avoid enlisting. It was a time when white feathers were being handed out indiscriminately by women on buses and in the street: often to soldiers wearing civvies who were on leave, and even to those who had been sent home wounded but not visibly so.)

As for Vickers, the 5th Battalion, in which he served according to his medal card in The National Archives, is on record as being held in reserve in Britain and never seeing action abroad, but there is a little more to Vickers' army service than that. One account says he was awarded the Silver War Badge, Victory Medal, and British War Medal, although his medal card shows only the Victory Medal and British War Medal.

The British War Medal was awarded both to men who had served in a 'theatre of war' (an area of active fighting) and those who had served overseas but not in an area of combat. The Victory Medal only went to those who had served in a theatre of war – and records show that Vickers certainly *had* been in the thick of it.

Before being transferred to the 5th (Reserve) Battalion, Harry Edward Vickers had been with the 9th Battalion, which had been sent to some of the most fiercely contested areas on the Front. In fact, the 9th took such a pounding that by 27 April 1918 it was reduced from a battalion (around 1,000 men) to a cadre, i.e., a small training unit (in this case, involving the training of newly arrived Americans).

Vickers joined the 9th Battalion in January 1916, and records show that this unit took part in two battles – Delville Wood and Flers-Courcelette – both of which came under the overall banner of the Battle of the Somme. He almost certainly saw action in both.

Delville Wood was not a single set-piece battle, but lasted from July to September in a number of separate attritional encounters that earned it the nickname 'Devil's Wood', initially with South African forces, and later British, fighting to retake the woods from the Germans. The 9th Battalion, Rifle Brigade, was part of the 14th light division, which suffered 3,615 casualties.

The Battle of Flers-Courcelette commenced in the same month that Delville Wood ended, and featured the first use of tanks. Between 15–22 September, the Allies gained a relatively small amount of ground but once again paid a heavy price – this time, 30,000 casualties overall.

Between February and March 1917, Vickers' 9th Battalion was one of the units engaging the Germans as they withdrew to the Hindenburg Line, and the 9th were subsequently involved in the first and second battles of Passchendaele. In 1918 they were back at the Somme, thrown into the battles of St Quentin and The Avre, in March and April respectively. This was the result of a major spring offensive by the Germans resulting in the Allies suffering very heavy casualties, and this action seems to have destroyed the 9th Battalion as a fighting force. It was just after this that they were withdrawn from the front line, and it wasn't much longer before the battalion's status was reduced to that of a training cadre. I suspect that Vickers, who was discharged in July 1918, received his wound at one of these last two battles. He was medically discharged from the army a few months before the end of the war.

Some accounts say that whatever Vickers' wound was and however he came by it, it left him with a permanent limp. As we'll see later, it's likely that even if it was severe at first, in later life the effects were outwardly very mild; if it did leave him with a limp, it was minor enough that he could hide it if necessary. And, of course, it certainly didn't hinder his nocturnal activities. The fact that he often stole bikes to move from one job to another, or make the first stage of his getaway, could feasibly be linked to some sort of weakness or mobility problem, but bikes were more likely to have been the means of a faster exit from the scene of the crime. It was noted in the Scotland Yard files that the location of recovered bicycles almost always indicated that the culprit was heading from the scene of the crime towards central London, and also that he cycled for an average of 5 miles before dumping the machine. In general, he seems to have been a physically fit and able man.

In some ways, the period after the First World War was difficult for the country as a whole, and Vickers' activities reflected what was happening nationally. Britain was changing, the staid Victorian era giving way to jazz music, short hair and daring dresses for women. The BBC began broadcasting radio programmes to the nation in November 1922. There were also major changes politically and economically. The year 1918 is famous for the landmark decision that allowed some (but by no means all) women to finally be allowed to vote in elections. What is less well known is that very many men didn't have the vote before that either. Vickers certainly wasn't eligible, but the fact that he had fought for his country was the reason why things changed for him and many others like him. Prime minister David Lloyd George said that 'The man who has fought must have the right to determine how the fruits of his peril are going to be dealt with.' This came about with the Representation of the People Act of June 1918.

But Lloyd George himself was to become the victim of the changes sweeping Britain. His Liberal Party and the Conservatives had long been the two major forces in British politics, but Vickers' release from prison coincided with the sudden and devastating decline of the Liberals, from which they have yet to recover, with Labour becoming the new rivals to the Tories.

And Vickers was unwittingly playing his part in another significant change in society – an unprecedented rise in crime. Recorded crimes in England and Wales had been at a pretty static level for decades, but after Vickers' return from war the figures went into an inexorable climb, virtually doubling every decade (apart from a hiatus in the 1950s).[3]

---

3. Howard Taylor, *The Politics of the Rising Crime Statistics of England and Wales, 1914–1960* (1997).

Vickers, unreformed and uncowed by his prison sentence, complete with its hard labour element, probably fell back into breaking and entering very soon after his release; there is every indication that he believed dull nine-to-five jobs were for other people, not the likes of him. In later years, when Flannelfoot's infamy had spread nationwide and beyond, it would be claimed that he came by the nickname as early as 1911, the very year of his release. However, throughout the course of my research the first occasion when a criminal with the 'Flannelfoot' nickname cropped up (at the time, it was usually written as 'Flannel Foot' or 'Flannel-Foot') came on 4 September 1921. This was in relation to the burglaries referred to earlier, involving the peculiar and perhaps mischievous theft of Mr Boulton's dentures. The culprit had also availed himself of a pair of Mr Boulton's gloves during the raid, as well as a pair of his socks to cover his shoes. The burglar went on to rob another house, which was where these items were discovered.

The interesting thing is that the newspapers of the day used the Flannelfoot name in such a way as to indicate that it would already be recognised by the general public, stating that he was 'up to his old tricks again'. One biographical piece on Walter Hambrook credits the *Daily Express* with coining the nickname, but this is a moot point. And even if that newspaper did first apply it to Harry Edward Vickers, it certainly wasn't a new term in itself. 'Flossie Flannelfoot' and 'Jemima Flannelfoot' were stage names appearing on music hall bills towards the end of the Victorian era; it was used as a character name in some plays; it may even have been a genuine surname, since it appears in a passenger liner's arrivals list in 1879.

Poor Mr Boulton, meanwhile, found himself confronted over the next few days with newspaper headlines such as 'Singer's Teeth Stolen'.

Reading between the lines, though, there are plausible candidates for earlier Flannelfoot jobs even where the nickname itself wasn't used in reports. Acton was a favourite stomping ground for Vickers, and a trawl of the *Acton Gazette* throws up several possibilities.

In June 1920, a series of five burglaries in one night along Shaa Road was put down to a gang of youths. The report, however, offers up no evidence of such a gang, nor does it explain why the youthfulness or otherwise of the criminals should be assumed. Various small items were taken this night, and the clues that Vickers *could* have been behind the spree (other than it being in Acton) are as follows:

• It was a Friday night event, which was always said to be one of Flannelfoot's preferred times.

- At the rear of one house, a bicycle was prepared as if for later getaway: it seems to have been a somewhat decrepit machine, but it had been oiled and its tyres pumped up – till the barking of a dog is thought to have caused the intruder to flee before getting the chance to use it.
- The burglar or burglars helped themselves to 'light refreshments' on the go – not unknown during a break-in, but again a known Flannelfoot habit.
- Most notably, an old kitchen towel was taken from the first house which was robbed, and discarded at the scene of one of the later burglaries. How many burglars, other than Flannelfoot, stole old towels in that way?

The only finding that militates against Vickers being behind these incidents was footprints and fingerprints in one of the houses. The large number of prints caused the owner to surmise that a gang was behind the robbery, but we can't be sure that one busy person couldn't have left them. While it's true that it was virtually unknown for Flannelfoot to leave fingerprints, and footprints were uncommon, if he had already abandoned his towel yet found himself tempted by further rich pickings, it is conceivable that he decided to throw caution to the wind for once.

In the same year, there was another break-in that bore several Flannelfoot hallmarks: a house was entered in a 'very dexterous manner' by way of a rear French window without causing any damage or breaking of glass, and a safe was ignored (contrary to some of the embellishments in Flannelfoot tales, he was no cracksman) but small items of jewellery were stolen. Interestingly, one of the things taken was a pair of gold-plated false teeth … Other burglaries in Acton around this time included the house of a newly-married couple whose wedding presents were stolen, and money taken from poor-boxes in the parish church. It would be nice to think that our Flannelfoot wouldn't stoop so low – but sadly, in fact, we shall see later that he would, and possibly even lower, depending on your take on such things. Perhaps also of significance is that the vicar's bike was also used by the perpetrator to flee on.

The following December, again in Acton, a house was entered through the fanlight over the kitchen door – as Flannelfoot sometimes did – and a great deal of jewellery went missing. The occupant's coat had been taken in this raid, with the burglar at least making it a (somewhat) fair exchange by leaving his old one behind. And this was another Friday night event.

In the same year that Flannelfoot was first identified by that name, and as we have seen was said to have been up to his 'old tricks' (1921), a girl was born to Harry and Alice who would go on to play a bizarre but absolutely crucial part in Harry's eventual downfall. The child's name was Elsie Vickers.

Chapter 4

The Monocled Mutineer

Meanwhile, the detective who had investigated the crimes leading to Vickers' first arrest was entering a busy time in his career, and had weightier matters to attend to than stolen false teeth. During the year that Vickers was serving his prison sentence, Walter Hambrook, still a sergeant, had been dealing with a relatively minor matter of fraudulent begging letters, but by the early 1920s he was a detective inspector with Scotland Yard. It was in this capacity that he became involved in what he described as the case of 'Britain's first gunman'. There had been shootings before, but he was referring to gunmen 'of the real American bandit type'.

The villain in question was Francis Toplis. He tended to go by his middle name of Percy, but he will be better known to many as 'The Monocled Mutineer', thanks to a popular 1980s TV series which in turn was based on a book of the same name. We shall come back to that in due course.

In early 1920, Toplis was a private in the Royal Army Service Corps, Mechanical Transport. One day, he hired a taxi to drive him from Amesbury in Wiltshire to the railway station at Andover, Hampshire: a journey of around 14 miles. Rather than pay the fare, Toplis – the man whom culture warriors of later years would endeavour to portray as some sort of misunderstood champion of the downtrodden – killed the unsuspecting driver with a single shot to the back of the head.

Hambrook didn't play a central role in the investigation on the ground, so to speak, since Toplis disappeared and the hunt soon went nationwide, but he and his team at Scotland Yard became the hub for a wide-ranging search involving several police forces.

The blood-soaked body of the taxi driver, his pockets left inside out after being rifled for cash, was found near Andover by a cyclist the following day. The victim was 27 years old, married with one child. Toplis already had something of a reputation, and his name soon cropped up in the investigation. Hambrook was aware of some of his historical exploits, including fraud and being found in possession of a loaded revolver, and that he had deserted from the army on more than one occasion.

Suspicions were heightened when it was discovered that he had returned to camp in a car and persuaded a fellow soldier to join him on a road trip. In fact,

Toplis had decided to head for Wales. They ended up in Swansea, but when Toplis read in the papers that he was the prime suspect in the murder of the taxi driver, he sent his companion back to Wiltshire by train, abandoned the car and vanished once more.

Hambrook learned that Toplis' army colleague had promised to send a letter to him addressed to the Union Jack armed forces club in Waterloo Road. He and other officers kept a watch on the place in case Toplis arrived to collect his letter, and although the murderer had the sense not to do so, Hambrook still suspected that he would be lying up in London somewhere and conducted exhaustive searches. However, the first positive sighting turned out to be over 500 miles away, in Scotland.

Disturbing news was passed to Hambrook of a new attack – this time in remote Tomintoul in the shadows of the Cairngorms. A farmer had alerted the local constable to smoke issuing from the chimney of an unoccupied gamekeeper's hut, and when they went together to investigate, they found a dishevelled man whom they took to be a tramp asleep on the floor. When the constable shook the man awake, he whipped out a revolver and opened fire on both policeman and farmer. As they lay wounded, their attacker cycled away with a breezy 'Cheerio!' It was Toplis.

After this, news trickled in to Hambrook of sightings elsewhere in Scotland and also northern England as Toplis kept on the move. The detective charted his movements on a map and tried to predict where he might be heading (foreshadowing one of the tools which would be deployed against Flannelfoot).

In Penrith, Cumbria (then Cumberland), PC Fulton spotted a man in RAF uniform. Believing there to be something suspicious about him but not wanting to put him on his guard, the officer engaged him in casual conversation and then left him alone. But once out of sight of the stranger, Fulton hurried to his station, where a quick check of 'wanted' descriptions and photographs confirmed that he had been speaking to the infamous Toplis. The unarmed constable set off on his bicycle to get his man. Toplis had moved on, but a local reported seeing a man in uniform on a country road some distance away. Fulton pedalled after him. Hambrook's description of the eventual encounter goes thus:

Fulton greeted the fugitive with 'Hello, old man ...'

'You're a smart lad,' came the reply. 'I am the man you were looking for – Percy Toplis. I shot a farmer and a policeman in Banffshire, and if there is any hanky-panky you go too.'

'Don't be silly. I have no chance against you – put the revolver away.'

Toplis kept his gun aimed at the policeman. 'I will kill you all or be killed. Throw down your handcuffs and truncheon.'

Fulton had little option but to comply. He probably feared the worst – but the cold-blooded killer allowed him to retreat, merely warning him not to follow. As Toplis himself knew, that was never going to happen. Soon after Fulton returned to Penrith, the county was swarming with police, most of them now themselves armed. Fulton was in a car with the local detective inspector and sergeant which caught up with Toplis, who had now changed into civilian clothes. They drove ahead of him, stopped the car and quickly jumped out. Toplis drew his gun and loosed off three shots – mercifully not hitting any of the men advancing on him.

The inspector and sergeant both fired back. Toplis crumpled to his knees for a second, then slumped face forward, dead from a bullet through the heart. Among the items found in his pocket was a gold-rimmed monocle – the affectation of Toplis's which inspired the naming of the book and TV series of the 1980s. But beyond that eyepiece, the directions taken between ugly reality and the portrayals in print and on film quickly begin to diverge.

In a desire to paint Toplis as some sort of oppressed working-class hero, rebelling against the useless and snobbish officer class, Toplis was represented as having led a mutiny in Étaples during the First World War. The problem is that Toplis almost certainly wasn't at Étaples when the mutiny took place; even the historical expert hired by the TV company which made *The Monocled Mutineer* said as much. There will always be those who, for ideological reasons, are prepared to distort some facts and overlook others in order to bolster the image of a plucky man of the people fighting back against the uncaring establishment. One academic described Toplis as being 'as much a victim of the times as he was a villain', a commonly heard plea in defence of criminals now, though rare back in his own time. But his record (which is much longer than given here, and includes strong links with two unsolved other murders) speaks for itself: Percy Toplis was a crook, conman and killer.

Back in London, it was Hambrook who was a key figure in setting up the Yard's famous Flying Squad. It was an elite, mobile unit formed specifically to investigate armed robberies and other serious crimes. In 1920, police cars were still relatively expensive and uncommon, but criminals had already cottoned on to the usefulness of motor vehicles. They could travel further afield to commit crimes, especially to places where their faces weren't known, but the main benefit was obviously speed of escape. The police realised they needed to literally catch up with them.

There was something of an antipathy among some of the older and more senior officers at Scotland Yard towards this modernising move, and initially the squad was provided with old, slow, cumbersome ex-army trucks with no radios. But as the new group gradually began to prove its worth in action, better and faster cars, and eventually radios, were introduced. It was the press who dubbed this team the 'Flying Squad', and the name quickly became so synonymous with the unit that it was even adopted officially by the Yard.

One of Hambrook's first big Flying Squad cases involved a shooting in Paddington. A report was received that a woman had been shot and seriously wounded in a hotel on Westbourne Terrace, close to Paddington Station. Hambrook visited the woman, Caroline Semmens, at nearby St Mary's hospital, where she was conscious and able to talk to him. He discovered that she was 30 years old and of French extraction, married to a Canadian called Edward Semmens, but Caroline had taken a lover and the pair had separated. Mrs Semmens had become so afraid of her husband that she employed a female private detective to accompany her when she went to fetch some clothes she had left behind. The seriously wounded Mrs Semmens couldn't have been more forthright when Hambrook asked her what had happened: 'My husband has done this,' she croaked. Her condition deteriorated, and she died not long afterwards. The full story of what occurred emerged at the inquest, in which Hambrook played a part.

With her private detective in tow, Caroline Semmens confronted her husband and asked for her clothing to be returned to her.

'Certainly you can have it.'

She followed him to the room where they had been stored, whereupon Mrs Semmens asked where her trunk was.

'It is here, or at least it should be.'

'If you want to keep these things, at least give me my mother's gift.'

At that, Semmens pulled a revolver from his pocket and said, 'Anyway, here's one for you to go on with.' He hit Caroline from close range, the bullet entering through an eye and lodging in her brain. Semmens fled, but was quickly tracked down and arrested in the locality. When Hambrook interviewed him, Semmens claimed, 'I did not know what I was doing.' By this he meant that he wasn't fully in control of his senses, and this would later be the story upon which his defence would be based.

The inquest verdict was one of wilful murder against Semmens, but at the trial defence counsel staked everything on their client's 'mental illness' and this argument received support from unexpected quarters. The medical officer of Brixton Prison said that Semmens 'seemed to have no clear impression of what had taken place'. He was in such a state that 'it would have taken very little to send him over the "borderline" so far as his reason was concerned …' Semmens, a well-travelled man, had contracted malaria in the past and a specialist in tropical diseases who had treated him was called to testify. Dr

MacAllister stated that Semmens was 'not mentally stable', and even offered the opinion that 'In such a condition, instinct often got the upper hand, and gave rise to crime.'

The medical evidence muddied the waters as far as the jury were concerned, and after discussing the matter for an hour they sent a message to the judge asking for clarification. They were unanimous, they said, in believing that there was no intent to murder – but, given the unusual circumstances, what verdict should they return? Mr Justice Lawrence told them it was not necessary for there to be intent to murder – if there was intent to do grievous bodily harm, then the verdict should be 'guilty'. If there was no intent to shoot so as to do grievous bodily harm, the verdict should be 'not guilty'. In what *The Times* – and no doubt Walter Hambrook – found to be a 'remarkable finding', Semmens was cleared of the charge and walked from the court a free man.

The Flying Squad officers were tough, and had to be – the kind of heavyweight organised crooks they often came up against weren't always prepared to come quietly. In September 1920 Hambrook and another inspector, along with eight other officers, were carrying out surveillance on a team of thieves known as the Elephant Gang (they sometimes used the Elephant and Castle area as a base). At this early stage, the crooks had no idea that the occasional drab, grey ex-army vehicle to be seen cruising around London contained Scotland Yard officers on the lookout.

As he and his men were driving around, Hambrook spotted a 'desperate rogue' well known to him jumping into a van in the Old Kent Road. His own wagon followed the van towards the Elephant and Castle, where six more men were picked up – half of whom were also familiar faces. The crooks didn't pull off a job that night, but they did lead the police to the garage where they kept their van, and it was put under constant surveillance.

This paid off a couple of days later when at 4 am, several gang members congregated at the garage carrying suspicious-looking parcels wrapped in newspaper. When the van set off, two Flying Squad wagons were following at a discreet distance. Hambrook looked on as three more men were picked up, bringing their total to eight.

After inspecting a silversmith's shop but evidently having a change of heart, the criminals parked near a clothes shop on Pimlico Road. Some approached the premises, while others loitered in the vicinity as if acting as lookouts. Hambrook now got his own team to disembark and spread out, hoping to cut off all escape routes.

With the Flying Squad looking on, ready to pounce, one of the gang members realised they were being watched and shouted to his accomplices,

'Quick – it's a tumble!' The gang scrambled into their own van and there was a brief chase, brought to an end when the Squad blocked the Ford the criminals were crammed into. A violent thunderstorm broke out just as everyone emerged from their vehicles, adding to the drama when the two sides clashed. A ferocious battle ensued, the villains wielding coshes, knuckle-dusters and even knives, while the police largely relied on their truncheons.

Hambrook had with him a heavy wooden walking cane, and managed to do a fair amount of damage until he was hit from behind by a thug swinging a life-preserver at his head and crying, 'Let's kill the bastard!' ('Life-preserver' was a term applied to various types of home-made weapons, but by this time usually meant a cosh.) Hambrook was knocked to the ground, but so was his attacker by a fellow detective with a truncheon. Prostrate and dazed, Hambrook was still clear-headed enough to see that the fight was going the way of his officers, even with a man down. None of the gang managed to escape; they were all arrested and ultimately convicted.

Hambrook's next prominent case was in February 1921, when he was called upon to investigate what was known at the time as The Empty Villa Mystery. This was the year in which Agatha Christie's first Poirot book, *The Mysterious Affair at Styles*, was published, but although The Empty Villa Mystery sounds like one of her novels, it was much more brutal and didn't have a neat conclusion which provided all the answers.

A young woman called Henrietta Weightman left her family home in the early evening, telling her parents that she would be back in an hour or so. When she hadn't returned by about 10 pm, her father retired for the night but left the door unlocked for her. Upon waking the next day, he found her still not back and began making urgent enquiries – unaware that by then a story had already hit the press of a girl's body having been found.

Henrietta was discovered in an empty, partly-built villa at Bushey Heath in Hertfordshire. She was lying on some sacks of cement; her corsets lay by her side, her hair was down and her skirt undone at the side. Inspector Hambrook was one of the investigating officers, and he was present at the inquest when a builder she was acquainted with, whose father owned the house, was questioned. There was something suspiciously defensive about the way he emphasised, unsolicited, that he had told Henrietta that he was married. He claimed that when they met on a recent occasion, she told him she was 'in trouble' and she said she would like him to take her out to dinner. 'Why on earth she should tell me [she was in trouble] I don't know,' the builder said somewhat disingenuously. He went on to explain that he knew someone who performed back-street abortions (terminations still being illegal then). It all sounded very suspicious, but it was also circumstantial: there were no signs of violence on Henrietta's body, and tests revealed no evidence of an attempted abortion.

The medical evidence was that Henrietta was four and a half months pregnant. The doctor who performed the post-mortem said that he could find no indication of poison, and although he couldn't rule it out, he didn't suspect it. His best guess was that *possibly*, a 'mildly depressed mind combined with a full stomach and being lightly clad caused heart failure'. Even to a lay person this sounds rather desperate, but it was all the inquest jury were presented with and an open verdict was returned.

Chapter 5

The Burglar with the Cat-like Tread

While Hambrook had been working on these cases, Flannelfoot had been widening his horizons a little.

On the night of 30 April 1922, or into the early hours of the next morning, he headed further west than before and entered a house on Aylett Road, Isleworth. His first task, of course, was to find something to put over his shoes, and it didn't take him long to come up with a napkin and a woman's overalls. So protected, he deftly gained entry to and prowled around several houses on the street, breaking into gas meters and hoovering up any cash left in coat pockets or which happened to be lying around.

Part of his haul was the whole monthly salary of an unfortunate shorthand typist, a sum of £10, which he found in her handbag. In one property, the family had made preparations for a wedding the following day and had laid out a wedding breakfast. Vickers helped himself to as much as he could manage before moving on. Interestingly, in one house he took a little boy's money box down from the mantelpiece, but left it unopened. He wouldn't always be so sentimental. Finally, he took what was becoming almost as much of a trademark for him as his 'flannel feet': a set of false teeth belonging to a 'well-known motorist'. At least this apparent celebrity, unlike the unfortunate singing artiste Mr Boulton, was allowed his anonymity and did not have to endure the sight of his name splashed across the newspapers. Whether there was a thriving trade in black market false teeth, complete with fences who specialised in them, is anybody's guess – but Vickers seemed to be attracted to them like a magpie to shiny objects.

He must have been pleased with his night's work because his next known job was also in Isleworth – this time just round the corner at South Western Terrace on London Road. Tellingly, both properties are almost equidistant from Isleworth's railway station. We have seen that Vickers often stole a bike to cover the initial part of his retreat, but he also used public transport for longer distances. This second Isleworth attack was carried out towards the end of November. At a time when Howard Carter was forcing his way into Tutankhamun's tomb, Vickers was breaking into semi-detached houses to acquire a rather more tawdry kind of treasure, with gas meters being his main target.

A couple of months later there was a series of burglaries attributed to a 'gang', but which had at least some of the hallmarks of Vickers' modus operandi, even though the location was some distance from his hitherto favourite stomping ground of West London. The main link with Flannelfoot was the use of cushion covers and towels to protect the footwear of the man or men behind the break-ins. These robberies were carried out in Enfield and Winchmore Hill in North London, in January 1923. Cash and jewellery were taken, but Vickers seemed to like quirky items, and although no teeth were missing this time round, whoever was behind the robberies liked the look of a boot brush and tin of polish. He also helped himself to a meal of beef, bread and cheese, with cake for dessert, and all washed down with both wine and whisky. If it was Flannelfoot, and he escaped on a bicycle as he was wont to do, it might have been a rather wobbly ride to the nearest tube station.

We don't hear of Vickers again until August 1923. The *Weekly Dispatch* told its readers that Flannelfoot, 'the burglar with the cat-like tread', was back after, it claimed, an absence of eighteen months. But even if he wasn't behind the raids in North London, I strongly suspect that he was at work somewhere. Burglary was steadily becoming a more common occurrence at this period, and it could well be that some of his simply weren't attributed as such because of a lack of the usual tell-tale signs for whatever reason.

Vickers next headed further east still, to Windsor Road, Southall. It was the same kind of quiet, pleasant-looking, tree-lined residential area that seemed to draw him, and it was just a ten-minute brisk walk from the railway station. Mrs Cleverley had put £10 aside to cover her forthcoming rates bill, but it was gone when she woke in the morning. The *Weekly Dispatch* said that Flannelfoot had gained entry by forcing windows using a gimlet. This is a small screwdriver-like tool for hand-drilling narrow holes in wood; it would no doubt have done the job, but something larger and stronger would surely have served him better, and since he didn't leave the tools of his trade behind, it's not clear how the newspaper could be so specific about it.

In other houses, Flannelfoot had, as usual, broken open gas meters and pocketed the money, and demonstrated his ready appetite again by scoffing a couple of bananas before moving on to commit more break-ins. He was soon in action again, staying on the western side of London but heading north this time.

On 8 September 1923, a fire broke out in a timber yard in Sutton, Surrey. In addition to the wood, there was also paint, oil and petrol stored in sheds in the yard, and the blaze soon became an inferno. People in nearby houses on adjoining Haddon Road began to panic as the flames crept nearer, and there was a frantic effort to remove furniture and valuables from houses, residents hauling everything as far as they could away from the flames that lit the night with a menacing orange glow. In some cases, window frames had to be knocked out in order to get furniture out. The homes of five workers at the yard did catch fire, but were saved from destruction by the heroic efforts of the fire brigade. The weary and bedraggled victims were provided with temporary shelter in the parish and municipal public halls. Haddon Road itself was a sorry sight, littered with broken glass and strewn with the rescued beds and other furniture. One of the victims of the fire, a widow, was rendered homeless and provided with short-term accommodation in Harrow. It would prove to be an unfortunate choice of location.

Towards the end of September, ten houses in Harrow were burgled during a four-night period – and the finger of suspicion was pointed at Flannelfoot. He was getting bolder, not just in coming back again and again to the same area, but in the lengths he was prepared to go to once inside a house.

In one residence, Vickers crept into a bedroom while its two occupants lay asleep. He quietly dipped his hand inside the pockets of a pair of trousers, and when he felt coins inside, took the garment downstairs so that he could empty out the contents without being heard. As he slipped out of the bedroom, he also noticed a key in the door (keys for internal doors seem to have been a more common thing then than today) so he took the precaution of locking the occupants in their own bedroom, giving him that extra level of security while he went about his work downstairs. Vickers bagged £10 in all, a typical haul for Flannelfoot in a single home. He was clearly clever and skilful at his trade, but although this is part of the reason why he was at large for so long, one wonders why, when it became clear that he was targeting one specific area night after night, the police weren't eventually able to concentrate their resources there. Perhaps they did and it simply wasn't reported, but if so, the quality of streetlighting might have played its part in allowing Vickers to elude any extra police on patrol.

As we shall see later, not all suburban streets – especially in the partly developed ones that Vickers liked – were lit at all. And any streetlighting that was in place would not have been nearly as effective as that which we are used to today. This was the 1920s, when gas streetlighting was still common; as regards electric streetlights, I recall that even in the road where I lived as a child in the 1960s, the lighting was quite feeble. (My dad and most other car owners left little hurricane lamps in the road beside their vehicles at night for safety's sake. I shudder to think what would happen to those lamps if they were left out today!)

This was a busy period even by Flannelfoot's busy standards. The *Uxbridge Gazette* attributed at least ten, and possibly twelve, burglaries to him during

September in Byron Road, Wealdstone, alone, and others in Harrow and Wembley. It calculated that he must by this point have committed between fifty and sixty crimes.

At just before 3 am, a Mrs Welsh was woken from her slumbers by a noise. As her head began to clear, she realised it sounded like a key being turned in a lock, and she urgently shook her husband awake. He leapt out of bed and rushed to the door – only to find that, like the 'trouser robbery' victims earlier in the month, he and his wife were locked in their own bedroom. Mr Welsh's niece was staying with them, and his cry of 'Burglars!' from behind the door brought her scurrying out onto the landing, where she saw that the key was still in the lock on the outside of her uncle's bedroom door.

Once released, Mr Welsh hurried out to see what had been taken, only to stumble over his own clothes, which had been removed from his bedside and left strewn about the landing. Flannelfoot had helped himself to £10 from the trouser pockets, and had then rifled through drawers downstairs before coming across Mrs Welsh's handbag, from which he obtained £15. In another house he found no money, but snacked on cheese and bananas from the larder. A pair of boots taken from one house were discovered in an old sack in a neighbour's garden.

A few days later he was working his way along Kingsley Road, South Harrow. Burglary must have stimulated his appetite because here he helped himself to a meal in one house, while elsewhere he robbed yet another widow, this time of her savings of 'several pounds'.

Once again, we note that Kingsley Road is virtually round the corner from the South Harrow Tube Station, and Bolton Road is no more than a mile from the North Harrow station. However, it is likely that Vickers either had further jobs in mind elsewhere, or found it more convenient to make his return journey home from a different station. A boy's bicycle stolen from a Kingsley Road address was later found in Hanwell, 5 or 6 miles to the south, an approximately thirty-minute cycle ride and a place with its own overground station. John Horwell, who was the then chief constable and who will figure again as the story develops, said in his memoir *Horwell of the Yard* that he believed the Flannelfoot method was to scout around before he burgled his first property to find a bike. Then as he went from one back garden to another, breaking in, he would haul the machine over the fence each time so it was there ready should he need to make a quick getaway.

It was again reported that Flannelfoot had, on most occasions, gained entry by drilling into the frame of kitchen or scullery windows, through which he fed a wire and used it to push or pull open the latch. 'Many residents,' bemoaned the *Uxbridge Gazette*, 'are now not leaving loose valuables or money downstairs.' But as we know, Flannelfoot had enough nerve to go upstairs and creep round the beds of sleeping people, so this precaution would not necessarily be enough. 'It would be a real source of satisfaction if he could be "laid by the heels",' said the *Gazette*, pointing out that such losses were particularly hard on the poor and only moderately well-off.

In fact, it seems that Vickers did come the closest so far to being 'laid by the heels' during his daring robbery from the Welshes' bedroom. Mr Welsh's cries woke neighbours; curtains were thrown back, windows thrown open. One person observed a man climb a fence and make off across some wasteland. But despite local rumours that he had been caught, Flannelfoot had long vanished into the darkness before any pursuit could be made. Either on this occasion or slightly later, still on Butler Road, Harrow, a man arrived home in the early hours of 19 October and saw a light on in his hall. He woke a friend and they went to investigate, only to discover that the intruder had fled out of the rear of the property just as they had entered the front.

Flannelfoot appeared to be getting more and more audacious, and surely it was only a matter of time before he pushed his luck too far? Sure enough, within a few months of his latest spree, the press would announce that the police had finally got their man.

But had they?

Chapter 6

The Man with One Leg

It was New Year's Day 1926 when Detective Inspector Hambrook, rather than recovering from the celebrations of the night before, was admitted through a police cordon outside 58 Arlington Road, Camden Town. He climbed the stairs to the top floor and cautiously peered into one of the bedrooms. He had been told what to expect by the uniformed officers who had already attended the scene, but it must still have been a shocking and harrowing sight.

A 16-year-old girl, dressed in her nightclothes, lay lifeless on the floor; her head rested in a pool of blood, and there was a stocking tied tightly round her slender neck. On the heavily bloodstained bed lay a stout poker and part of a broken pair of fire-tongs. Stepping carefully into the room with a police surgeon who had joined him, Hambrook examined the bed more closely. The end of the eiderdown was saturated in blood, as were the sheets beneath, and there was a bloodstained overcoat on a chair by the end of the bed. Hambrook went through the pockets and produced a set of keys on a keyring. A small amount of loose change lay about the bed, and there was more on the floor beside the corpse. The detective moved over to the window, pulling the curtain back to reveal a large piece of broken tong which corresponded with the smaller part he had seen earlier.

Hambrook believed that the tongs had inflicted fatal head injuries. However, although the girl had certainly been savagely struck, the doctor thought the cause of death would prove to be strangulation.

The victim of the brutal attack was Polly Walker; her mother had already alerted the police to the identity of the person she felt sure was the killer, and told them where he lived. Taking the keys he had found at the scene, Hambrook made the two-minute walk round the corner to No. 32 Delancey Street. The suspect wasn't present, but Hambrook was able to confirm that the keys did fit the door. Acting on a hunch or information received, Hambrook returned to Arlington Road and tried the keys in the front door there. After much trial and error, he discovered that one of them, with a little deft wiggling, could have been used to open it. The man on the run was Ewen Stitchell, who was passing himself off by the fanciful name of Eugene de Vere. He had been a friend of the Walker family for a short time, albeit a troublesome one. The hunt was on to find him.

Mr W.E. Sims was an air force man currently staying at a small temperance hotel in Hitchin, Hertfordshire, called The Acacias. On Saturday, 2 January a man arrived at the hotel seeking accommodation, and was allocated the shared room in which Sims was staying. The newcomer wore Oxford bags, horn-rimmed glasses, and was clean-shaven. What struck Sims as odd was that the man didn't take his glasses off when he went to bed. When Sims read about the Camden murder in the following day's paper, which featured a picture of the wanted man, he became suspicious. The suspect in the photo wore a moustache whereas the new arrival was clean-shaven, but otherwise there was a strong similarity: around 5 feet 9 inches, light brown hair, slim build, mid- to late-twenties. Sims discreetly approached the landlady, and they devised a plan.

The newcomer had busied himself with a crossword puzzle, and the landlady hovered near him, engaging him in small-talk in order to make sure he stayed in the house. Sims, meanwhile, slipped out and rushed to the police station. Sergeant Saunders hurried back with the air force man, and they found the suspicious character still sitting in a chair working on his crossword. Saunders sidled up and sat in a chair next to him on his left-hand side. By this time, descriptions of Stitchell/de Vere had been circulated, and the constable knew that he had a wooden left leg. Three times he surreptitiously bumped the man's left leg with his foot, and when the crossword puzzler didn't seem to notice, the policeman was sure he had his man.

Now, it seems that there must have been a little more to this scenario than meets the eye. We don't know whether Saunders was in plain clothes or not, but either way it would be odd for a person not to at least take notice when someone came to sit close beside him. And wooden leg or not, it's almost impossible to believe that Stitchell wouldn't have felt the effect of the knocks, no matter how gentle, at the point where the prosthesis was fitted to his thigh. My guess is that he was putting on an act akin to burying his head in the sand – *if I don't take any notice of you, you might just go away*. But there was no chance of that, and Stitchell was marched off to Hitchin police station. Inspector Hambrook was summoned, and after satisfying himself that it was the right man, he formally charged him, saying, 'I am arresting you for the wilful murder of Polly Walker.' Stitchell merely complained that his artificial leg was hurting him, as, being unable to afford bus or train fare, he had walked the 32 miles from Camden. Hambrook escorted his prisoner back to London by train that same evening.

The story that emerged was that de Vere, as they knew him, had befriended Polly and had started to visit the house on a regular basis, soon becoming acquainted with the family, including her widowed mother. De Vere, who spoke with a pronounced Scottish accent, was an unemployed tailor currently trying to eke out a living by busking with an accordion outside West End theatres. The kindly Mrs Walker took pity on him and often gave him food. Relations between the three initially grew quite amiable. Things changed when Polly became friendly with another young man. De Vere and Polly were not in a 'relationship' of any kind beyond friendship, but he quickly became jealous and began hounding her, and even turned on her mother when she upbraided him about his behaviour; the ensuing row resulted in Mrs Walker telling him to leave and not come back again.

Early on the morning of the murder, Mrs Walker left the house while Polly was still in bed, locking the front door behind her. The building was actually a lodging house run by Mrs Walker, and a few minutes later another woman who was staying there heard a scream followed by retreating footsteps. She recognised it as de Vere from his distinctive gait. For some reason she didn't think to investigate, but witnesses in the street saw the limping man making off in a hurry. When Mrs Walker returned she found the front door unlocked, and before she even went inside she had a chilling premonition that something terrible had happened. Sadly, she was right.

That Polly had been killed by strangulation was later confirmed. The blows had probably knocked her unconscious before the stocking was tied round her neck, since there were no signs of a struggle. It later emerged that de Vere had been sneaking belongings from the house for some time and pawning them to line his own pockets. It was Hambrook whose inquiries led to de Vere being exposed as Ewen Stitchell, originally of Brechin.[1]

There was a dramatic incident just before the inquest. As Stitchell was being led by two police officers from the taxi they had taken to the St Pancras Coroner's Court, a man pushed free from the onlookers on the pavement and floored the suspect with a single blow to the jaw, shouting, 'You [expletive – we don't know what word he used], you have murdered my sister!' Polly's brother Frank was restrained by other officers, while Stitchell was carried inside. Hambrook was later to comment, 'I cannot pretend I was sorry to see the scoundrel knocked down …'

---

1. He was commonly referred to as 'John' Stitchell, and even Hambrook got it slightly wrong in his memoirs, calling him 'Stitchwell'. His real full name, as it appears in various official records from before the murder, was Ewen Anderson Stitchell.

When the case eventually went to trial, Stitchell's story was that he had visited the house when Polly was alone, they ended up quarrelling, she had called him a 'beast' and had bitten his finger, and he had run after her and hit her with the tongs. His feeble defence was that at the time he didn't know what he was doing, nor did he recall subsequently using the poker on her – which makes his 'recollection' of the finale to this tale all the more surprising. In his version of events, he simply laid her on the bed, picked up the stocking and tied it round her neck, while she said, 'Eugene, I love you forever more.' A penny dreadful author would have been proud of such a scene.

Unsurprisingly, the jury were unmoved by his melodramatic account and found Stitchell guilty after a short deliberation. The only possible sentence at the time was death, though the jury had added a recommendation of mercy to their verdict on the grounds of 'strong provocation and the peculiar mentality of the prisoner'. The sentence was referred to the Court of Criminal Appeal, but it did not save Stitchell's neck. He was hanged at Pentonville prison, and Walter Hambrook's last duty as far as this case went was the gruesome task of attending the execution and formally identifying the body afterwards.

Chapter 7

The Lure of Pastures New

In November 1923, Flannelfoot struck again, this time breaking in to a number of properties on Carlton Avenue, Kenton, in the district of Harrow. Perhaps feeling lazy or in a hurry, the houses he chose were within a stone's throw of Kenton Station on this occasion and no bicycle was taken. Otherwise, it was the usual scenario: small, low-value items and loose change. He again filled his belly while he was at it – indulging in what was described as a 'hearty meal' in one house. At another property, he repeated his bold tactic of entering the bedroom of a sleeping occupant and taking money from trouser pockets – the wrappings around his shoes no doubt ensuring that he was able to work in near-silence. However, the fourpence he obtained from the trousers may well have made him think it was barely worth the risk on this occasion at least.

But then, on 12 December 1924, a headline in the crime columns of the *Uxbridge Gazette* triumphantly declared:

FLANNELFOOT CAUGHT

On an early December morning in 1924, in New Malden, south-west London, Hilda Baker's husband slipped out of bed and left his wife dozing while he readied himself to set off for work at Covent Garden. It wasn't long before Hilda was woken by someone touching her face. Believing her husband had returned for some reason and was playing a trick on her, she sleepily groaned, 'Don't play about ...' There was no reply, and before she could even think of dropping back off to sleep, through her closed eyes she was aware of a torchlight being aimed at her face. Blinking against the bright light, she saw a silhouetted figure standing over her.

'Put your hands behind you,' he growled.

She did as he ordered, and the man proceeded to tie her wrists together. 'If you make any noise, I will knock you senseless. I will knife you.'

It is likely that he had staked out the house on previous occasions and knew who lived there and their habits, so was aware that Hilda's husband left for work very early. The cord he used to tie Hilda had been cut from a washing line in the garden before entering the property.

Leaving Hilda tightly bound in her own bed, the intruder prowled round the bedroom looking in drawers, eventually amassing goods and cash to the value of £15. Satisfied with his pickings, to Hilda's horror the man came and sat beside her on the bed. When he attempted to kiss her, she struggled against him and he turned rougher. He kneeled on the bed before her, and when she tried to cry for help he clamped his hand to her mouth, swearing violently.

'I'll have you before I go!' he threatened. Luckily for Hilda, he either lost his nerve or it was an empty threat, and before long he said, 'The time's getting on. I shall have to leave you, you little devil, after all.'

Hilda, who hadn't long been married, said she hoped he hadn't taken any of her wedding presents.

'I've only taken your money.'

To her intense relief, the man walked out of the bedroom and went downstairs, but he still wasn't finished – she heard him exploring the dining room for more money. While he did so, she struggled with the cord round her wrists and managed to free herself. She ran into the bathroom and locked the door, then threw the window open and screamed for help. At that moment, she saw the burglar pedalling away on a bike.

No one seemed to be responding to her cries, so she slipped her dressing gown and shoes on and ran out of the house, soon finding a policeman up the road.[1] This led to Detective Inspector Walker coming to examine the scene of the crime, where he found that the burglar had bored a hole in the window frame of the scullery door to access the catch.

'He made enquiries,' the press reported enigmatically, which must mean that he either recognised a known offender from Hilda's description or had received a tip-off. In company with Detective Sergeant Loring, he went straight to a specific address in Shepherd's Bush some 10 miles north of New Malden, where he found his suspect, whom he knew by name, in bed. When Inspector Walker told him he would have to come along to take part in an identity parade, the man leapt out of bed 'in a fighting mode', but he soon calmed down and accompanied the officers to Malden Police Station. When he was searched, officers found his coat had a home-made inner pocket made of blue serge, about 10 inches long and 2 inches wide. When he was asked what it was for, he replied defiantly, 'You find out.'

The police gathered together seven other men and lined the arrested man up among them for Hilda to inspect. Without hesitating, she went right up and touched him on the shoulder. 'That's the man.'

---

1. What are the chances of that happening today?!

'The police believe that Flannel Foot and the man now under arrest at Maldon [*sic*] are one and the same person because of the similarity of the modus operandi,' declared the *Uxbridge Gazette*. And there were some very good reasons for both the police and the public to think and hope that they *had* finally caught the notorious burglar, whose true identity they didn't yet know. There were indeed some strong similarities to his methods, such as drilling a hole in order to open a window latch, prowling in a bedroom containing a sleeping occupant, and escaping on a bicycle. And although by far the majority of Flannelfoot's burglaries took place north of the Thames, New Malden near Kingston upon Thames was only a few miles from territory in which he had operated previously. But the Flannelfoot we have come to know took pains to *avoid* waking people, and had certainly never made threats of violence.

In fact, the man they had caught was George Humphries, aged 39, described euphemistically as a 'dealer'. He pleaded not guilty when his case came to trial, but was convicted on two counts: burglary, for which he received five years' penal servitude; and assaulting Hilda Baker, which added twelve months with hard labour, to run concurrently.

The search for Flannelfoot was back on.

Vickers, who at this time was living at 151 Lyndhurst Road, Wood Green (a very similar-looking area and type of house to the places he mostly targeted) seems to have lain low for a lengthy period, because there were no reports in his old haunts of crimes bearing the Flannelfoot hallmarks until the late summer of 1927. It would be unusual for a habitual criminal like Vickers to suddenly and completely stop working like that, and I would suggest that the answer lies in one of two alternatives.

It's not impossible that, just as with his first arrest in 1910 when he passed himself off as 'Henry Williams', he *had* been caught at around the same time as Humphries, using yet another assumed name. A short prison sentence would then explain his disappearing off the radar.

The second and more likely possibility is that he worked much further afield for some reason, perhaps fearing that local police were getting used to his ways and might be lying in wait. The police – and, thanks to the press, even the British public as a whole – were by now aware of Flannelfoot and his methods, and he would surely have been aware of this. As we shall see later, any crimes of even a loosely similar nature (and occasionally even some that were barely similar at all) tended to either be ascribed to Flannelfoot directly, or were described as being 'Flannelfoot' in nature.

There don't seem to be reports in any part of the country between the beginning of 1925 and late May of 1927 of burglaries suspected to have been committed by Flannelfoot. On 10 April 1927, Scotland Yard received a phone call from the Stoke-on-Trent police regarding several break-ins the previous night which bore some of the hallmarks associated with Vickers. Did they know whether he was currently active in the Metropolitan area?

The note of the call eventually found its way into the hands of Inspector Hambrook, who told his Stoke colleagues that 'Nothing is known respecting him since his last conviction of January 1911…' (i.e. they knew he had been active, but not where he was).

When Flannelfoot did strike again, he was back in familiar territory: Harrow, more specifically, Kenton Park Crescent. This was a recently completed estate of the kind we know Flannelfoot preferred – and he happened to be living during a boom time for such property developments.

After the First World War, David Lloyd George famously promised a 'land fit for heroes', and the government provided money to local authorities in a move designed to stimulate a big increase in the number of houses being built. As the 1920s wore on, but especially into the 1930s, there was a massive expansion in house-building, and even today, very many of us in Britain are living in homes built at that time.[2] Existing districts expanded (by the time Walter Hambrook retired, Ealing, where he lived, had doubled in size since he had moved there), and new estates were created.

The kind of new developments that Vickers headed for on his night-time expeditions were created to house people fleeing smoky, overcrowded London. People who had been living in overcrowded rented rooms discovered that at a stretch, they could afford to own their own three-bedroomed house with a small deposit (sometimes as little as £1!) and a modest, low-interest repayment plan after that.

There was even a name for one such region, invented by the Metropolitan Railway, the company transporting people to and from the North-West London area prized by Flannelfoot: 'Metroland'. This was allied with a surge in picturesque publications by developers and those railway companies with new housing along their lines, all designed to lure Londoners. In 1930, George Moss & Son tempted prospective buyers with houses around a village green with a 'beautiful old church, a little moss-grown churchyard, long vistas of green fields'.[3] This was Northolt, where Flannelfoot plied his own particular trade on several occasions. Various gimmicks and inducements were employed to attract people to see new houses, such as vouchers for trains, and sometimes

---

2. By the end of the 1930s, one family in three was living in an interwar house. *Findmypast.com.*
3. *Thirties Housing*, Routledge Library Editions.

cars were even laid on to ferry people from the station to the new estate. For those thinking of moving to Bexleyheath, south of the Thames, a free rail season ticket was available for a limited period. Vickers was living there at the time his son Jack was born, and his father and brother also had homes there – is it possible that it was such offers that brought them there? Is it even possible that it was Vickers' early visits to his family that opened his eyes to the attractions of such locations as potential targets?

The pleasant imagery conveyed by the developers and railway companies wasn't misleading; areas which are today indistinguishable from any other part of the Greater London sprawl were then more village-like, and some, such as Flannelfoot favourite Greenford, actually were still villages, surrounded by pleasant countryside.

It wasn't just the scenery that developers had in their armoury to tempt Londoners. The houses themselves had modern amenities, the likes of which many of those moving in would never have had before. (These included novelties such as third bedrooms, bathrooms and inside toilets.) A Mrs Vaughan achieved her goal of escaping Brixton for a 'nicer life' in 1934 by securing a Swiss Chalet-style house in New Malden.[4] The fact that Flannelfoot had paid the area a visit in the past and would do so in the future probably wouldn't have put Mrs Vaughan off buying her dream home, even if she had known.

The houses were built on greenfield sites on the periphery of the metropolis, and the very effective marketing campaign helped to make them very desirable for city folk, especially those living in the grimmer and more run-down districts of the capital. Both the developers and the railway companies, whose services would-be commuters would use, made effective use of attractively illustrated advertising, complete with bucolic imagery and the lure of moving to the 'country'. The builders weren't selling 'houses' but 'cottages' and 'villas', often with the mock Tudor design much derided by modern architects but preferred by countless home-owners to the featureless, soulless homes that were usually the alternative at such prices.

Other criticism of the style of such urban developments came from writers and thinkers of the day. Poet Hilaire Belloc called the homes 'Miserable sheds of painted tin/Gaunt villas, planted round with stunted trees'. Graham Greene was of the opinion that 'red-bricked, Tudor-gabled, half-timbered suburban homes' represented 'something worse than the meanness of poverty – the meanness of spirit'. J.B. Priestley wrote of 'miles of semi-detached bungalows, all with their little garages, wireless sets, their periodicals about film stars, their

4. *Daily Mail*, 29 January 2010, extracted from *The Thirties: An Intimate History of Britain* by Juliet Gardiner (HarperPress, 2010).

swimming costumes and tennis rackets and dancing shoes', but this sounds more like snobbery than constructive criticism of the new estates themselves. It would be nice to know what kind of areas and properties those well-to-do gentlemen lived in themselves. No doubt the people who were escaping from cramped London terraced housing would have been happy to hand their old homes over to the critics. The new estates provided cheap, decent houses for the masses – something modern Britain, ironically, has been crying out for, for decades.

John Betjeman seemed to have a special hatred of Slough, writing in his eponymous poem: 'Come friendly bombs, and fall on Slough/It isn't fit for humans now'. Which, appearing as it did shortly before the Second World War, was unfortunate timing, though he can hardly be blamed for that and, in fact, he is said to have later regretted writing it. And in later years, almost as if in an act of penance, he presented a more sympathetic, almost affectionate view in a 1973 BBC documentary (called, appropriately enough, *Metro-Land*) which quickly became a classic of its kind and is still repeated to this day.

One of the things that attracted Vickers to such places was that even those estates tacked on to the edge of greater London would have had fields and open land on one or more of their borders, unlit at night, of course – ideal initially as a place for lurking when planning a raid, and later for disappearing into in case of emergency. As we shall see elsewhere, there was something about the window frames of these new-builds which made them relatively easy to penetrate with a thin instrument. And although Vickers eschewed the diamonds and paintings of the truly wealthy, he knew that the families moving into these new estates weren't poor, and did possess modest valuables and ready cash, hence his arrival in Harrow on 15 May 1927.

Flannelfoot was back with a bang, breaking into eight houses on that single night. The poor occupants had only been living in their new homes for six or seven weeks – not the ideal start to life on Kenton Park Crescent. In every case, a hole was drilled or bored in the window frame to facilitate clean and almost silent access. Baby clothes were taken from a washing line in one of the gardens to cover the burglar's footwear, and found discarded in the last house visited. Small amounts of money and jewellery were taken, along with a bike, and the press were quick to highlight the similarities with Flannelfoot's methods and mark him down as the likely suspect. In fact, he may have increased his total had it not been for the presence of dogs in some of the homes. He visited four adjoining properties, missed two out, then entered the next four. The two which were spared were the only ones with dogs.

Some of the more flowery descriptions of Flannelfoot (including one from John Horwell, who would in time be the chief constable in overall charge of the team assigned to catching Flannelfoot) claim that dogs were no obstacle to him – he could 'charm' them. But there is no solid evidence for this and it sounds fanciful (as do many of the claims in his memoir, unfortunately). There are some potential Flannelfoot burglaries in houses where there were dogs which didn't raise the alarm, but also ones like those above where he seems to have avoided them solely *because* there were dogs. We shall see that there was a case in later years where an owner believed their dog had been poisoned or drugged to keep it quiet. Vickers may have been able to befriend them once inside, but most dogs would surely have barked before he got the chance, as soon as they heard him entering.

(The only thing we can be sure of is that his favourite type of dog ran very quickly around a cinder track in pursuit of a mechanical hare.)

Dogs aside, perhaps Vickers made enough during that one night to give himself another break, because things once again went rather quiet again for a time. He doesn't seem to have returned to action again until the following year, 1928.

Chapter 8

The Margate Mystery

By 1929, Walter Hambrook was a chief inspector and head of the Flying Squad. Having been one of the founder members of the Squad when its total strength was six men and one inspector, he was now in charge of a unit of fifty, with further recruitment imminent. It wasn't long before he was involved in a tricky and complicated case that would occupy a good deal of his time.

In what became known as The Margate Mystery, the body of 63-year-old Rosaline Fox was found after a fire in her room at the Hotel Metropole in that south-eastern coastal town. At first it was assumed to be a case of accidental death. It was said that the woman, who had seemed to be in robust health when she first stayed in Margate, looked sickly in the days before her death, and had fainted on one occasion. The doctor who examined her body was happy to confirm that she had died from suffocation as a result of the dense smoke, so no post-mortem was carried out. The inquest agreed with his findings, and Mrs Fox's body was transported to her original home in Fransham, Norfolk, for burial.

However, the local police began to hear rumours that all was not as it might seem, and an insurance investigator also questioned the accidental death theory. The local police took the drastic step of asking Scotland Yard for their help and expertise.

Writing after his retirement, Hambrook explained that at that time the Yard had a rota consisting of pairings of chief inspectors and sergeants to be on standby should a provincial force request assistance on a big case. This is how Hambrook and Detective Sergeant Ambrose Ayto found themselves driving down to Margate in November of that year.

Hambrook learned that hotel staff had been alerted to smoke emanating from beneath Mrs Fox's door at around midnight, and had hurried to investigate. They found the room full of thick smoke, and Rosaline lying on the bed. Local police were summoned and upon arrival attempted to resuscitate her, but were unsuccessful. It appeared to them that her clothes had been placed too close to the gas fire and had caught fire, but her son Sidney, aged 30, would later say he believed the fire had been caused by a newspaper she had been reading before going to bed.

In fact, Sidney himself quickly became the prime suspect for what the police soon suspected to be a case of murder. Mrs Fox's son was already in prison on remand after being arrested over unpaid bills in hotels and lodging houses. Hambrook immediately recognised the name. Sidney Fox not only had 'previous' when it came to matters of fraud, but by a remarkable coincidence he had been arrested by Hambrook himself thirteen years earlier: during the war, he had masqueraded as a Royal Flying Corps officer, paying bills with cheques he himself had forged. For now, though, Hambrook made sure not to see Fox or let him know he was on the case. One thing of interest to Hambrook was insurance policies which had been taken out with three separate companies not long before Rosaline's death, but first Hambrook and Sergeant Ayto visited the hotel to see the room where Rosaline had died for themselves.

By now, it had been cleared and cleaned, but Hambrook carried out a detailed inspection anyway – and behind the gas fire he found a screwed-up lead capsule from a port bottle. Sidney Fox had been staying in the room next door to his mother, and in there Hambrook found a half-bottle of port hidden in a cupboard. To Hambrook, who thanks to his previous dealings with Fox knew about his criminal history, these seemingly unimportant things took on great significance. Fox had once managed to worm his way into the affections of a very rich Australian woman who was living in Southsea, and within a short time had not only talked her into taking out a life insurance policy with him as the beneficiary, but to make out a will with him as the sole inheritor of her fortune.

One night soon afterwards, Fox plied the woman with drink, then turned on the gas tap in her room as she slept. By good fortune something woke her before she succumbed to the fumes. She survived, but even though Hambrook was sure that Fox had been behind it, there had been insufficient evidence to build a case against him. Now, though, Hambrook felt sure that Rosaline Fox was the victim of the same trick – and fate had provided him with another crack at his man.

Not put off by the fact that his crime scene had been completely sanitised, Hambrook tracked down the tip where everything had been dumped, and with the help of a team of council workers managed to retrieve the charred and dirty clothing and other items. Calling upon the recollections of all who had witnessed the scene, he went about reassembling everything as it would have been when Rosaline's body was discovered, and had the whole scene photographed for his own research as well as with a view to a future court case.

His next job was to work with the local fire chief to put under the microscope Sidney Fox's version of how the fire came about. He had claimed that his mother had been sitting reading a newspaper in an armchair by the gas fire and must have left the paper too close to the fire when she went to bed. It had ignited, and the fire had spread while she was asleep. But after examining the scene and carrying out their own experiments, Hambrook and the fire officer were of one mind: the fire had been started deliberately, and it had started *under* the armchair. The area between the chair and the fire showed no evidence of burning at all.

Hambrook's next step was to apply for an exhumation of the body, as well as requesting that Sir Bernard Spilsbury should carry out a post-mortem.

Permission to dig up Rosaline's body was granted, and Hambrook rendezvoused with Spilsbury in London. The latter drove them both to Norfolk in his own car, where they arrived at noon on a mild November day. Hambrook, Spilsbury, several local constables and others gathered by the as yet unmarked grave in the picturesque, isolated churchyard, and watched as the gravediggers began the unpleasant task of undoing their earlier work. The coffin was taken to a disused schoolroom, which had been converted into a temporary mortuary so that Spilsbury could commence his work. Poignantly, this very place had, in happier days, been attended not only by Rosaline as a child, but also her own four children after her.

Spilsbury's investigation turned the whole case on its head. He found no evidence of soot or smoke in Rosaline's airway, and no carbon monoxide in her blood. What he did find traces of, with Hambrook and the Chief Constable of Norfolk looking on, was a big bruise on her larynx, and another on her tongue – she had died, he said, not from the effects of the fire, but manual strangulation. The external bruise was from pressure to that area, and the injury to her tongue was the result of her biting her own tongue as she fought for her life.

It was an eventful drive back to Margate in more ways than one. First, Spilsbury took a wrong turn as it got dark and they found themselves driving along narrow, winding country lanes which took them deeper and deeper into the Norfolk countryside. Looking for someone to give them directions, the only person they could find out and about at that time of night proved to be what Hambrook described as 'a true simpleton. We could get nothing out of him except vague conversation in the broadest of Norfolk dialects'. Hambrook was reduced to shinning up a series of roadside signposts and striking matches to get some idea of where they were and which direction they needed to take.

The more important development along the way back to London was when Spilsbury got to play detective. At one point, he suddenly turned to Hambrook and asked, 'Where are the old lady's false teeth?' Hambrook told him they hadn't found any teeth, but Spilsbury insisted that she must have been wearing them. The body he had examined was toothless, but when she was strangled, she had bitten her tongue. Hambrook speculated that the pressure from her gums could have made the mark, but Spilsbury was positive that they were tooth marks.

Thus, when he returned to Margate Hambrook focused on the false teeth. Not only did they back up Spilsbury's theory that she had bitten her tongue while being strangled, but their absence from her mouth indicated that someone had interfered with her body after death. He tracked down a chambermaid who had found them in a basin, and they were retrieved as an exhibit. (There was no mention of whether the teeth might have been removed by those first on the scene who tried to resuscitate Rosaline, but Hambrook was far too clever and experienced not to have taken this into account, so presumably his enquiries ruled this out.)

To further bolster Spilsbury's findings, Hambrook next made himself a guinea pig in a rather extreme and unpleasant experiment. He, Sergeant Ayto and some local officers found a derelict building with a room of a similar size to that in which Rosaline had been killed. Here, they started a fire much like the one that had broken out on the night of the murder, then stood steadfastly breathing in the smoke just as Rosaline would have done had she been alive when it started.

After standing their ground for as long as they could bear it, they staggered out coughing, spluttering, blowing their noses and clearing their throats. The resultant black sputum, absent from Rosaline's airways, confirmed that it would have been impossible for her to have been alive and breathing when the fire broke out.

Hambrook and Ayto now set about tracking down as many people as they could who might be able to further their enquiries. They learned: that Sidney Fox had complained of the cold in the hotel rooms he and his mother had originally been allocated, ensuring that they were moved to ones with gas fires; that a few days before Rosaline's death, Fox was known to have read a newspaper story about a woman who had burned to death while sitting reading a paper close to a gas fire; that the foolish Fox had, when approaching insurance companies, asked questions such as 'Will the policy cover my mother in the event of her being drowned in the bath?' and 'Will it cover her if she dies as a result of ptomaine poisoning?'

Hambrook did a lot of travelling, visiting various towns Fox and his mother had stayed in recently, and everywhere he went he found that they had absconded without paying their bills. Whether Rosaline knew what was going on is a moot point, but it seems likely that her son was telling her he had settled the bill each time they moved on.

Hambrook finally decided he had amassed enough evidence to make his move. When he visited the remand prison to formally charge Fox with murder, the young man remained impassive upon seeing that the lead detective on the case was the same officer who had investigated him years previously, and simply murmured, 'I must consult my solicitor.'

At the trial, Fox remained composed and unwavering in his claims of innocence – even when, almost as if he had incurred the wrath of God, a thunderstorm of Biblical proportions broke out as he was speaking, nearly drowning out his words and eerily illuminating the courtroom with sporadic flashes of lightning.

The medical evidence of Spilsbury and other experts, although fiercely contested by the defence, carried the day. When sentence of death was passed on Fox, he simply bowed his head and muttered, 'Amen.' According to Hambrook, this was the first ever case in Britain where a son had murdered his mother for financial gain.

In 2021, the excellent BBC programme *Murder, Mystery and My Family*, in which two barristers re-examine historical murder cases, looked at the Rosaline Fox case. A pathologist pointed out that although Spilsbury saw a bruise on Mrs Fox's throat (the one on the tongue wasn't mentioned), others who also subsequently looked at the woman's body found no such bruising. It was stated that since bruising on a corpse doesn't dissipate or clear up, Spilsbury must have mistaken a rare but naturally occurring bruise-like phenomenon for the real thing, and that it had faded away or been masked by decomposition by the time the other pathologists examined the body. Present-day forensic investigators also decided that the fire had probably started accidentally, and that Rosaline died from existing heart problems, the fire being an unfortunate coincidence. However, it was not mentioned on the programme that at the trial her health was described as 'good', nor that Spilsbury found some 'disease of the arteries to the heart' which he believed to be not unusual for someone of her age, and had stated categorically that he did not believe it to have been the cause of her death. The day before Rosaline's death, her son had visited an insurance company to extend the deadline till midnight of the following day on one of several short-term policies which he had been taking out against his mother's accidental death over a period of weeks. Despite this fact, the programme concluded that Rosaline *had* died of natural causes and that Fox should have been found not guilty.

Spilsbury has his modern critics, but he had examined hundreds of corpses and was the leading expert of the day, and the programme, deliberately or otherwise, omitted certain pertinent facts. One was Fox's previous attempt to gas a victim. That is purely circumstantial, but for the programme not to mention that Spilsbury wasn't looking at the body of a recently expired person – his examination took place after an exhumation almost three weeks after death – was a significant oversight. Nor was there any reference to the bruised tongue or the missing false teeth. The opinion of those who examined the scene that the fire started *under* Rosaline's chair – hardly the sort of place one would expect – was also not brought to light.

Hambrook probably didn't mourn the passing of Fox when the sentence was carried out, but he certainly did that of Sergeant Ambrose Ayto, who fell ill and died a couple of years after this case: a man whom Hambrook said had been 'destined … to high rank' had he lived.

In September 1930, Hambrook was on his travels again, this time to Ramsgate, where he would face the challenge of what was described as his 'most baffling case' – and one of the biggest obstacles came in the form of the victim herself. He might, in fact, have called it his most *frustrating* case, since because of the obstacles he faced, the killer was never caught and it became one of his few unsolved murders.

Late one Saturday afternoon, 12-year-old Ellen Marvell was sent by her mother to buy something from the shop opposite, run by Margery Wren, a woman in her eighties. The shop should have been open at that time, but Ellen found the door locked. Peering through the glass, she saw the owner sitting in a chair in her back room. The girl rattled the door so as to jingle the bell which was hanging on the inside. Mrs Wren slowly raised herself from the chair and came to open up, but now the mystery only deepened.

She normally wore her hair up, beneath a cap, but this afternoon it was hanging loosely down her back. More significantly, young Ellen noticed cuts and bruises to her face, and blood trickling down. She asked Mrs Wren what the matter was, but the rather vacant shopkeeper barely seemed to hear the question, and simply asked Ellen what she had come to buy. Every time Ellen tried to explain what she wanted, Mrs Wren's replies were incoherent, and she eventually got down several boxes of goods so that she could choose for herself. Ellen hurried home to tell her father, and after going to see Mrs Wren for himself he called on the local doctor while sending Ellen to summon the police.

When questioned at the house and again at the hospital where she was taken, Margery Wren repeatedly insisted that she had fallen. Eventually, though, she admitted that she'd been attacked. She said a man had grabbed her by the throat and hit her about the head with her fire tongs. But all the pieces of the puzzle still weren't in place. When she was asked who had done it, she gave several names but none of them seemed like likely candidates and little she said by way of explanation seemed to make sense. The doctors felt sure she was holding something back.

'He's escaped,' she said at one point, 'and you'll never get him. He had a white bag.'

With little information to go on, and much of that contradictory and confused, Scotland Yard were asked to send assistance. Hambrook, along with Detective Sergeant Carson, arrived in Ramsgate three days after the attack. By now Mrs Wren's condition had deteriorated, and doctors told Hambrook that there was no point in trying to question her – she was on the brink of slipping into a coma from which she was unlikely to emerge. He was left to try to sort through the wildly differing statements the old woman had given to various officers and medics: to one she said she was alone, felt giddy and fell over; to another, that nobody had hit her as she had no enemies; then to the same officer, she proceeded to relate a tale of being attacked by two men.

When, before Hambrook's arrival, the chief constable himself tried to gently extract more details, asking her if she knew who had done it, she admitted that she did but refused to be pressed further. Hambrook would come to feel sure that Mrs Wren was protecting someone, but it's odd that the subject of concussion never seems to have come up as an explanation for these garbled stories.

The poor woman died the day after Hambrook and Carson arrived in town, and as he was prone to do, Hambrook arranged for Sir Bernard Spilsbury to come and carry out the post-mortem. The eminent doctor was soon able to rule out a fall as the cause of death. Margery Wren had been badly beaten, and he provided a list of injuries to her head and face, including fractures to bones near her windpipe which were suggestive of attempted strangulation. Hairs of a similar colour to Mrs Wren's were found on the fire tongs, and there was no doubt in Spilsbury's mind that this was the weapon which had caused the blows to her head.

Hambrook was left with two difficult tasks. The first was a search of the back room of the shop where she lived. Sadly, they discovered that Mrs Wren had let herself go in her final years. The place was so dirty and evil-smelling that even these hardened detectives had to spray disinfectant and vermin-killing agents around before they could linger there for any length of time. The other headache was following up on the pages and pages of notes recorded during her ramblings, including the list of named suspects: not all of whom lived locally. It was almost as if she had named everyone she knew or at least had seen on the day of her death. Hambrook even tracked down the man with the white bag Mrs Wren had accused – a soldier with his kit bag who was out and about in town that day. Like the others, though, he had a perfectly good alibi and was ruled out.

Although there simply wasn't enough to go on, Hambrook did eventually whittle the list of suspects down to three decent possibilities. He felt sure the killer was one of those three, whom he never named, but there was no evidence which would warrant pursuing any of them further. He did, though, remain adamant to the rest of his days that Mrs Wren knew his identity.

Chapter 9

An Epidemic of Flannel-footed Burglars

Flannelfoot fever was increasing towards the end of the 1920s and into the 1930s, and all sorts of burglaries or attempted break-ins led to speculation that the criminal of that nickname was behind them, even when there was little evidence to justify such claims. In August 1928 a number of unsuccessful break-ins occurred in Millet Road, Greenford. It was certainly Flannelfoot's patch, but unless he was losing his touch, they were probably the work of other nocturnal prowlers. The attempts to gain entry to several properties were noisy enough to wake occupants and set dogs barking; this sounds too crude for Flannelfoot, but concerns that it was him were not unreasonable, and one resident told the local press that 'We are not actually afraid but we don't like to feel there is someone prowling about at night. It is a pity that a trap cannot be set for him.'

The following month, however, a number of crimes committed very nearby were more justifiably attributed to Flannelfoot. Three houses on Kings Avenue, Greenford Park (Nos. 66, 74 and 78) were all broken into on the night of Friday, 21 September (a favoured Flannelfoot day) and into the early hours of Saturday morning. Probably starting with No. 78, he made his way in via the French windows and gave the house a thorough going-over, albeit for a fairly small return. Just over a pound in cash was taken, along with postage stamps, fountain pens and, somewhat bizarrely, a whistle and some hankies.

During the burglaries of the previous month which were put down to Flannelfoot but which may not have been his handiwork, barking dogs were one of the reasons for the failure. There is, however, one reason for thinking it just may have been Flannelfoot – and that he had learned a valuable lesson.

This is because there was a dog at No. 78, but not only didn't it bark, but it was ill all the following day. The owners, who had only lived in the house for a week, suspected that their pet had been poisoned or sedated by the intruder.

Two doors down at No. 74, home of Mr C. Elton, Flannelfoot had used one of the tools from his kit to force open a rear dining room window. He seems to have been foiled on this occasion, since despite an extensive search there was nothing of worth in the dining room, and the internal door leading to the rest of the house was locked. Perhaps believing that breaking it open would be likely to wake anyone asleep upstairs, he moved on, taking with him only a knife, which he left behind inside No. 66 after using it to force entry. Again, the house was thoroughly searched, but little was taken – not even, according to the owner, small items that might have been worth selling on. It was unusual for Flannelfoot to ignore minor articles, but by now he would have been at work in the street for a good while and perhaps felt he was pushing his luck – something he rarely did. In order to escape, he stole, in his customary fashion, a bicycle and pedalled off into the night. What he didn't realise in the darkness was that it had a puncture; it was found abandoned just over a mile away in a garden – ironically enough, near the police station. Looking at his route, it could be that he was making his way to South Greenford Railway Station, or, further still in the same direction, the Greenford tube station.

Just over a year later, in October 1929, the *West Middlesex Gazette* alerted its readers to 'Burglarious Entries into Three Northolt Houses', complete with 'The Interesting Career of a Cigarette Case'. It cited Flannelfoot as the culprit, calling him 'the sinister nightbird whose exploits about that district during the last year or two form a formidable list'. The robberies, the paper said, featured the 'usual wrapping of feet ... the silent and thorough ransacking of ground floor rooms, the curious taste displayed in the choice of articles for removal, the theft of a bicycle from an outhouse, and its subsequent abandonment', which all pointed to the notorious criminal everyone was talking about.

This spree featured three consecutive houses on Church Road, very close to his earlier Greenford raids, and the bike referred to in the piece was later found in Southall. This was the scene of at least one of his prior crimes, and close to where he had once previously left another getaway bike – almost certainly because it was close to whatever form of public transport he preferred to take him the 16 or so miles back to his then home in Wood Green.

He probably was heard during his burglary in one of the properties. A Mr Jones was disturbed by a sound during the night, but assumed it must be another member of the family who couldn't sleep. When he came down in the morning, he saw obvious signs that someone had been inside, searching, but he couldn't see an obvious method of entry. It was only later that he realised the intruder had forced the lock to a rear door, but had then taken the trouble to put the disc back in place that protected the keyhole, thus in a sense covering his tracks. Flannelfoot did the same thing at the next house, but although it sounds clever, in reality it's hard to see what he hoped to gain by this. It delayed discovery of his method of entry, but it didn't buy him any extra escape time – in fact, it extended the time he spent at work – and his means of entry was bound to have been discovered eventually anyway. From Mr Jones's house Flannelfoot took a 'Druidical emblem' and broke into a child's money box to help himself to a few shillings' worth of threepenny pieces. He again ignored things that did have some monetary value, yet took books which Mr Jones said were virtually worthless. Perhaps he just liked reading.

Then there was the Holmesian-sounding mystery of the silver cigarette case. Flannelfoot had found and examined this item in one of the other houses he visited, the home of a Mr Walden. However, rather than take it he left it open on a table – and it transpired that this article had an interesting past. It had been a gift to Mr Walden to mark his army service in Mesopotamia and had an inscription inside to that effect. It had been stolen in another burglary a year previously, but three months later it came back into his possession when some unknown person tossed it into his garden and vanished. The *West Middlesex Gazette* had reported on the case at the time, and now speculated that the original burglar had read about the great sentimental value it held for Mr Walden, and of the way he had served his country, and had felt moved to return it to its rightful owner.

But this idea could, without stretching plausibility too far, be taken further. Is it possible that Vickers, an ex-army man himself, had read about the earlier theft, recognised what he was holding in his hands and found himself unable to subject Mr Walden to yet another loss of his precious memento? We shall never know, but it's an interesting scenario, and if true would add to our knowledge of Vickers as a man. But this idea could even be taken a step further – what if Vickers recognised that cigarette case because he *was* the man who had stolen it previously? The original theft did happen on a Friday, but on the other hand there are a few aspects to it which would have been completely out of character for him. Not only did the original criminal initially try to force open the *front* door, but he did so in the early evening. Vickers, to the best of our knowledge, operated exclusively late at night or in the early hours; he rarely, if ever, attempted to enter premises from the street at the front, where, of course, the possibility of being seen, no matter what time of the night or day, was that much greater.

The person who first took the cigarette case may have been keeping watch on the house because he pounced soon after Mrs Walden had popped out to do some shopping. In fact, the house backed on to the grounds of an unoccupied old rectory, which again brings to mind Flannelfoot and his liking for such uninhabited spaces for reconnaissance and escape. Whoever *was* responsible on that first occasion, they got away with a coat which was to have been a Christmas present for the Waldens' daughter, a small amount of cash, and, of course, the silver cigarette case.

'It's a bit heavy,' said Mr Walden ruefully after it was returned to him, 'but I shall carry it with me in the future.'

Back to the current Flannelfoot raids, mindful of the rash of burglaries in the Northolt area, some residents were reportedly barricading doors at night. But one resident, Mr Ferrie, took the opposite approach. He deliberately left his bedroom door wide open – if anyone was in his house, he wanted to hear them at work and tackle them. Perhaps he was a heavy sleeper because his strategy didn't work. He came downstairs one morning to find his dining room floor covered with documents and papers 'thick as the driven snow'. Twenty-eight shillings had been taken, along with an opal ring and two watches.

Baby clothes, used for Flannelfoot's usual precautionary measures, were taken from the Jones residence and found in the garden of a Mr Denison, and Mr Walden of cigarette case fame became the gainer of a dirty towel for whom an owner was never found.

All in all, it was a typical night's work for Flannelfoot.

This wave of criminal activity prompted residents in Greenford and Northolt to call for more policemen for the district. There was an increase in numbers, but this was put down to a need to match the steady increase in population as more and more houses continued to be built. It will be seen that sending additional police officers to a district would, anyway, prove no deterrent to Flannelfoot. But something far bigger than the loss of shillings and trinkets was looming on the horizon at this time.

Two weeks after the Church Road burglaries, something happened in America whose effects would ripple outwards and very quickly engulf Britain: the Wall Street Crash, which triggered what came to be called the Great Depression, the worst economic crisis ever known. Unemployment, hunger, malnutrition and associated illnesses soon devastated this country. As ever, the less well-off, the class to which Vickers belonged, were hardest hit. Its effects would last for virtually the whole decade – and there was a concomitant surge in the already growing crime figures, as desperation hit the poorest in those days before the introduction of state benefits. Between 1930 and 1938, the number of prosecutions in England and Wales virtually doubled. Flannelfoot would figure among those statistics, but not yet …

In 1931 there was what was described as an 'epidemic of flannel-footed burglars' in the Greater London area. The *Surrey Mirror* reported that there were four raids in one week during February, with Kingswood, Ashtead and Guildford being hit. Plenty of jewellery went missing – 'the more valuable the better', it declared. But this doesn't sound like *the* Flannelfoot, who tended to target the homes of people who couldn't afford especially valuable jewellery, and anyway although he made exceptions, the towns mentioned were quite some way beyond his normal range. The 'more valuable the better' phrase may simply have been journalistic licence, and, of course, not all of those many burglaries in the West London area could have been down to Vickers. A high proportion undoubtedly were, but it's quite possible that other criminals had read about his methods and decided they might work for them too.

The *Daily Herald* said that Scotland Yard detectives were 'baffled' by the mysterious burglar known as Flannelfoot. It said he was recently thought to have been operating in Cheam, Surrey, which was a little closer to his habitual territory.

We are on much surer ground with the next reported Flannelfoot activity. In May, houses on a recently built estate in Norwood Green were targeted, taking him back to Southall. He visited properties on three adjacent streets, all within a few dozen metres of each other. A house on Manston Avenue was on the list, where he took, in true Flannelfoot fashion, small, portable articles and a little cash from a money box. Marks on the window frame of a house on Cranbourne Avenue belonging to a local headmaster indicated that he had attempted to break in, but had failed or been spooked. But on the next street, Wimborne Avenue, he at least obtained his common mode of getaway transport – a bicycle – on which to ride away at his leisure.

We are definitely back on Flannelfoot's turf in October 1932. The Belvue Estate in the town of Northolt, where he had made 'burglarious entries' a couple of years previously, was the subject of his attentions again. The *West Middlesex Gazette* was almost admiring in its description of the 'neat manner' in which he made his holes in order to get at the window catches on the inside – 'the work of an expert, always in silence … the handiwork of an experienced "craftsman".'

Needless to say, towels had been used to conceal his footprints and deaden his tread, and a bike had been found discarded some distance from the scene of his crimes. The occupant of 26 Sandringham Road came down in the morning to find all of the downstairs rooms in 'utter confusion'. The whole place had been rummaged, leading to a decent haul by Flannelfoot's standards: £4 taken from a coat pocket, 30 shillings from an electricity meter, and 5 shillings each from two children's money boxes. Two watches – one gold and one silver – were also stolen.

A couple of doors down, he entered through a small window above the French doors, exhibiting 'remarkable agility' (especially bearing in mind Vickers' old war wound). There was a dog in the next-door property, but this didn't stop Flannelfoot, who grabbed brandy, whiskey, cigarettes and a chicken breast. Round the corner on Belvue Road, he took £7 in cash and two watches. Flannelfoot seems to have taken an interest in paperwork because this was another place where letters and documents were found strewn on the floor. We know he took postage stamps if available, and he may also have been looking for postal orders and the like. It was here that he dumped the towel he had been using to cover his footwear.

This year, 1932, featured significant events in the lives of both Vickers and Hambrook. In the case of Vickers, something happened that was to set off a chain of events which would ultimately lead to his downfall.

First, though, Walter Hambrook, who had risen up the ladder again and was now a superintendent, would be faced with possibly the biggest and most controversial murder case of his long career.

Chapter 10

Murder in Knightsbridge

The residents of swanky William Mews in Knightsbridge (an address where various celebrities, including the Beatles, would one day reside) had grown used to the parties and disturbances at No. 21, so it was a matter of irritation but no great surprise when raised voices were heard coming from the open window of the first-floor apartment, echoing around the quiet, narrow cobbled street at 3 am on 19 May 1932. Neighbour Mrs Hall, woken by the shouting, dragged herself from her bed and peered out.

She saw the sometime-boyfriend of the occupant of No. 21, Thomas William Scott Stephen (known for some reason as Michael, as if he didn't already have enough names) in the street below being assailed on two fronts. The taxi driver was accusing him of damaging his vehicle, while the occupier of the troublesome flat, 28-year-old socialite Elvira Dolores Barney, stood at her window apparently naked, shouting that she would never let Michael into her house again, and that she would shoot him if he came near her.

Despite this, once Stephen had pacified the taxi driver, he crossed the street and proceeded to ring the bell of No. 21, while Elvira screamed at him to go away or she would call the police. Stephen persisted, but Elvira had withdrawn and, seeing he was getting nowhere, the man started to walk away. Before he had gone far, though, Elvira reappeared. She leaned out of the window brandishing a revolver, and cried, 'Laugh, baby, for the last time!' There was a loud *crack* as she opened fire, the bullet missed and Stephen nonchalantly told her not to be so foolish. Nevertheless, he decided not to push his luck any further. Instead, he sauntered over to a parked van, and finding it unlocked, opened the door and spent the night inside. But this wasn't the end of the matter.

The pair were seen together again the next day, acting as if nothing had happened, and two weeks later Elvira threw a party at her flat which was attended by around thirty people, including Stephen. There were drinks at the flat, then at 10 pm everyone went off to a West End club. Residents of William Mews were no doubt relieved that only Elvira and Stephen returned to the flat – little knowing that this was just the calm before the storm.

At around 4 am the peace of the Mews was shattered again when a new violent argument erupted at No. 21. A neighbour heard Elvira yell 'Get out of my house at once! I hate you! Get out – I'll shoot you!' She heard Stephen tell her he was leaving – quickly followed by the sound of a gunshot. Elvira screamed, and Stephen was heard groaning 'Oh God, what have you done?' There was another scream from Elvira, who then yelled 'Chicken! Chicken! I'm sorry. Come back to me. I'll do anything you ask me ...' A few minutes later she was heard to cry despairingly, 'Michael! Michael!', then all fell silent until first a doctor, and then the police arrived. They were all too late to save Stephen.

Elvira Barney came from a wealthy family who owned a house in nearby Belgrave Square and a country retreat in Battle, Sussex. She was, in fact, married. Her husband was American John Sterling Barney, a popular singer and member of a trio which had been performing in London at the time the pair met. They had married in 1929 within a short time of meeting each other, but it was a rash and hasty move, and it wasn't long before things turned sour. John Barney returned to the United States little more than a year after the wedding.

The woman he left behind was born Elvira Enid Mullens, a sometime performer who became Barney after her marriage and who also adopted Dolores as her middle name in real life, taken from her stage name of Dolores Ashley. Her father was, albeit with some misgivings, happy to finance Elvira's extremely hedonistic lifestyle. As is apparently usually the case with 'socialites', she depended on these handouts and never had to stoop to anything so low as gainful employment; she was ostensibly an actress, but seems to have appeared on the stage on very few occasions. Interestingly, she is quoted as being 26 rather than 28 in almost all accounts of this story – and even agreed that she was 26 when it was put to her at the subsequent trial. There is absolutely no doubt that her birth was registered in Chelsea in January 1904, so there can equally be no doubt that she was 28 in the summer of 1932.

Elvira and Stephen were perhaps well suited to each other in a sense because he, too, was the black sheep of his family. He at least did work for a living at one time – as a dress designer in Paris. When that came to an end, his father, like Elvira's, had financed his partying lifestyle for a while: the difference being that his patience ran out. When the money stopped, Stephen's mother and brother helped, but even they became tired of 'lending' him money they knew they would never see again. Not long before his death, there was a tense encounter between Stephen and his brother in the latter's office over Elvira, with whom the family believed he was living despite his (almost certainly spurious) denials. Stephen was supposed to be marrying her once she got a divorce, but the brother told him that their father did not approve of his association with her. Angry words were exchanged, resulting in the brother ordering Stephen to leave. It was the last time he saw Stephen alive.

The first person to arrive on the scene at William Mews was Elvira's own physician, Dr Durrant, whom she had telephoned, screaming, 'Come at once! There has been a terrible accident here. Jump into a taxi and come at once. A gentleman has shot himself!'

When Durrant arrived, he found Stephen lying with his right hand across his chest, and observed a bullet hole close to his left lapel. A revolver lay by his left hand. As he examined the victim – whom he soon realised had been dead for at least an hour – Elvira pleaded, 'He's not dead is he? Don't let my parents know. If he is dead let me die too … I will kill myself!'

As soon as she said this, while the medical man was trying to calm her he strategically placed his foot over the gun, though taking care not to actually touch it. He told Elvira that she needed to telephone the police, but she sank to her knees beside the body.

'I love him so! I love him!'

She claimed that she and Stephen had quarrelled about another woman she believed he was seeing, and that she had threatened to kill herself. Stephen, she said, knowing that she kept a revolver underneath a cushion on a chair, rushed to get it before she could, saying, 'At all events, you won't do it with this.' She then, she told Dr Durrant, wrestled with him for possession of the gun, and it went off. Death wasn't immediate – Stephen staggered into the bathroom to inspect his wound, but soon she heard him shouting to her to fetch a doctor.

The police were at last summoned: first a constable who was nearby, then Detective Inspector Winter, who took possession of the revolver and unloaded it. He found Elvira to be in a hysterical condition. She seemed to resent his 'intrusion', and her agitated state, no doubt coupled with her innate sense of entitlement, led her to assume that she could simply order the lowly policeman to leave. He managed to calm her enough to get some of the story from her, she saying that there had been a struggle over the gun and it had gone off.

Once the seriousness of the situation was appreciated, it was not long before other officers began to arrive. Hambrook himself was one of them, becoming the senior officer on the scene, although a later visitor was Norman Kendal, Assistant Commissioner of Scotland Yard, and it didn't go without mention that it was highly unusual for someone so senior to personally visit the scene of a crime, even a murder. Hambrook found Stephen's body sprawled partly on the landing but with his legs on the stairs, in a kind of huddled posture, clearly shot in the chest. He could detect no signs of a struggle.

Another arrival was Detective Sergeant Campion, who became the next victim of Elvira's wrath. When he informed her that she needed to accompany him to the Gerald Road police station in order to provide a statement, she flew at him, hitting him in the face and crying, 'I'll teach you to put me in a cell, you foul swine!'

At some point, her phone rang. She tried to answer it but the uniformed officers present wouldn't allow her to, leading to a further volley of abuse. Whoever was trying to get through to her rang again, and this time she forced her way to it, with the officers allowing her to get her hands on it and shout into it rather than inflame matters by fighting with her any further.

The caller was her mother, Lady Evelyne Mullens, and after Elvira had told her what had happened she turned back to the policemen.

'Now that you know who my mother is, perhaps you will be a little more careful what you say and do to me. I'll teach you to take me to a police station!'

Acting with great restraint, the officers gently persuaded her that she had no choice, and finally she went along with them to give a full statement. On 4 June, the day that Stephen was cremated, Elvira Barney was picked up from her parents' home in Belgrave Square and taken back to the Gerald Road police station. There, in the presence of Hambrook, she was formally charged with Stephen's murder. She spent the night in a cell, and the following day was taken to the Westminster Police Court (the precursor of today's Magistrates' Courts). Despite this being little more than a pre-trial hearing, a crowd, which had begun to gather an hour before the scheduled start time, strained to get a glimpse of her as the police car whisked her into the yard at the rear of the building. Hambrook, Winter and other detectives also had to force their way through the throng.

Barney, with fair, straw-coloured hair peeping out beneath a black hat, was described as being as 'pale as marble' and visibly distressed. She sat with her mother in an ante-room until called, then they, accompanied by a female court officer, made their way into court. Elvira was in such a frail state that she could only walk with the support of the two women either side of her, and buckled at the knees several times before she had reached the dock. There, she sat with her head in her hands.

Winter very briefly ran through the arrest, ending with Elvira's response: 'I did not shoot him. I am not guilty.' She was remanded to Holloway women's prison for seven days, pending trial. Elvira rose unsteadily to her feet, ready to be taken away. She looked dazedly around the courtroom for a moment, tottered to the steps down from the dock, then half stumbled, half collapsed. Only the waiting arms of the quick-thinking female court officer saved Elvira from crashing face-first to the floor. She was revived with smelling salts, but upon her arrival at Holloway, Elvira Barney was taken straight to the prison hospital. Some women spectators in court had been moved to tears at her plight – though probably not the mother and female relatives of Michael Stephen.

The newspapers had been full of the shooting of Stephen and arrest of Elvira, so predictably, interest in the trial was at fever pitch by the time it commenced on 4 July, with the police again struggling to control crowds outside the Old Bailey.

The presiding judge was Justice Travers Humphreys, and unsurprisingly given her previous statements, Elvira Dolores Barney pleaded not guilty. The first day of the trial was taken up with the opening statement by the prosecution, during which Elvira collapsed once more. She was called to give evidence on the second day, repeating much of what we have already heard, but adding that it had never been in her mind to shoot him, and that there was no one of whom she was fonder.

The circumstances of what happened on the night of 19 May were examined in great detail, with Elvira sticking to her story of a struggle for the gun and an accidental discharge. Sir Bernard Spilsbury was in action again, describing the bullet's trajectory as horizontal, passing through one lung (the cause of death) and embedding itself in a rib at the back. He pointed out that although the revolver was quite light in weight, the trigger required a 14lb pull, meaning an accidental firing was less likely than with some other guns.[1] The weapon had been discharged at a distance of between three and six inches, and Spilsbury suggested that it would have been practically impossible for Stephen to have shot himself. (In a sense, this last point was something of a red herring since neither the prosecution nor the defence were suggesting that it might have been suicide.)

Elvira's story was that 'our hands were together ... his hands on mine ...' when the gun went off, upon which he 'wore an astonished look' and went into the bathroom. 'I did not think anything serious had happened – it seemed quite all right,' she said (until she heard him calling for help from the bathroom). This sounds disingenuous to say the least. Regardless of who was to blame, a pistol had been discharged at close quarters during a tussle and her lover had immediately rushed to the bathroom (surely, clutching his chest as he did so).

One expert witness said the circumstances could indicate a struggle, or at least that it couldn't be ruled out, while another said that if someone had been handling the barrel when the gun went off, they would have staining or

---

1. As a comparison, based on a range of sources it appears that the average 'pull weight' of modern pistols is between five and seven pounds.

blackening to the hand. It had been noted at the scene that Stephen's hands were perfectly clean.

Doctor Durrant weighed in on Elvira's behalf, saying that in view of the hysterical state she was in when he had arrived, he did not believe she could have made up her story. He had not the slightest doubt that she was telling what she thought was the truth. It has to be borne in mind that this was her own personal physician and quite possibly the family doctor too. (But it must be remembered that Elvira had had around an hour to dwell on what had happened before his arrival.)

The Holloway Prison doctor found bruising on Elvira's arms, which he thought may have been caused by the grip of human fingers, and she also had other minor abrasions.

Elvira claimed that Stephen said he wished the doctor would hurry so he could say it wasn't her fault, and she denied having shouted that she would shoot him, as a witness had claimed to overhear. Rather, she told the court that she had threatened to shoot herself. It was put to her that it would have been impossible for Stephen to have held the gun pointing towards himself *and* to have pressed the trigger. Elvira could only say that she had no idea whose finger was on the trigger when the gun went off (yet she had said earlier that 'his hands were on mine'), nor from whose hand the pistol fell after being fired. It is perhaps not unreasonable to observe that Elvira was conveniently unable to recall the details to any question whose answer might incriminate her, but remembered with clarity everything that bolstered her innocence. She further denied that Stephen had cried 'Good God, what have you done?', as witnesses had testified to.

Her barrister complained about the focus that had been put on his client's wealth and extravagant lifestyle. He put her temper and slapping of Inspector Winter down to her being understandably fraught over her lover's death, and in typical defence counsel fashion, he tried to find an innocent variation on the words the witnesses claimed to have heard: Elvira did not say 'I will shoot you', but 'I am going to shoot', implying that it was related to her claim to have threatened suicide. Judge Humphreys praised the Defence speech, extolling it as 'one of the finest speeches' he had ever heard at the bar. This is worryingly reminiscent of a scene from *Rumpole of the Bailey*, though his lordship did balance things somewhat when he criticised the lawyer for making 'sneering' comments regarding the prosecution witnesses.

The jury took two hours to reach its conclusion. To the astonishment of many, Elvira Barney was cleared of both murder and manslaughter. She walked free from court, and press photographs of the day show her getting into a car, a bunch of flowers from well-wishers in hand, smiling broadly and looking remarkably relaxed, almost as if setting off on an outing to the seaside.

She had escaped a lengthy stay in prison, not to mention a possible death sentence, and although the jury were perhaps justified in believing there was not sufficient evidence on which to convict someone on such a serious charge, grave doubts must hang over Elvira's version of what happened that night. It's true that her sybaritic lifestyle should not, in a legal sense, have influenced the jury's thinking; but there was clearly something off about the woman – not least her casual firing of the gun into the street about two weeks previous to the death of Stephen, which surely says something about her character.

After the trial, Elvira was driven directly from the Old Bailey to her parents' Belgravia home, but within days she was back at the same Westminster Police Court in which she had dramatically collapsed some weeks previously. This time, she was being prosecuted for illegal possession of a firearm. In some circumstances, this might have seemed like a petty vendetta by the police, who presumably had some discretion as to whether to pursue such a matter against someone who had very recently faced the trauma of a life-or-death trial. However, another way of looking at it is that the police were angered by what they saw as a murderer walking free.

Whatever the thinking behind the prosecution, Elvira was this time found guilty and fined £50 plus costs. But even this was not the end of her troubles, nor her final court appearance.

She quickly fled to France, but within weeks, while driving recklessly in Cannes, she caused an accident in which the driver of another car was seriously injured. This time, though, not only was she in the playground of the rich and famous where her own status counted for little, but she had injured someone richer and more privileged than herself: one Countess Karolyi. Elvira was again convicted and fined.

This proved to be the beginning of the end for Elvira Barney. Weeks later one of her friends committed suicide and left a letter specifically blaming two people, one of whom was Elvira. She did not say why, but she was a heroin addict and Elvira herself was by now addicted to cocaine, and the reference was almost certainly to do with the debauched scene they both inhabited.

By December 1936, Elvira – still only 32 – was a drunken, drug-addled wreck, and her body could take no more. She was found dead and alone in a Paris hotel room on Christmas Day.

Walter Hambrook wasn't the only link between this case and Vickers. The man who would one day lead the prosecution case against him would be one Christmas Humphreys – son of Travers Humphreys, the judge at Elvira's murder trial.

Chapter 11

The Norfolk Woman

A major event had occurred in Harry Vickers' life in the same year that Hambrook was involved in the Elvira Barney case, and it was one that would have repercussions he could never have envisaged.

On Christmas Day 1932, Harry Vickers walked out on his wife of twenty-two years.

By this time the family had moved to Essex, living at 4 Russell Gardens, Wickford. He was to move from address to address quite frequently from now on, mostly but not exclusively in London – *and* there was another woman in the picture.

There is no evidence as to whether the new relationship began after the break-up of the marriage or was the cause of it, but it's highly likely that Vickers met his lover while living his secret burgling and gambling (and no doubt socialising) life away from the marital home. Michael Innes, writing in *Great Cases of Scotland Yard*, weaves a story of an unnamed woman who lived in North Norfolk but who was a regular visitor and sometimes stayed overnight with Vickers but didn't live with him. As the police pieced together the Flannelfoot story, they would find that Vickers and his new woman did actually live together as man and wife from an early stage – probably as soon as he left Alice.

When Vickers walked out on Alice, he didn't leave alone. He was accompanied by his and Alice's 11-year-old daughter Elsie. Their son Jack had died in infancy, as we have seen, and there was an elder daughter Vera, who stayed with Alice. Details of what exactly happened on that December day would emerge in time, but the question of whether Vickers took Elsie forcibly or whether she was happy to be with her father would never quite be cleared up, though both sides would one day have their say. Elsie would have left her friends and relatives behind, but Innes portrays the Norfolk woman, whom he labels 'Mrs A', as having a daughter called Alice, claiming that Elsie told police that Mrs A often used to bring Alice to London, and she and Elsie would play together.

Michael Innes doesn't seem to have consulted the police files on the case, not unreasonably, since he was writing a broader general history of crime of which Flannelfoot was but one case; nevertheless, his whole Flannelfoot story has to be treated with some caution. It is, frustratingly, a highly fictionalised account featuring much invented dialogue, making it impossible to sift fact from fiction. It's likely that he didn't know the real surname of the 'Norfolk woman' (which didn't begin with 'A'). Elsie would, in time, tell of a niece of hers, not a daughter; the Scotland Yard notes of her statements make no mention of them playing together and anyway she was probably too old for that. What's more likely is that Innes misinterpreted the details of a story, which we shall examine in its proper place, of a niece of the Norfolk woman who without doubt did visit Vickers while Elsie was with him – but she was a young woman who travelled alone to join them, not a child who would have made a playmate for Elsie.

Vickers taking his daughter seems an odd move on several levels. Even now it is relatively rare for a man to take, or be allowed to take, children with him when a marriage breaks up, but it was highly unusual then. And it's even stranger that he would take a child along when setting up home with a lover. It might make sense if Vickers had in some way been 'saving' an unhappy Elsie from a mean and horrible Alice Vickers, but there are no hints that she was a bad mother in any way or that there was any problem with their relationship.

Did Elsie go willingly? She was not a baby, and it isn't easy to imagine that Vickers could have forced her to both accompany him and stay for an extended period against her wishes. One thing we do know is that the move caught Alice Vickers completely off guard, and she had no idea where the pair of them went. Her later accounts give the impression that Elsie *was* virtually abducted, but as I've said, there isn't a great deal of clarity about the full circumstances surrounding this traumatic event. It does seem that Vickers started his new life under his old pseudonym – Henry Williams – though whether his new partner in life knew his true identity isn't clear.

Chapter 12

Enter Inspector Thompson

'Locked room' crime stories were very popular in the 1930s, the heyday of what we now call 'cosy crime' fiction and authors like Agatha Christie and Dorothy L. Sayers. The challenge for writers was to construct a plot whereby a murder had been committed in seemingly impossible circumstances, such as a room locked from the inside with no one but the victim present, or other such baffling situations. The challenge for readers, of course, was to try to guess the ingenious solution before the detective revealed it.

Luckily, in real life locked room murders were rare and relatively easily solved – the hard part was catching the killer.

At about 8 pm on 17 May 1933, a street trader on Churton Street in Pimlico, Westminster, heard what sounded like a prolonged and violent argument between a man and a woman in one of the flats above. He was concerned enough to hurry to nearby Rochester Row police station and alert the police. When they arrived at the house – No. 5 – and knocked on the door, the occupant shouted that he couldn't open it because he had lost the key earlier that day. A young Indian man came out onto the little balcony that overlooked the street and explained that his wife had been drinking, and the disturbance had been 'just a little domestic dispute' which was now resolved. Despite the dubious-sounding lost key story, and even one of the policemen thinking he heard a woman's cry, they merely warned him not to cause any further breaches of the peace and went away

Less than an hour later, Mrs C.J. Graham, whose third-floor flat on the opposite side of the relatively narrow street looked down onto the first-floor flat where the commotion had taken place, witnessed a bizarre, and what at first appeared to be an amusing spectacle – what she described to her husband as a 'pantomime' when she called him to come and see. The Indian resident was chasing his young English wife in and out of the flat's two rooms, sometimes through the internal doors, sometimes even by means of the narrow, iron-railed balconies outside each window. But Mrs Graham's laughter quickly subsided when it became clear that this was no stage farce. The woman was, in fact, fighting for her life.

She began to scream for help. Cries of 'Police!' and 'Murder!' echoed around the street. The man was trying to grab the woman as the chase continued, and Mrs Graham thought he was also hitting out at her with his fist– but this would prove to be wrong. It was not an empty fist with which he was striking his wife.

The tussle eventually brought them to the window, and the neighbour now saw how sickly white the young woman's face was, and how frenzied the man's. The window was broken during the struggle, but then the pair moved away from it, out of sight, and things went quiet for a time. It wasn't to last long. More sounds of breaking glass brought Mrs Graham back to her vantage point, and now the full horror of what was really taking place hit her. The woman was on the floor with the man standing over her, raining down blows on her prostrate body. Finally, he drew the curtains and the room light was switched off.

The Grahams called the police.

When the first officers arrived on the scene accompanied by a police surgeon, the door to the bedroom was locked and they could only gain access by climbing over from the next-door balcony. Inside, they found the lifeless body of a young woman and a constable was dispatched to Scotland Yard. Inspector Thompson would be in charge of this case.

Thomas 'Tommy' Basil Thompson was 43, from a humble Croydon family. He was an experienced officer by this time, having joined the police in 1911, becoming a Scotland Yard detective after ten years' service. Walter Hambrook would in time give the Flannelfoot case the nudge it needed, but it was Thompson who was to take the lead.

By the time he arrived at Churton Street, a crowd of onlookers was beginning to gather outside and a police cordon was formed to keep them away. Thompson made his way upstairs and examined the fully-clothed body of the person who would be identified as Mona Lavinia Hussain. She was just 20 years old, a native of Cumberland. Mona was heavily bloodstained, lying face down, and clutching a clump of black hair in her left hand. Thompson and the doctor observed numerous stab wounds to all parts of her body, and the detective was then shown a large, long-bladed knife which had been found in a cupboard.

Mavis Elwood, Mona Hussain's cousin, appeared on the scene and was able to provide some context regarding the events of the evening, as she had been living with the couple until recently. The person Inspector Thompson needed to look for, she said, was Nessar Hussain, 27, an Indian chef who had been married to Mona for around five years. Thompson had men sent out in search of him, and arranged for Mavis Elwood to be taken away by police car to make a full statement.

The hunt for Hussain went on through the night. Ports were put on alert, and his description, furnished by Miss Elwood, was circulated nationally – a move which was to pay off quicker and more satisfyingly than Inspector Thompson could have expected.

The following day, he received an urgent call from police in Liverpool: a man fitting the suspect's description had been picked up from a seamen's lodging house in the docklands district of that city. He had denied being Nessar Hussain, giving his name as 'Mohammed Hamid'. However, he had bloodstains on his shirt and coat, a cut to his knee, another to his trousers, along with abrasions to his hands that appeared to have been made by fingernails. Thompson, accompanied by Sergeant Smith, rushed north that evening.

At Liverpool Central Police Station the next morning, the detained man was brought before the two Yard men.

'We are police officers from London,' Thompson began, then asked the man if he understood English.

'I understand very well.'

'At 11 pm on Wednesday last, the seventeenth, I saw the dead body of Mona Lavinia Hussain on the first floor of 5 Churton Street, Pimlico …'

Notwithstanding the false name he had previously given, Hussain chipped in, 'Yes, my wife.'

'I am taking you into custody for wilfully murdering her with a knife … You are not obliged to say anything, but anything you do say may be given in evidence.'

'Yes, I don't care what happens. Here I am – take me.'

Which is exactly what Thompson and Smith did. Hussain was escorted back to London, where things continued to move quickly. The inquest was held very soon after the arrest, and Sir Bernard Spilsbury, who had carried out the post-mortem, told the court of his findings. Mona was found to have had thirty-six knife wounds inflicted on her in an attack involving 'great violence'. Hussain had not been punching her as Mrs Graham looked on, but stabbing her. His wife had cuts to the head, neck, chest, both arms and legs. One wound to the neck, five inches in length, had severed an artery, and Spilsbury pronounced the cause of death to be heart failure due to blood loss.

Mavis Elwood was then called, through whose testimony more was learned about the couple. Mona was the daughter of a Cumbrian miner, and had been just 16 when she married Hussain, who was a 'Mahommedan'. They had been married for five years, but Mavis described the marriage as a troubled one, and didn't shirk from telling the inquest about Mona's own part in that.

She regularly went out socialising in the evenings, often not coming back till the early hours and sometimes not for days. She had left her husband 'permanently' on three or four occasions, blaming the way he treated her, but she kept coming back to him.

A couple of days later, Hussain made his appearance at the Westminster Police Court charged with murder. He made a nonchalant entrance, smiling to friends in the public gallery as he walked to the dock, but this jaunty mood wasn't to last long.

At this session, there were further revelations about the state of the Hussains' marriage. He swore an oath on the Koran, and all communication was carried out through an interpreter. Inspector Thompson was the only witness called, and he went through his arrest of Hussain in Liverpool and what the prisoner had said to him. When Hussain was asked if he had any reply, his demeanour changed. He poured out a 'torrent' of words in Hindustani, which went on so long that the magistrate had to ask the interpreter to put a halt to it. The tirade amounted to Hussain telling the magistrate, somewhat ironically, that he had nothing to say, before going on to claim that 'the whole thing was a lie', and that he had been drunk when he made his admission to Thompson in Liverpool. The case was adjourned, and Hussain was remanded in custody.

On 26 May, a stained oak coffin was taken from the Westminster mortuary to Streatham for the burial of Mona Hussain. The only family present were her father and brother, who had travelled from their home village in Cumberland to attend the funeral and had been looked after by church authorities. Mona's father tearfully told a reporter that Mona's mother had died some years previously, adding perhaps pointedly, that 'she had lost her guiding star'.

Hussain was back in court the following day, now claiming through his interpreter that he did not fully understand the evidence which had been presented against him during his previous appearance. The clerk of the court dutifully read through Thompson's statement.

A new dimension to what lay behind the events on the day of the murder now came to light. Mona had been conducting an affair with a German called Sigfried Robertson. Hussain was alleged to have told Thompson and Smith in Liverpool: 'I cannot understand what I do ... She was bad woman [sic] and went with other men.' And on the train journey to London, he had declared, 'One thing only I regret: I cannot find the German Sigfried. My wife was bad woman and went away with that man.' A witness said that Mona had lived with Sigfried for a while, but that he had gone to Paris before the murder had taken place.

Mavis Elwood, who as we have heard had been staying with the couple, said that Mona used to receive letters from the German. She told her husband they were from a girlfriend, and although he appeared to accept this explanation, he must have had his doubts because it was one of these letters which seemed to tip him over the edge.

He surreptitiously took it from her handbag and, unable to read it himself, took it to a friend who could. The contents led to a heated confrontation in the flat, during which Mona threatened to leave Hussain and he responded by threatening to kill her if she did. Before he could make good his promise, Mona managed to grab a few things and dart out, and now Hussain turned his attentions on Mavis Elwood, no doubt seeing her as an accomplice. He threatened to kill her too, and Mavis hurriedly followed Mona out of the flat.

At one point while she was giving evidence, the stress of the trial got to Mavis. She began to sway unsteadily in her seat for a moment, then fainted. Police officers rushed to her aid and helped her out of the courtroom.

Meanwhile, another witness who had known Mona was questioned about her 'ungovernable temper', and was asked about three separate occasions when she had smashed her employer's window, and another when she had been carried by four constables to Bow Street station on a stretcher (presumably meaning under restraint). The witness said that her husband sometimes gave her his wages so that she could pay the rent and buy food, but that she would spend it on socialising and leave the bills unpaid. This inevitably led to rows, and during one of these Hussain had told her that if they lived in India, he would have killed her, but in this country he could not touch her.

Shortly before she was killed, Mona and a friend were in a cafe when they encountered Hussain, who was working there. Having calmed down, he told her he loved her and wanted her to come back. Her reply is unknown, but the following day, the day of the murder, she again bumped into him at Piccadilly tube station, and this time he gave her little choice, seizing her by the arm and hauling her away.

The knife used in the killing was identified by the owner of the cutler's shop where it had been purchased, who remembered Hussain saying he wanted a 'keen edge' on it.

On the final day of the hearing, which had resumed on 8 June after another adjournment, the proceedings took a curious turn.

Hussain arrived at court in a dishevelled state, his hair a mess, and no collar to his shirt (shirt collars in those days were removable). As soon as he was in the dock he kicked off his shoes and put his feet up, and when the magistrate told him to sit up properly, he demanded in Hindustani, 'What have you brought me here for?' and tried to leave the dock. He was restrained by police officers, and advised by his counsel that it was in his own interests to settle down. However, as the hearing progressed and witnesses were heard, he muttered to himself, sang, whistled, and generally behaved as if he was anywhere but in a court which would determine whether he should be tried for murder. Every now and then he shouted something out loud in his own language, and then made a second attempt to get out of the dock, this time over the rail at the rear. He was forced back, and two policemen were assigned to stand either side of him.

Despite the interruptions, the hearing was brought to a conclusion and the magistrates were satisfied that enough evidence had been put forward to warrant Hussain being committed for trial. But Hussain's behaviour in court had been the precursor to an unexpected twist to the story.

At the end of June 1933, Nessar Hussain appeared at the Old Bailey before Mr Justice Humphreys, the same judge who tried Walter Hambrook's Elvira Barney case, and, as we have heard, whose barrister son would one day play a part in the Vickers story. But for now, all attention was on Hussain, who arrived at court in a similar state to that which he had presented a couple of weeks earlier: ruffled hair, shoeless, coat torn. He was brought in under the firm grip of two warders, but when things got under way this time there were no attempts to escape; in fact, he affected not the slightest interest in proceedings. However, behind the scenes, there had been developments.

The senior medical officer of Brixton Prison, where Hussain had been held pending trial, took the stand and expressed the opinion that the prisoner was insane and incapable of instructing counsel or following the proceedings of the trial, a view with which Hussain's own defence concurred. Mr Justice Humphreys had little choice but to find the prisoner insane and unfit to plead, and to be detained at His Majesty's pleasure.

Far be it from me to question the judgement of these eminent men at such a distance. It may be that flashbacks relating to the brutal and bloody murder of his wife, no doubt in a fit of rage which he later regretted, allied with an impending trial which might result in his hanging, tipped Hussain over the edge. But it might strike some as suspicious that he seemed to be completely transformed by mental illness just in time for his final court appearances. Before his arrest, he was able to concoct a lie about losing the key and calmly and smoothly charm his way out of having the police enter his flat; when he was arrested he was compos mentis enough to know he was in trouble, and sharp and articulate enough to invent a false name. It was only when he realised that he wasn't going to be able to bluster his way out of trouble that his mood turned first to anger and contempt, and, finally, the bizarre display in court.

Amy Bell, in *Murder Capital*, says that the police were, unsurprisingly, sceptical about Hussain's sudden descent into 'insanity', but there was little they could do to prove it was an act.

An interesting postscript to this story is a throwaway comment by Mavis Elwood that when her cousin married Hussain in 1929, she did so using the name Mafalda Emily Bosi Dognarelli. On the face of it, this sounds quite outlandish – but a look at the marriage records for that year confirms the story. In fact, she must have used even more middle names than that, since the entry for the event, which took place at St Giles', London, lists her as 'Malfada [*sic*] E.M.A.M.L.B. Dognarelli'. The truth was that Mona had been born with the rather more prosaic surname of 'Smith', but there must be something in the fact that she chose such an apparently authentic yet uncommon name. It's hardly the kind of thing a teenage miner's daughter from a Cumbrian village is likely to have plucked out of thin air. The only clue we have comes from cousin Mavis, who, while admitting that there were no family members of that name, suggested that it was one she might have used to 'go on the shows'. This indicates that she may have been an actress, singer, or performer of some kind. It would make sense that she would want or be advised to find an alternative to 'Smith', and perhaps the exotic alternative was copied from a European performer known to her or her agent or manager.

The most likely reason for her using a name other than her own at the wedding ceremony, regardless of how she came by it, is that she had eloped with Hussain and was marrying without her parents' consent.

So, in a sense, and thanks to the good work of the Liverpool police (who were praised both by the court and Thompson himself) Thompson had got his man. The end result wasn't quite what he was expecting, but although it hasn't been possible to ascertain if and when Hussain was released, it's likely to have been a lengthy period of incarceration. Thompson was carving out a reputation for himself, and it wouldn't be long before his bosses decided he might just be the man to succeed where others had failed – and catch Flannelfoot.

Chapter 13

Flannelfoot on Tour?

No doubt to the relief of the police, not to mention London householders, there was a lull in Flannelfoot burglaries as the year 1933 got under way. This was not because Vickers' new woman had had a reforming effect on him. What the police weren't to know for quite some time was that the pair, with Elsie in tow, had temporarily forsaken London for the south coast.

They did return, though, and there was a report of nine burglaries in a single night in the London area in July. They were laid at Flannelfoot's doorstep, but specific details are scarce so it's hard to make a judgement. In February of the following year, break-ins took place on Wood End Lane and Ribblesdale Avenue, Northolt. Flannelfoot had struck here on numerous occasions; the two roads are close together, and less than a mile from the tube station – it would be discovered later that by this time he was living in Fulham, the district where he had married Alice all those years ago, which was around an hour's ride from Northolt.

'The signs point the finger of suspicion at the now almost legendary figure of "Flannelfoot",' the *West Middlesex Gazette* announced. Vickers usually waited till the early hours and targeted occupied premises where the inhabitants were asleep. His first raid on this night was at the house of a Mr Kay, who was out at the time. The burglary had to have taken place before 10 pm because this was when Kay arrived home. This was most unlike a Flannelfoot job, but he did tend to take up position relatively early and settle down to wait to strike, so perhaps he saw his opportunity and went for it. It was winter, so it would have been dark well before he even arrived in Northolt.

Mr Kay opened his front door to find a house in complete disarray. The paper speculated that a clue to it being the work of Flannelfoot was the distribution of mud, which was not only on the floor but smeared on furniture legs: 'No ordinary footwear could have been have so distributive,' thus it probably came from rags wrapped around the feet and lower legs. It was, however, unusual for the careful Vickers to leave *any* footmarks, since he normally covered his shoes with clean cloth before moving around the property. Flannelfoot – or whoever it was – forced open the French windows at the rear with a spade or other implement (again, rather crude-sounding by his standards), broke open the electricity meter from which he took a small amount of money, and also found a book of stamps.

On Ribblesdale Road, Mr Miller's gold watch was taken, together with an overcoat, three pairs of shoes, £6 in cash and the customary contents of the gas meter. At a third house, the burglar raided a gas meter yet again, and here refreshed himself with a couple of bananas. Perhaps surprisingly, considering that it had reported on his activities for some years, the *West Middlesex Gazette* on this occasion declared, 'It is of course doubtful whether the said "Flannelfoot" is a single individual', a theory it had never espoused before but one which did crop up from time to time.

We do know that by 27 October 1933, Flannelfoot was on familiar territory. Greenford police were alerted to a spate of six burglaries on Cavendish Avenue in the Sudbury Hill district of West London. To gain entry to the first house the usual Flannelfoot method was used, and from this place he stole scullery and French door keys and used them to unlock doors in some of the other houses. In one case he carefully unscrewed the metal plate covering the lock of the French doors and inserted one of his handy implements into the keyhole, with which he was able to turn a key left in the lock on the inside.

Now we explore the possibility that Flannelfoot ventured much further afield, particularly north of Greater London. The only burglaries with which he was associated in the second half of 1934 occurred in the eastern and central parts of England.

'Is Flannelfoot, the notorious safe-breaker, who has eluded the whole of the Metropolitan Police and Scotland Yard, operating in Leicester?' asked the *Leicester Evening Mail* in early September when reporting on a number of recent robberies in the city. Even the local police said they couldn't rule it out, claiming that he carried out 'similar jobs' in London. But, of course, he didn't. For all his 'legendary' reputation, Flannelfoot cracked nothing tougher than utility meters and children's money boxes. Perhaps he had broadened his skill set; perhaps he came all the way to Leicester because he had heard of easy pickings, and richer ones than those he was accustomed to in West London – but probably not. One of the things that made the Leicester force think of Flannelfoot was that in at least one case, the burglar must have worked either barefoot or had covered his outdoor footwear. They were presumably able to deduce this because of a wet and perhaps muddy environment outside the premises, yet a lack of footprints inside.

Very soon afterwards, an office break-in and another safe robbery, again said to have been carried out with covered footwear, took place in the same city. But if Flannelfoot had come to town in search of easy money, he had been sadly mistaken on this occasion. There were 10 shillings in loose change in the office, but the safe, after all his hard work in opening it, contained only paperwork. And opening it did involve hard work, because it weighed one hundredweight (112 pounds, or just under 10 stone) yet had been pulled out and turned on its back to better enable the thief (or thieves) to work on the door.

On 15 September there was a safe-breaking in Coventry which the local police were so confident had been committed by the same person as the ones in Leicester (and thus Flannelfoot in their estimation) that they contacted the Leicester force so they could swap notes. This time the offender – whose feet again were believed to have been wrapped in some material or other – had to work even harder, dragging the safe out of the office in which it was located into a workroom, leading the police to believe he must have 'prodigious strength'. This time all the effort paid off, since once the safe was cracked it coughed up £30.

Attention now turns to Grantham the following month, where the offices of three builders' firms were targeted in quick succession. Here, in at least two instances entry was gained by the use of a ladder, apparently to access a high ground-floor window. Once inside, workmen's tools from within the premises were used to get into locked cupboards and drawers, and £10 together with postage stamps was taken. There was evidence of a failed attempt to open a safe in one place, while in another the safe was opened with a pick.

The offender certainly wasn't 'flannel-footed', because in one property police found numerous footprints on the linoleum-covered office floor – actual footprints, that is, not shoe or boot prints. Of course, it's possible that in commercial premises as opposed to domestic residences, Vickers would be less likely to come across handy textiles of any kind and so might have chosen to go barefoot. But the other problem in this case was that the police called in an 'expert shoe-fitter', who was of the opinion that the footprints indicated the villain would wear a size 5 shoe. This would normally indicate a female, which is highly unlikely, which leaves us with a small man or older child. We don't know Vickers' shoe size, but he was neither short nor slightly built, and we can safely rule him out in this case.

This theory that it was a small man or a juvenile is supported by the fact that the burglar had squeezed through a window little more than one foot square. That these crimes were laid at Flannelfoot's door was probably due to the heightened awareness that his publicity had engendered, leading to an element of paranoia.

A more interesting suggestion of Flannelfoot at work outside London came in October, when another building firm's property was burgled. There was again an aborted attempt at picking the lock of a safe, this time involving the use of nails, and when that didn't work a more brutal attempt to force it open or even dismantle it was employed, using screwdrivers and a chisel. The perpetrator managed to bash part of the outer skin of the safe off, but the stronger inner layer remained intact.

Consequently, only a small amount of cash was taken from the property. Again, this sounds not only crude but not exactly the work of a bright, experienced criminal. Unless Vickers had drastically changed his ways, which can't be ruled out, this is unlikely to have been his handiwork. What makes this an interesting case – and one which, based on the modus operandi, could easily have been linked to the crimes in Leicester, Coventry, and especially Grantham – is that a suspect was afterwards spotted on the Peterborough to London road (which, in effect, would also probably be the Grantham to London route). He was described as being between 5 feet 6 and 5 feet 8 in height, thickset, clean-shaven, with a swarthy complexion. He wore a bowler hat and dark overcoat, and his age was estimated to be early forties. This sighting sparked a major manhunt, which included civilians, but no further sightings were made.

In some ways these crimes don't sound as much like the work of Flannelfoot as the newspapers would have us believe, and, of course, we associate him almost exclusively with London. We also associate him with extreme caution: he broke into houses in areas he was familiar with and from which he knew the best exit routes for getting safely home. It was a tried and tested formula, and he never got caught. Why change it and randomly start operating in places unknown to him?

Nevertheless, there are some clues suggesting that he *could possibly* have been the man behind some, if not all, of the jobs described above. In the last case, for example, the height and age would have been about right for Vickers, and in one of the police pictures in the Scotland Yard files he is wearing a bowler-like hat. These things are, as I say, merely suggestive and would fit many other men (though if we narrow it down to those making their way on foot from the vicinity of a burglary along the London road in the middle of the night, the list becomes considerably shorter). But there is a much more promising piece of information to add to the mix. Although Scotland Yard didn't know it at the time, conclusive evidence would emerge – which we shall explore in detail later – that for a period commencing in the spring of 1934, Vickers *did* travel around the country, and he *did* head north of London. What we don't know, unfortunately, is how many months he was away for. It was ostensibly a holiday tour, but where Flannelfoot is concerned, who knows?

Vickers' reign didn't have much longer to run. He must have known that each successive raid raised his statistical chance of being caught, especially if he continued to target the same relatively small area, and this line of reasoning may just have pressured him into rethinking his plans. But there is another reason for believing that Vickers might have been feeling the heat by this point. We know now that the net was beginning to close around him, and he may well have been aware of it.

Chapter 14

Duncan Joins the Hunt

Retracing our steps somewhat, in the summer of 1933, another of the officers who would play a key role in bringing Flannelfoot to justice, Inspector James Duncan, was in action. He was from Kincardineshire in Scotland, having been in the force for fourteen years, an experienced officer but ten years younger than Vickers. Like Vickers, though, he had been wounded during the war, in his case while serving with the Gordon Highlanders.

In this year he found himself embroiled in a far more violent case than anything featuring Flannelfoot – more violent than most common crimes of the day other than murder – involving not only a brutal attack on a police officer, but a shotgun hold-up, described as the first of its kind in London and something normally only seen in America.

There had been a series of vicious attacks on women in the spring of 1933, mostly robberies featuring gratuitous physical assaults. Five females, including a mother and daughter, had been robbed in the streets of London – most being struck about the head and face in the process. All of these crimes featured young men driving around in a stolen car, and on 8 April, Inspector Duncan, accompanied by Detective Sergeant Ronald Bailey, were cruising in an unmarked police car in search of the vehicle when they spotted it in Golders Green and gave chase, soon forcing it to come to a halt.

Bailey approached the car, whose number had been provided by witnesses, and when he noticed four handbags on the back seat he asked the driver, Reg Rogers, to get out. Instead, Frank Miller, his passenger, cried 'Drive like hell!' and Rogers obliged. But when Rogers put his foot down, Sergeant Bailey jumped onto the running board, and as the car began to pick up pace, he somehow managed to scramble inside through the open window. This put him in a vulnerable position, however, sprawled on the laps of the two criminals. Before he could twist into a position to defend himself, Miller grabbed him by the coat collar, while Rogers leaned across while still driving and pressed him against the back of the seat. Bailey managed to free himself from the driver's grasp, but as he did so, Miller rammed the detective's head through the glass partition between the front and back seats. Bailey ended up on his back, still sprawled on the front seats, with Miller raining blows against his face. The sergeant, by now bleeding profusely from cuts to his head and face, kicked out in desperation, smashing the windscreen and losing his shoe in the process.

'Shall I stop, and we'll do him in?' shouted Rogers.

'You drive the car and leave the [expletive excluded from newspaper account] to me,' Miller told him. 'I'll strangle the [...].'

Miller tightened Bailey's collar around his throat till the detective was fighting for breath. Luckily for him, the crooks decided to dump their damaged car and steal another before squeezing the life out of Bailey. In Hampstead, the car pulled up, Miller and Rogers jumped out, and the semi-conscious officer heard another car nearby roar into life. Bailey was somehow able to stagger out in time to get the registration number of the latest vehicle as it drove away. By this time Inspector Duncan had caught up in his vehicle and came to the aid of his bloody and exhausted colleague, later described by the police surgeon as being in a state of severe shock.

The pair were caught a few days later. Frank Miller of Tottenham, 19, was sentenced to four years' penal servitude and eighteen strokes of the cat for the robberies and assaults on four women, car theft, and actual bodily harm on Sergeant Bailey. Rogers got five years and eighteen strokes.

Chapter 15

The Penny Drops

Walter Hambrook was not one of the detectives assigned to the Flannelfoot case, but, like most of the country, he was well aware of it. In fact, something about it rang a bell with him, but he had dealt with countless criminals in his long career and he just couldn't quite put his finger on what it was. Then, on his way home from the Yard one evening in early 1934, a man who clearly recognised Hambrook stopped him as he was walking through Notting Hill, wanting to talk. Hambrook couldn't place the stranger, but after a brief introduction it transpired that the man (whose name Hambrook did not record) had led the prosecution in a burglary case over twenty years ago, when Hambrook had been a mere sergeant. The details of the case slowly came back to him – he hadn't been the arresting officer (as is sometimes claimed) but had visited at least two of the homes that had been burgled, and also attended the Old Bailey for the trial of the prisoner.

The case in question, the barrister reminded him, was that of 'Henry Williams', who had served his nine months' imprisonment and had then apparently dropped off the radar.

Or had he?

The more Walter Hambrook thought about the scenes of crime he had investigated all those years back, and the details of the burglary methods which had emerged at the trial, the more certain Hambrook became that Henry Williams was Flannelfoot.

He took his theory to the Yard officers dealing with the case, explaining what had happened, and telling them, 'Catch Williams, and you have caught Flannelfoot!'

Despite Hambrook's rank and reputation, however, neither Thompson nor his fellow officers were initially convinced that the youth sentenced in 1911 for a couple of minor burglaries must be the man responsible for a plague of break-ins in 1934. How old must he be? How could they not know about him by now? The Met police, like most other forces, were familiar with the names and faces of the habitual criminal fraternity in their area. But Hambrook persisted. He had studied the crime scenes and methods of entry, and his copper's instinct told him that he was right.

After a study of all the available information, Hambrook's hunch must finally have been believed. There can be no doubt that detectives traced Alice Vickers through the electoral register or other records to her address in Reading (she had returned to her home town after Vickers had deserted their home in Essex) and arranged for her to be interviewed. They soon discovered that not only had Vickers vanished, but that he had taken his daughter with him.

On 25 May 1934, the *Daily Herald* ran a front-page banner headline:

FLANNEL-FOOT HUNTED: GIRL'S PICTURE AS CLUE

The *Herald* (but apparently no other newspaper), announced that Scotland Yard had taken the unusual step of publishing the picture of a 13-year-old girl whose father, it declared, 'is the notorious burglar known as Flannel Foot'. Note the confident assertion that the girl 'is' the daughter of Flannelfoot: not suspected, not may possibly be, but *is* the daughter of the long sought-after man. Both father and daughter had gone missing, the *Herald* told its readers, and 'it is thought she may be with him and so give a clue to his whereabouts'.

The 'inside' information regarding the girl wasn't the only telling detail made public. His age and details about his background were published – and his name. Or at least *a* name.

It's surprising how much confusion Vickers' use of the easily checkable and verifiable 'Henry Williams' pseudonym caused everyone. Even this announcement boldly announced that 'his real name is Henry Williams'. In what is a rather disjointed article (or rather series of articles – it was considered a big enough story to be spread over several pages) there is a sort of postscript towards the end which adds that 'his daughter is known as Elsie Vickers', yet the writer or writers don't seem to have been capable of putting two and two together as regards his true surname.

Whatever they chose to call him, the press told readers that Elsie, aged 13 and 5 feet in height, was believed to be with him, and the articles provided a little bit of background.

'Williams' was 45, had eluded the police for more than twenty years, and had previously been a butcher in Reading. He was called 'Flannelfoot', the *Herald* confided to its readers, because of a club foot that he had had from birth which forced him to drag one foot in a limping fashion. 'However, it is believed that he has so schooled himself that he can walk without this limp being noticeable.'

This is a further example of the muddled nature of the story: he had become known as Flannelfoot because of a club foot which caused a limp, but he had trained himself not to limp. Of course, we know that he served in an infantry regiment during the war and there is absolutely no possibility that a man with a congenital condition like club foot would have passed the initial medical, let alone been allocated to such a regiment. He had no such disability, and as we know, the nickname was given him because of his burglary methods.

The *Herald* article described 'Williams' as the 'Business Man', inferring that most of his crimes being committed at weekends meant he was legitimately engaged during the week. 'He is thought to lead a Jekyll and Hyde existence,' claimed the writer, 'working as a respectable business man through the week, then making his real livelihood by crime at weekend.'

Again, the 'businessman' idea was a fabrication, and certainly couldn't have come from Scotland Yard itself, where such a notion had never been entertained. It seems that in trying to make a big splash out of issuing Elsie's photograph, the paper had taken to guesswork and embellishment to make up for the relatively few solid available facts.

It was claimed that one of the reasons Flannelfoot targeted new estates was because the locks of internal doors and the keys issued for these new properties were identical – once Flannelfoot got hold of the key to one house, he could move about freely in any he cared to burgle on that particular estate. Here, the *Herald* was on firmer ground. Flannelfoot certainly did take keys, and there is every reason to think that their explanation for it was correct. However, even this idea may have been overstated; I am only aware of a single story of him using the keys from one house to open internal doors in another, and there *are* occasions on record of him being foiled by locked inner doors.

Other 'facts' about Flannelfoot's methods are also more plausible. We are told that sometimes, when a key had been left in the lock on the other side of the door, he was able to manipulate it in order to unlock the door using one of his specialist tools, and he was also known to remove the keyhole plate. Both of these things, without doubt, featured in some Flannelfoot break-ins.

Perhaps the biggest piece of hokum in the whole series of articles is that the police had managed to identify the place where he was staying and had launched a raid – only to find that he had already fled. He had left behind some items of his burglar's toolkit, and even some photographs, which makes it sound as though he left in great haste and that the police must have come tantalisingly close to catching him. Of course, this is nonsense. The police had obtained the photographs from Alice Vickers, and still had absolutely no idea where to find the man himself – but from now on, Flannelfoot was a known and marked man.

Chapter 16

The Unfortunate Misses Watson

A soon-to-be retired Walter Hambrook's memory for criminal names and faces pointed the Yard in Vickers' direction, but in the early 1930s the serving officer who would actually lead the team on the ground was a new rising star at the Yard.

In John Horwell's book *Horwell of the Yard*, the then chief constable described how he made catching Flannelfoot a priority, and how he thought about who might head the team that would achieve it. 'I had in my mind a youngish, quiet, reserved and deep-thinking officer … I know him as a very persistent officer, one of the bulldog breed, who having fastened his teeth into a case would never beg off until he had captured his man.'

The detective in question was Inspector Thomas Thompson.

Horwell largely gave him free rein as to how he should go about his task, and allowed Thompson to hand-pick a team of both male and female officers. He also procured several cars ('supercharged', unlike the standard police vehicle) for this new team's use.

Just over a year after Scotland Yard went public with the news about Flannelfoot taking off with his daughter Elsie Vickers, Thompson was on the trail of a heartless serial fraudster.

Annie Forman was a 45-year-old East Ender from a decent family who had taken to a life of crime. She was a clever and calculating woman who developed a skill for spinning yarns which induced people to part with their money – lots of it. But she wasn't so clever that her crimes didn't eventually catch up with her. By the time she crossed paths with Inspector Thompson she had already served four sentences, although the most recent, a four-year stretch, had been ten years earlier. She had the air of someone who had finally gone straight; she had eyesight problems herself, and after her release in 1924 she became involved in a scheme which involved her visiting blind prisoners and helping to teach them Braille.

However, it was this very disability of her own – which Thompson soon came to believe she exaggerated in order to gain both sympathy and money from her victims – which was one of the planks in the case against her on this occasion. She met and fell in love with a young man, and, wishing to impress him, portrayed herself as 'a person of substance' who could help him financially and find him employment.

In order to live up to this role she needed a ready source of cash she didn't currently have, so she turned to the Misses Watson: two elderly spinsters of Tooting, whose parents she claimed to have been acquainted with. She arrived wearing dark glasses, claiming to be recovering from blindness, and hoping that they might let her have £12 in order to start a little knitting business to provide for herself and her aged mother. The sisters agreed to let her have the money. But as so often happens in such cases, once Forman realised she had gained the confidence of the sisters, her stories and demands began to escalate.

Among her numerous tales, Forman at one point said that her current employers had sent her a cheque for monies owed to her amounting to £300, but that she had lost it and they had refused to send her another. She had sued the employers, she told the sisters, and judgement had been awarded to her in the total of £15,000. All she needed was £3,000 in order to first settle a counter-claim which had to be paid before the £15,000 could be paid over to her. Again, the Misses Watson were taken in and handed over the money. It took several more such sob stories before the penny dropped and the Watson sisters turned to the police.

When Inspector Thompson pounced, Forman was indicted on seven separate charges for obtaining £3,740 in total. This was a huge amount then, but Thompson told the court that there was evidence that she had actually obtained around £18,000 from the sisters over a two-year period, 'which was in effect the whole of their property in the world'. The prosecution counsel bluntly remarked that the case 'showed the astonishing credulity with which people would swallow the most astounding stories not supported by evidence'.

Thompson said it was the most callous fraud he had ever dealt with. He had managed to recover between £3,000 and £4,000 for the Watsons, including deeds to some houses. Forman's defence claimed that his client did not tell the Watsons that she was blind, but partially blind, along with inflammation of the eyes which caused her to wear dark glasses. She had perpetrated the fraud not out of greed, but because of her infatuation with the new man in her life. Almost all the money went to him and his parents. It didn't help her case that she asked for seven other offences of obtaining 'considerable sums' of money to be taken into account, and the Common Serjeant declared her a 'very wicked person' and a 'very dangerous person to have about in society', from whom the public must be protected. He sent her down for seven years.

Very soon after Thompson had finished with this case, it was a telephone operator who played both the detective and heroine of a story featuring a young man called George Gothard, 24. He made a telephone call to palatial Zetland House, Kensington, and got through to a maid. He informed her he was Colonel Mayhew and said that a young man named West (whom, one suspects, would look strikingly like Gothard) would be arriving to pick up 30 shillings that the colonel had promised in order to enable him to get a job. He added that he had contacted the maid's employer, Mrs Houghton, who had said that it would be all right. But Gothard made a big mistake.

In those days, telephone operators manually put calls through and were able to listen in to what was being said. When Gothard told the maid that he was calling from a certain address, the operator immediately knew it was a lie – her system told her that he was phoning from a telephone box. She called the police straight away and Inspector Thompson nipped to Zetland House as quickly as he could, in fact, arriving before Gothard. He instructed the maid to put the 30 shillings in an envelope as requested, and assured her that he would be in an adjoining room listening in.

Sure enough, Gothard, calling himself West, arrived to collect the money. While the maid engaged him in conversation, Thompson made his dramatic appearance like a character from an Agatha Christie play. When the detective told the man who he was and informed him that he was being arrested, Gothard didn't go quietly. There was a violent struggle, but that sort of thing was meat and drink to Yard officers, who spent a good deal of their time taking on hardened organised criminals. The young man was subdued and taken away to meet his fate.

Chapter 17

The Plight of Alice Vickers

In the early hours of Saturday, 21 April 1934, it is highly likely that Flannelfoot took up a covert position at the rear of some houses on North Hyde Lane, Norwood Green, about 6 miles south of the Cavendish Avenue crimes, watching till all the lights had gone out. When morning came, the occupiers of Nos. 4, 5, 6, and 11 discovered that they had been burgled. In all cases, a thin instrument had been inserted through the woodwork of the casement windows and the catch had been opened. The haul comprised mostly cash from utility meters, and a bicycle stolen for the thief's escape was not recovered. It must have been a long and patient vigil for Flannelfoot before striking, since the occupant of one of the houses didn't go to bed until 1 am.

Thompson's Flannelfoot team were in no doubt that both the Sudbury Hill and Norwood Green crimes were committed by the same person – and that it was their man. The assistant chief constable sent a memo to his boss John Horwell, to that effect: 'We have not yet found out what the subject of this file is doing', (i.e. where he might be found) he said, and made a number of suggestions as to how they might track him down. First and foremost, they should send someone to talk to his wife in Reading, whom they believed had been deserted by Vickers in 1932. She had already been interviewed by local police, turning up the story of how he had abandoned her and taken Elsie with him, but there must be more they could learn from this crucial connection. Thompson knew Alice Vickers was keen to trace the daughter he had taken with him, and was thought to be instigating proceedings against her husband for desertion. 'If the woman's statements are true, we ought to be able to get her to tell us much more than she appears to have told the Reading officer,' said the memo.

The Yard was also aware that Vickers' father and brother were living in Bexleyheath, but had been interviewed and also claimed not to know of their relative's whereabouts. The assistant chief constable wondered whether a warrant might be obtained which would allow them to intercept mail addressed to both men to see whether Vickers was writing to them. Other than this, he concluded, the only other strategy would be to choose likely locations that might appeal to Vickers and assign officers to keep watch at weekends until he was caught.

On 7 May 1934, DI Mitchell of Scotland Yard was duly sent to Reading to talk to Alice Vickers and try to wheedle more information out of her. She maintained, however, that she had no idea where her husband was, and Mitchell was of the opinion that she was telling the truth. She told him of how when, as we have heard, they had been living in Wickford, Essex, in 1932, Vickers took Elsie out supposedly for a walk on Christmas morning and neither of them returned. Alice swore she had not heard from them since, and the emotions she experienced, especially on the day itself – Christmas Day, of all days – can only be imagined. For a spouse to walk out without warning is one thing, but for her daughter to also vanish while Alice was presumably preparing the family Christmas meal, expecting them to be all sitting round the table and enjoying it together, is on another level entirely.

Does this hint at the true character of Vickers? The best slant that can be put on it is that his unhappiness had been festering for a long time and, Christmas being the emotionally charged time that it can be, he reached breaking point. Love can also lead to people doing things they otherwise wouldn't dream of. We have no idea of the strength of Vickers' emotional attachment to the 'Norfolk woman'. They did stay together for several years, but as we shall see, there is good reason to believe that he was quite prepared to be casually unfaithful to his new woman less than a year after taking up with her.

Emotional turmoil notwithstanding, the indications point towards Vickers' act – not just of walking out on Alice, but taking into account the timing and the way he did it – as being a callous and self-centred one.

In spite of that, though, DI Mitchell got the impression that if it had not been for Vickers taking Elsie, Alice wouldn't have been keen to help the police track down her wayward husband. As it was, she provided them with five photographs (the Yard had been concerned that the only one they had was from his original arrest in 1910, when he was a very young man). After some rummaging, she was able to furnish them with one snap of Elsie and four of Vickers. The latter batch included one of him in 1918 when he was still in the army, and there was a photo in which he featured among a group of *Sunday News* machine managers, taken at a works outing to Hindhead in 1924. The consensus of opinion was always that Vickers never got a proper job after leaving prison; it would be interesting to know why he should be part of a works outing, but I have been unable to find any evidence that he worked for the *Sunday News*, and something Alice was to later say would seem to confirm that he never stooped to anything as prosaic and inconvenient as regular paid employment.

Mitchell's investigation might not have turned up Vickers' whereabouts, but it did provide some interesting little snippets that add somewhat to our picture of the man and his life.

Inspector Hambrook aged about 30.
(*Courtesy Hazel Price*)

Renowned pathologist Sir Bernard Spilsbury.
(*Wikimedia Commons*)

SIR BERNARD SPILSBURY.

When arsenic has closed your eyes,
  This certain hope your corpse may rest in :—
Sir B. will kindly analyse
  The contents of your large intestine.

MR. PUNCH'S PERSONALITIES.—LXIV.

Spilsbury as portrayed in *Punch* magazine – an indication of his celebrity. (*Wikimedia Commons, originally from Wellcome Images*)

Burntwood Asylum, converted to an emergency hospital during the Second World War. Vickers died here on 9 December 1942. (*Wikimedia Commons*)

Elvira Barney after her acquittal. (*Wikimedia Commons*)

Tempting prospective homeowners away from London. Flannelfoot struck at least two of the mentioned locations. (© *TfL from the London Transport Museum collection*)

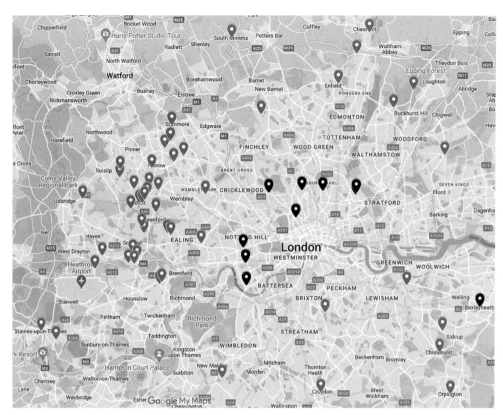

Tracking Flannelfoot. Grey dots – known burglary locations (note that there were numerous burglaries in most locations); black dots – places he lived. (*Google Maps*)

Rifleman Vickers. (*Patrick J. Vickers, Wikimedia Commons*)

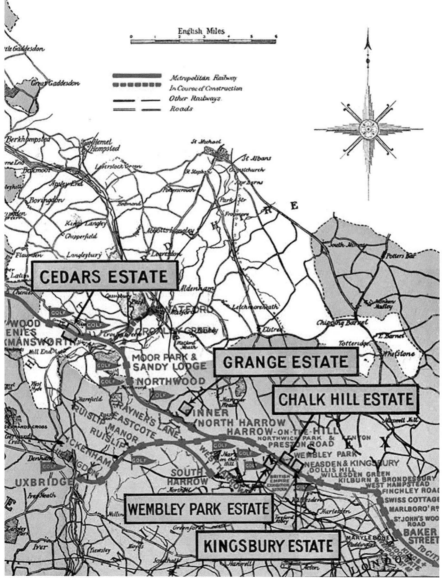

Metropolitan Railway map of 'Metro-Land' – which might just as easily have been called 'Flannelfoot Land'. It includes Eastcote, where he was finally cornered. (*Wikimedia Commons*)

Vickers unwittingly led detectives to his lodgings in the marked property, and surveillance was carried out from an adjacent building. (*Google Maps*)

Sidney Fox, executed for murdering his mother Rosaline after a painstaking investigation by Hambrook and Spilsbury. (*Wikimedia Commons*)

Vickers' 'wanted' notice from his Scotland Yard file. (*The National Archives, ref. MEPO3/1312*)

Alice Hanslip, whose rendezvous with her lover Vickers ultimately led to his arrest. (*The National Archives, ref. MEPO3/1312*)

Elsie, the Vickers' daughter. When she was identified after being found wandering the streets, police were one step closer to catching Flannelfoot. (*The National Archives, ref. MEPO3/1312*)

Chief Inspector Thomas Basil Thompson, who led the Flannelfoot team and played a central part in tracking down Alice Hanslip in Norfolk. (*Courtesy Alan Moss/Metropolitan Police*)

According to the police and prison records, Harry Vickers was 5 feet 5½ inches in height, but both his father and Alice insisted that he was appreciably taller than that. The other noteworthy thing that came out of the interviews with those who knew him best was that, despite his war wound, he was capable of walking without a noticeable limp. Just for good measure, he took pride in his appearance and was almost always smartly dressed when out and about.

Before his disappearance, Alice told Mitchell, Vickers only came home at weekends – but not because he had a job to go to. She believed that he spent his days travelling to race meetings: 'punting'. She was specific that she had 'never known him to follow any occupation', and during his weekday absences he never contacted her. If he literally didn't come home at all on weekdays, this implies that he either slept in paid accommodation or with friends – or that he was already making extended stays with the other woman in his life.

Finally, Alice told Mitchell that although Vickers had made no attempt to support her financially since his abrupt departure, she was aware that he used to send small amounts of money to his mother using his brother Stan as an intermediary.

Several weeks later, Alice Vickers had to badger DI Mitchell to let her have the photographs back 'as you promised to do' (which he duly did), adding that she had been 'hoping to hear from you before this long time, that you had been able to find my little Elsie for me, but I am beginning to lose all hopes of ever seeing her again. Will you please do all you can for me, as I've no other help of finding her but through you and your men.' From this final heartfelt plea, we can see why Mitchell was so sure that Alice wasn't withholding knowledge of her husband's whereabouts.

All in all, the chat with Alice didn't provide a lot for the Yard to go on, but enquiries were made at the *Sunday News* (which had since been taken over by the *Sunday Graphic*) to see if anyone remembered or was still in touch with Vickers. Many of the old staff had lost their jobs because of the takeover, so hopes weren't high – but eventually someone was identified, and this led to one of the more significant breakthroughs of the whole case.

Dennis Whitehead, who lived in Hammersmith, had been a friend of Vickers for a number of years. It's not stated specifically, but it seems he worked at the old *Sunday News*, and presumably it was through that friendship that Vickers came to be on the works outing. Vickers and Whitehead had other things in common: the latter also had one previous conviction, and was a follower of horse racing.

Whitehead confirmed Alice's report that Vickers travelled the country attending race meetings; he never missed Brighton, yet for some reason Whitehead had not seen him there that year (1934). More interestingly,

Whitehead was able to tell the police that Vickers had been 'associated with' a fair-haired woman for around nine years, about whom he had always been very cagey. He was aware that he had lived in the Maida Vale area, but the last time Whitehead had seen him was some months back when he bumped into him on a tram near Hammersmith. During the course of their chat, Vickers had mentioned that he was then living in Fulham. Sadly, no specific address came out in the conversation, but it was something to go on, and in time the Yard would apply a little more pressure on Whitehead.

Chapter 18

The Scotland Yard Dossier

Thanks to a detailed list compiled by Scotland Yard of Flannelfoot's known crimes, which covers the period October 1934 to May 1936, we can see some interesting facts and patterns begin to emerge about the man and his methods.

Flannelfoot was fairly quiet during the middle of 1934 – at least as far as London was concerned. It would eventually be discovered that he was on his travels from May or June, ostensibly on a pleasure trip. But from what we know of his love of trackside betting, these jaunts may have been timed so that Vickers could attend race meetings around the country. He appears again in Yard crime records in October, not only active in places we might associate him with to the north of the City, such as Enfield and Hounslow, but popping up in Ashford in Kent, around 20 miles and about an hour by train from the centre of London, and Sidcup in the same county, 12 to 15 miles south of the Thames. After the Ashford raid, where he burgled three houses, Vickers left his stolen bicycle in Hounslow as he made his way east back towards London. Sidcup may have been a more rural area than his more usual haunts, but even there new housing developments were springing up at this time, and news of this is perhaps what drew him beyond his normal area of operations. After breaking into two houses on Margaret's Way, his getaway machine was eventually abandoned near Greenwich Railway Station. This means he pedalled for around 7 miles, half the distance or more to where he was living, before switching to public transport.

For the first few months of 1935, Vickers went out at least once a week, sometimes twice but rarely more, sticking mostly to familiar territory such as Hounslow and Enfield (again), but with the odd expedition to other new and more distant places thrown in almost as if for the sake of variety. During this period he made another of his relatively rare trips south of the Thames, this time to Petts Wood, one more rural location where new houses were expanding the village. He broke into two houses on Eastbrook Road, Shooters Hill, which handily had, and still has, a large area of parkland on one side. Vickers would return to this district again in January 1936, undoubtedly drawn to the new Shrewsbury Park Estate, where he entered two more houses by removing putty from the window frames. Yet another area being developed in the 1930s was Monks Park, near Wembley. He found this estate profitable, moving between four houses in one March night on Park View, before leaving his stolen bike beside the tram tracks on Harrow Road – no doubt, if the lighting allowed, taking in the famous twin towers of the nearby old Wembley Stadium.

Before that, still in 1935, he was back in full swing, venturing all over London and beyond, mostly on Monday and Saturday evenings during this period. In addition to his customary western haunts, Flannelfoot struck as far north as South Mimms and Cheshunt, both beyond the modern M25 circle, Croydon to the south, and Barkingside near Ilford to the east. All of the above expeditions between 1933 and 1936, amounting to 189 homes in forty-two places, were spread over sixty-seven nights, and involved investigating officers from no fewer than forty-five police stations – and this with a six month break in 1935!

There is a marked pattern to the nights Flannelfoot chose to work on. (The proviso is that the Yard lists don't make it clear whether the days recorded refer to the evening he set out, or the early hours of the following day when he might have actually struck. I'm assuming they refer to the evening of the day quoted.)

Monday was by far Flannelfoot's favoured day. He notched up twenty-seven Monday night expeditions during this time. Saturday came a close second with twenty-one. The total for these two days is larger than all the other days of the week added together: Tuesday, five; Wednesday, nine; Thursday, six; Friday and Sunday, just one occasion each.

He visited a number of the streets named in this survey twice: Crosslands Avenue, Norwood Green on New Year's Day 1936 and again at the end of April; Templedene Avenue, Staines in March and December 1935; Apple Grove, Enfield in December 1935 and April 1936; Bullsmoor Lane in the Enfield area in December 1934 and February 1935.

The most number of break-ins in one night was six on unlucky Curzon Avenue, Wealdstone. This was on 25 November 1935, and according to the Yard records it was his first job after the six-month break, so perhaps he was making up for lost time. On only two occasions did Flannelfoot confine himself to a single housebreaking in an evening, both within a few weeks of each other. On 30 January he only managed one house, on Downing Drive, Greenford, and on 3 February the same thing happened on Tudor Way, Uxbridge. It's highly likely that he was either disturbed or noticed activity which caused him to abort the mission for safety's sake on these nights. One of the burglaries on the list took place on Pavilion Way, Eastcote, in February 1936. Eighteen months later, he would revisit this location too – little knowing that within spitting distance of the road where he first struck, his career would finally and abruptly come to an end.

Perhaps surprisingly, he managed to find a handy bike on every one of the night-time raids except for one, when he visited Barkingside near Ilford in March 1935. The majority of bikes were recovered for their owners: fifty-three out of sixty-nine, most being found at or near a rail, tram or bus station.

Vickers regularly cycled 5 miles or more after committing his final burglary of the night. On a few occasions he did twice that distance. One of his longest was from Kenilworth Avenue, Harrow, in January 1936, where he had found two houses with windows left conveniently open rather than having to resort to implements from his array of tools. When he had taken all he wanted, he pedalled for just over 10 miles to Ethelden Road, Shepherd's Bush. What makes this excursion a little more interesting is that we know that the following year, Vickers was living just a five-minute walk from where he left that bike. He may even have already been living there at this time – which would make it one of the few, if not the only occasion, where he cycled all the way home rather than completing his journey by public transport. I suspect this was not the case, however. The obvious risk in doing such a thing, and the reason why he almost never cycled all the way home, was that if a stolen bike were linked to Flannelfoot burglaries (as they often were) it may well have helped police to zoom in on where he lived.

During that year, he confined himself largely to West London: places like Hounslow, Greenford, Uxbridge and New Malden, all of which places he would have been very familiar with. There were, though, a few forays elsewhere, like Chingford to the north-east and Chislehurst to the south-east.

He seemed to be getting a little bolder, or alternatively perhaps luckier as regards the opportunities which presented themselves, since there were more instances of four- and five-house raids in one night now. But time was running out.

Chapter 19

The Net Closing

In January 1936, Chief Constable John Horwell issued a 'Secret Confidential Notice' which featured a photograph of 'Henry Williams alias Harry Edward Vickers, alias Flannel Foot'. It was accompanied by a description: 5 feet 6½ inches in height, pale complexion, brown hair, blue eyes, birthmark on left hand. It was also pointed out that the photograph dated to 1924, so our man may now be 'fuller in face'. It was circulated to officers 'only with a view to arouse their enthusiasm and to assist them in the special observation which has been arranged'. The notice went on to provide some background on what was known about Flannelfoot's methods and habits: he targeted – usually on Friday and Sunday nights – houses of the '£400-700 type' from among the numerous new estates springing up around London, said Horwell. These had windows 'usually of the casement type' with frames made of 'new and soft wood' through which he is able to insert his thin, sharp tools at such an angle as to be able to push the fastener open. 'This man seems to be able to make friends with any dog at scene [*sic*] of his crimes and has been known to take the joint from the larder and give it to the dog.' It was stressed that the contents of the notice should be kept in the strictest confidence, since although the Yard was in no doubt that Vickers was behind these crimes, there was no actual evidence against him – thus it was imperative to catch him in the act. (Besides which, should it leak to the newspapers, it might cause him to move his operations outside London before he could be caught.)

Officers were also alerted to the fact that should they see someone they believed fitted Vickers' description, he would prove 'a most difficult criminal to follow'. An occasion was referred to when he was being followed onto a train, he leapt back off the moving locomotive just before it reached the end of the platform, then casually sat on a seat to check whether he was being followed. On another occasion he was riding away from a crime he had committed on a bike he had stolen when he came across a constable patrolling his beat. It was four in the morning, but instead of pedalling like fury, he 'politely stopped and asked the constable whether he desired assistance. The constable being unaware of the crime, thanked him and he passed on'.

These final points are intriguing because all other internal discussions regarding Flannelfoot stress that they had no idea where he might be found and only knew where he had been *after* the crimes had been committed. Quite how it came about that he was supposedly being followed isn't clear, and it presents a conundrum. Every other reference to him categorically states that the police simply did not know where to find him up to this point, and there is not a shred of evidence in the Yard files that he was ever seen or followed by an officer until the end game was played out.

Horwell's closing comment: *It is believed that when caught he will put up a very stiff fight to escape from custody* not only doesn't sound like Vickers from what is now known of him, but proved to be very wide of the mark when the time came. As chief constable, Horwell was in nominal charge of the hunt for Flannelfoot, but it's likely that he had little, if any, hands-on involvement and this isn't the only occasion when there is a suspicion that he was prone to error and exaggeration, as his memoir would testify to. It wasn't an officer following Vickers which proved to be the next big leap forward in the case, but the discovery of someone else entirely.

Early the following month, the attention of a policeman patrolling his beat was drawn to a young girl walking the streets. It probably didn't seem much to him at the time – but it would prove to be the most significant breakthrough in the whole investigation.

A teenage girl wandering along, aimlessly kicking stones in the road, wasn't so strange, but there was something about her troubled, faraway expression that attracted the officer's attention. He approached her and asked her if she was all right, and in performing this charitable act he set in motion a chain of events which would lead to the capture of Flannelfoot. It wasn't long before a newspaper headline was imploring:

DO YOU KNOW HER?

This was the call for assistance the *Weekly Dispatch* of 16 February made to its readers. Beneath the headline was a grainy picture of a girl it described as being around 18 years old, sitting in a Highgate Hospital bed with a nurse by her side. She was around 5 feet 6 in height, with a fair complexion, brown hair and a round face – and she was suffering from amnesia.

She could tell neither the police nor hospital staff where she came from, nor anything at all about her background. She didn't even know her own name, though something she had mumbled indicated that her Christian name might sound like 'Inez'. The board above her bed simply recorded her as 'Patient Number 27' – and for the next few days, that was the name she became known by as the press throughout the country put out calls for anyone who might recognise her to come forward.

There was no further progress for over four weeks, and then, in early March, the long-awaited breakthrough came.

Alice Vickers clearly wasn't a regular reader of newspapers in her Reading home, but she claims she did come across a copy of one of the dailies featuring the story and picture of Patient Number 27, and instantly recognised that it was Elsie, the daughter whom she hadn't seen in four years.

Alice immediately wrote to the matron of the ward on which Elsie was being looked after, explaining who she was and providing proof that she was the girl's mother. As soon as she received a reply inviting her to visit, she took the first train to London, accompanied by her sister for moral support.

At the hospital she was invited into the matron's room, where the girl was waiting for her. Alice later said that when she entered, Elsie – whose memory had still not fully returned – looked at her blankly for a moment, then sprang to her feet and ran to her, crying 'Mummy! Oh, Mummy!'

The pair were too overcome with emotion to speak further at first, with Elsie still recovering from her own trauma and Alice having almost given up hope of ever seeing her daughter again. But they were served tea and given time to compose themselves, and before long they began to chat about their experiences.

Alice Vickers, now in her mid-forties, was described as a 'kindly, grey haired lady' by the *Daily Mirror*. Elsie was a 'pretty girl, looking much older than her fourteen years'. Alice told reporters that it was almost as if Elsie had come back from the dead, while Elsie, with 'tears in her big, dark eyes', said 'I am so happy to be going home again with Mummy.'

Inspector Thompson tried to talk to Elsie; she was in no state to be interviewed properly yet, but he did manage to get an address: she had been living with her father at 23 Tufnell Park Road, Holloway, in North London. When officers were hurriedly dispatched to investigate, it came as no surprise that Vickers had vanished and left no forwarding address, but they were able to glean a few things from neighbours. The occupant had been living there with a child and an adult female. They had kept themselves to themselves, so little was known about them, but two men who had been in the habit of going to greyhound meetings with Vickers did so in the company of plain clothes officers for the next few visits. The wily Vickers, though, did not make an appearance.

A few weeks later, on 12 March 1936, Tommy Thompson and Inspector Knight travelled to Reading to try again with Elsie, now she'd had time to recover. Initially, the family were reluctant to let them see the girl – though one suspects that it was more to protect Vickers than Elsie herself. The two Scotland Yard men finally got their way – and the 14-year-old provided them with an itinerary of her and her father's movements from the fateful Christmas Day when she had been whisked away from the family home.

After their disappearance in December 1932, they lived at 28 Brunswick Road, Brighton; in May of the following year, they moved to a place called 'Woodlands', in Woodingdean, about 4 miles from the centre of Brighton. They stayed there till September, when they moved back to London: initially Edith Road, West Kensington, then 95 Drive Mansions, Fulham Road until May of 1934. Vickers then took Elsie on a little tour of Britain (though the chances are, as I've already said, that it was in pursuit of horse or dog racing meetings rather than the 'holiday' that Elsie described the trip as). They travelled to Leicester, Manchester and Liverpool. On their return to London, Elsie found herself living at 32 Oakley Square, Camden Town, then 2 Sotheby Rd, Highbury, and finally the 23 Tufnell Park Road address from where she had gone missing, and where they had lived under the name of 'Howard'. Needless to say, Elsie didn't attend school at all while she, her father and his mystery woman were leading this nomadic lifestyle.

All in all, Elsie demonstrated a remarkable memory for precise addresses and dates for someone so young *and* who had recently been suffering from trauma and amnesia. And her dates throw up some interesting possibilities, one of which was that even while away, Vickers commuted to London in order to continue his burgling career; the other is that he really did carry out his night-time work further afield.

We have seen that in July of 1933 there was a rash of burglaries in Northolt, London; they were carried out in the Flannelfoot style, and it was an area with which he was associated. However, according to Elsie's detailed account of their movements, she, Vickers and the woman he had taken up with were living in Woodingdean just outside Brighton at the time.

Elsie said that Vickers took her travelling around the country from May of 1934. Leicester is one of the places she names, and again we have seen that the Leicester police suspected Flannelfoot of paying them a visit in that year. This was four or five months after their departure from London, and unfortunately Elsie doesn't say exactly when they were in Leicester, nor when the 'tour' ended.

Elsie gave the detectives some idea of what life was like at this time. She said she wasn't allowed to go out, and described herself as being practically a prisoner till she finally ran away (something Vickers would vehemently deny).

Like her mother, she had no idea what her father did for a living, but she did know how keen he was on dog racing. He tended to go out on Sunday, Wednesday and Friday nights, and didn't come home until around 7.30 am, when he would go straight to bed. After these nights out, he would sometimes empty the money from his pockets and let her count it when he got home. She estimated that it usually came to between £5 and £7 (at a time when the average weekly wage was just under £5).

'This information fairly conclusively proves we are on the track of the right man,' said Chief Inspector Thompson.

But he was also suspicious that Elsie hadn't told them everything she knew. She claimed to know very little about the woman who was living with her father. She described her as being around 35 years old, about 5 feet 5 inches tall, with curly black hair, a round face, hooked nose and blue eyes. Elsie was able to recall one small but tantalising piece of background information: the woman was said to have a niece of a similar age to Elsie, who had a deformed leg, and who lived with her grandparents between Thetford and Brandon in Norfolk.

A Miss Stockhardt, who lived in the same Tufnell Park Road lodging house, agreed to be accompanied to Reading to try to jog Elsie's memory regarding the identity of the elusive woman, but the family wouldn't allow the visitor to see the girl alone. Alice Vickers was now stating categorically that she couldn't see why she should help the police find her husband. This was surprising loyalty indeed from a wife who had been callously abandoned for another woman, and she had changed her tune somewhat since begging the police to help her track Vickers down so that she might be reunited with Elsie.

The Norfolk police's enquiries failed to trace a likely family, which was hardly surprising with so little to go on. But Tommy Thompson wasn't so easily beaten – and his persistence and dogged detective skills regarding the Norfolk connection would eventually pay off.

At around this time, Inspector Thompson sent a note to his chief constable, John Horwell, with some suggestions for future tactics. Any officers encountering a cyclist in the early hours should stop them, and if they are found to be in possession of galoshes, thin-bladed knives or pliers, they should be required to prove their identity and occupation. Thompson knew that most ticket collectors at outlying rail and tube stations were familiar with their regular early morning workers, so they could be asked to point out 'strangers' to officers undertaking surveillance duties. The same might be done with tram conductors. Horwell then called a conference of 'crime chiefs' and arrangements were made to increase observation in Flannelfoot's regular haunts during the times when he might be expected to make an appearance. This initially meant extra patrols at weekends, but when Flannelfoot struck in New Malden on Monday, 20 January of that year, Horwell ruefully reflected that his already stretched manpower might need to start increasing surveillance on at least some weeknights too.

The idea that Flannelfoot *only* struck at the weekend didn't hold water anyway. There is a memo dated 20 May 1936 in the Scotland Yard files in which someone had analysed his crimes so far that year. This showed the following pattern (the night on which he would have commenced operations is quoted, even though his work may have continued into the early hours of the following day):

- Sunday nights, on ten occasions
- Monday nights, twice
- Tuesday, five times
- Wednesday nights, three times
- Thursday nights, once
- Most surprising of all, he had never committed a crime on Friday night or in the early hours of Saturday during this period. This was not his pattern of earlier years, but perhaps even burglars need a day off.

This is only a few months in a single year out of a long criminal career, but it goes to show that Flannelfoot was far less predictable than most people seemed to assume.

At around this time, Horwell issued a revised and expanded description of the wanted man. His height was now given as 5 feet 6½ inches, just an inch more than earlier estimates, despite the family's insistence that he was 'much' taller. Vickers, the 'special confidential notice' said, had deep-set blue eyes; large prominent ears ('left one noticeable so'); a square, heavy chin; long straight nose; full lips; wide mouth; 'cynical expression'; lower eyelids pouch; hair lightish brown ('well-oiled, straight, grows well back from forehead'); and a 'good figure'. By 'eyelids pouch', Horwell presumably meant what we would now call bags under the eyes. It was now revealed that it was his left leg which had been the reason for his medical discharge from the army during the war, the cause given rather vaguely as 'injured sinews'. And finally, there was a reminder that Vickers always 'dresses smartly'.

Thompson, meanwhile, had been working on Dennis Whitehead, the friend of Vickers who had been tracked down through the *Sunday News* works outing photograph, and was able to give Horwell an update. Whitehead had last seen Vickers at Kempton Park racecourse fourteen months previously, before Elsie had run away from him, where he had admitted he knew the police were hunting for the pair of them. Thompson's enquiries also revealed that Vickers was still not drawing the army pension that he was entitled to – almost certainly because he knew it entailed providing an address which might lead to his capture.

Flannelfoot was becoming something of an embarrassment for a Scotland Yard force famed for its expertise and reputation for getting results. Elsie's story may have galvanised them into ever greater efforts, but they were a long way from being able to put their man in cuffs just yet. And there were, of course, other and more serious criminals to be caught.

Tommy Thompson was promoted to chief inspector in August 1936, and by the following month he featured in a big press splash about what was called Scotland Yard's 'Big Eight'. As we have seen, The Yard had been sending experienced men to help provincial forces deal with more serious crimes, mostly murders, for some time. The 'Big Eight' idea seemed to be a way of putting it on a more formal footing. Six senior officers, including Thompson, were to be available to pack their bags and travel to any part of the country; the other two, still of at least inspector rank, were based at the Yard and worked on things like criminal records and fingerprints.

When this announcement was made, Thompson was, in fact, already engaged on such a case, probably the biggest of his career thus far. Police in Yorkshire had called upon the assistance of Scotland Yard to solve the brutal murder of a teenage girl. This is a disturbing case for two completely different reasons. The first and most obvious is that an innocent young girl was taken from her family in such a horrific fashion. The other is that the man arrested by Thompson after his investigations, who was eventually hanged, may well not have committed the crime.

Irene Hart was a 16-year-old Rotherham girl who lived with her father, stepmother Avice, and her stepmother's disabled brother, Ambrose. At the time of the following events, Avice's father, 62-year-old Andrew Bagley, was also staying at the house. The house had only two bedrooms, so Bagley slept on a mattress on the floor in Irene's bedroom.

On the morning of 12 September 1936, Irene went missing. She was found murdered later the same day. At the request of Rotherham Chief Constable R. Hall, Thompson, accompanied by Detective Sergeant Tasker, travelled north by train to take charge of the investigation, staying in a local hotel. After making their own inquiries they attended the inquest, where the story unfolded. Avice Hart told the court that she had last seen her stepdaughter alive at 9.30 am on Saturday. Avice left the house to do some shopping, leaving

Bagley in the kitchen reading a newspaper. She assumed that Irene would soon go upstairs to wash and dress the disabled Ambrose.

When Mrs Hart returned home at about 11 am, Bagley and Ambrose were still in the house, Bagley still downstairs and Ambrose upstairs. Bagley told Avice that he had given Irene £1 to buy herself a dress and a hairband from a local shop. He then left, saying he was travelling to Sheffield and would be back later that night. When the girl still hadn't returned by the time her husband came home from work at 11.45 am, and an enquiry at the local shop proved that she hadn't been there, the pair began to worry and commenced a search of the house. Inside a closet in her bedroom, they noticed that the trap-door leading to the attic had been left partly open, and Mr Hart climbed up to investigate. He saw some of the clothes that Irene had been wearing that day beside a large tin trunk, and, fearing the worst, rushed out to find a policeman. Meanwhile, Avice Hart took a closer look and noticed a portion of Irene's cream-coloured skirt protruding from beneath the lid of the 4-foot-long container. She lifted the lid, revealing the gruesome sight of Irene's lifeless, partially clothed body curled up inside. A ball of newspaper had been stuffed into her mouth, and she had been strangled with a piece of rope which was still tied round her neck.

Initial reports spoke of police interviewing Avice's brother Ambrose: 'a deaf-and-dumb dwarf, unable to walk'. But their attention quickly turned to Avice's father Andrew Bagley, especially when he didn't return as expected that night. Thompson and Tasker called on lodging houses and Poor Law institutions in search of him, and when that failed to turn anything up a major nationwide hunt was set in motion.

Numerous supposed sightings of Bagley proved to be false alarms, and there was brief excitement when a man was found dead on a railway line 10 miles from Rotherham. He fitted Bagley's description, but this also turned out to be a case of misidentification.

Thompson and Tasker stayed on for a couple more weeks, but with Bagley, their chief and indeed only suspect on the run, there was little more for them to do in Rotherham and they returned to London.

Bagley was caught in Nottinghamshire several weeks later, when he was recognised from the detailed descriptions which had adorned numerous newspapers during the course of the manhunt. He tried to explain that although he *had* vanished because he knew the police would be arriving on the day of the murder, it wasn't because he had killed Irene but because he knew he was liable for prosecution over debts accrued by his late common-law wife.

Nevertheless, he was arrested and charged with the murder of Irene Hart. The prosecution put forward jealousy as a motive: Irene had been to the pictures with her uncle and a young man not long before her death, and Bagley, who slept in the same room as Irene, had been angry about the youth accompanying them. Irene had been killed by a piece of washing line which had been taken from a bowl, and this bowl had Bagley's fingerprints on it.

The jury took less than three hours (not an especially short time for that period) to decide that Andrew Bagley was guilty of murder, and he was hanged early the following year after an appeal was rejected out of hand.

However, crime writer Jeanette Hensby, in her fascinating book *The Rotherham Trunk Murder*, makes a good case for the true murderer having been Ambrose, the same deaf-mute man who was questioned before Bagley became the prime suspect. Her theory is that before fleeing, Bagley and Avice Hart found Irene in her bedroom, having been killed by Ambrose who was still beside the body. Bagley, not wanting Ambrose, his son, to face the death sentence, colluded with Avice to cover up the truth. They put Irene's body in the trunk, and Bagley, knowing he was wanted for other matters, fled before the alarm was raised.

Bagley's actions certainly made him appear to be guilty, and Inspector Thompson was no doubt satisfied that justice had been served. However, evidence uncovered during Jeanette Hensby's detailed investigation into the case strongly suggests that the wrong man may have been hanged.

Chapter 20

Hambrook's Last Case

Hambrook's recollection of the conviction of Henry Williams/Harry Vickers was crucial to the Flannelfoot investigation, but he was not destined to be the man who would arrest him, since the 60-year-old detective's days at the Yard were nearly numbered after a long and illustrious career. And, as ever for a man in his position, weightier matters took priority over the activities of a small-time crook.

Superintendent Walter Hambrook's final murder investigation before his retirement took place in 1936, a few months after the sensation of Elsie and the 'Patient Number 27' story. It would prove a difficult one to crack, and would, in fact, drag on frustratingly beyond Hambrook's already set retirement date.

In August of that year, a woman in a London lodging house became worried when she noticed that her neighbour, 66-year-old Ada Fortescue, hadn't taken in her daily delivery of milk bottles for two successive days. The neighbour telephoned the police, who, after knocking at the front door of the four-storey house but getting no reply, went round to the rear where they found an unlocked door. Making their way down to the basement, where Mrs Fortescue had her own apartment, they found her lifeless body, bound and gagged. A pair of cotton pyjamas had been tied tightly around her neck, and her head was wrapped in a sheet with a woollen jumper on top of that. When all of the wrappings were removed, the officers saw that there were severe wounds to the woman's face. The murder was discovered on Friday the 13th. Scotland Yard was immediately informed, and Superintendent Hambrook hurried to the scene with colleague Inspector Rawlins.

What Hambrook couldn't have known – but, thanks to the publicity this case received, Harry Vickers almost certainly did – was that he and his colleagues were swarming all over Flannelfoot's home territory. The murder happened in Shepherd's Bush, and this was almost certainly where Vickers was living then – literally just a short walk from the crime scene. It's tempting to think that when he read about the investigation and who was in charge, Vickers nipped down the road to gain the satisfaction of watching Hambrook at work, hovering just out of sight.

If so, he would have witnessed police photographers and fingerprint experts coming and going, as the investigation team tried to piece together what had happened and who might be responsible. Neighbours described Mrs Fortescue as a very reserved woman who tended to keep herself to herself, but she wasn't a recluse, enjoying trips away and visits to the theatre and cinema. She also had a sideline as a freelance 'patent food demonstrator', which took her around the country giving talks. One of the first things Hambrook discovered was that Fortescue wasn't her original name. She was a widow and her husband had been called Fortschunk, but because this was a Germanic name, she had decided to change it during the last war. Initial reports said that she was 'comfortably off', always well dressed, and gave the impression that she was the landlady of the house in Roseford Gardens. A somewhat different picture was to emerge later: rather than being the owner or landlady of the building in which she lived, she merely sub-let a basement room of the property she herself rented in order to bring in a little more income. She was, in fact, not very well off, which was why, in her mid-sixties, she still had to work. At the time of her death she was standing in as the rent collector for other tenants while the woman who normally did the job was on holiday, and because of this she had a stash of cash which she had hidden in a box under a table.

The ransacked room led Hambrook and Rawlins to believe that this had been a robbery which had turned into a murder, but the only initial lead Hambrook had to go on was that a young couple had hastily moved out of the house at around the time of the killing. Hambrook appealed to other lodging house owners to keep an eye out for a man in his early to mid-thirties, and a woman in her early to mid-twenties. He also assembled a large team of detectives to visit lodging houses and shops where such places were advertised, in the hope of finding sightings. He was hindered by the fact that only Mrs Fortescue knew the names of the young couple – even assuming they gave their real names – and the descriptions given by neighbours were too vague to be of much use. It was believed that the pair had rented a furnished room in the Roseford Gardens property, but had left abruptly on the day of the murder after staying there for just eight days. Police later learned that they probably had a young child with them, approximately 4 years old.

Hambrook faced another setback when the fingerprint team told him that the prints found were smudged and of no use for identification. It was believed that the murderer or murderers assumed, as did many others, that their victim was reasonably wealthy: whereas in the event they got away with the paltry sum of £3.

Many locals were questioned, and various people came forward voluntarily with reports of strange activity in the vicinity of the building, which was situated on a quiet thoroughfare off Shepherd's Bush Green. A boy who lived nearby said he had been playing with his ball when it accidentally bounced down the steps towards the basement where Mrs Fortescue lived. As he was going to retrieve it, a man he didn't recognise climbed out of the basement apartment window, threw the ball back to him, then clambered back inside. A woman who lived in another flat in the same street noticed a man loitering outside the house in the days before Mrs Fortescue's body was found. He appeared nervous, and kept looking up and down the street; when he realised the woman was observing him, he appeared to position himself so that his face couldn't be seen. She provided the police with a description.

Hambrook and his team issued several appeals in the press regarding the young couple they wanted to talk to, but time dragged on and no new lead was unearthed. It didn't help that the vague descriptions could have applied to thousands of young couples: he was about 5 foot 10, medium build, dark hair; she was about 5 foot 5 with a pale complexion and hair which curled at the back. The observation that she was supposed to 'walk with a quick step' added very little of worth.

Chief Constable John Horwell added his own appeal particularly directed at landladies in the Greater London area who let rooms at between 10 shillings and £1 a week, the kind of budget it was believed the couple would be able to afford. The downside of this publicity was that the couple themselves would have been highly likely to hear about it and, if they had the financial means, move as far out of London as possible. In the meantime, the inquest on Ada Fortescue's death was held in Hammersmith.

The ubiquitous Sir Bernard Spilsbury, who had performed the post-mortem, described her as being stoutly built, about 5 feet 1. Despite a mark right round her neck indicating that she had suffered some degree of strangulation, this wasn't the cause of death. Her face was badly bruised: eyes, cheeks, nose, jaw – and although the skull itself wasn't fractured, it was this severe beating to the head which had been the primary cause of death, with smothering by the sheet and jumper speeding up the process. She was also badly bruised on various other parts of her body. The police surgeon who had been called to the scene believed that the smothering had taken place about half an hour after the brutal injuries had been inflicted, and this conjures up a nightmarish scenario where the murderer, believing he had beaten Ada Fortescue to death, was getting on with ransacking the room when groans, movement or both alerted him to the fact that she was still alive, so had finished the job off by a different method.

The only development on the police's side was the discovery that someone had been filming in the streets of the general area at the time. They had been able to take stills from the footage and distribute them to locals 'in the remote hope,' said *The Times*, 'that one may be that of the man whom police wish to interview.

But progress was slow, and time had run out for Hambrook. The Ada Fortescue murder became known as 'Hambrook's Last Case', but it was an unfinished one, and 7 September 1936 saw the end of his thirty-eight years' service. The job was handed over to his successor, Superintendent John Sands.

As we have seen, Vickers was virtually a neighbour of Mrs Fortescue at this time, and in another bizarre coincidence the police finally discovered that the couple they were after had given the name of 'Williams' when taking the room; as with Vickers, it was believed to be false.

The police came by a source of more specific information on the couple, though it's not clear how, and were now saying that as well as giving the name 'Williams', the man had provided a birth date of 1901 and his occupation as a general labourer. They also had more detailed descriptions: 'Mr Williams' had broad shoulders, dark hair greying at the sides, and a prominent nose – Roman or pointed. He walked erectly, with long steps and a swinging gait. His wife was of medium to plump build, with dark hair cut in the bob style then fashionable. She also walked erectly, and very quickly, and regarding her clothing, had 'a decided preference for blue colours'.

The case was finally cracked in early October with the arrest of a man and woman in Dalston, less than 10 miles from the Shepherd's Bush location of the crime. It won't come as a surprise to learn that their name wasn't Williams – they didn't share a surname. He was Alfred Stratford, who had left his wife and the surviving six of their seven children. She was Mary Ann Flynn, who proved very talkative after her arrest – even when the officers cautioned against it, at least until she was formally charged, they couldn't stop the torrent of incriminating statements. 'We are both as much to blame ... I want to make a clean breast of it,' she told them.

At the trial, the counsel for the prosecution pointed out that the police had initially very little to go on, and praised their work in finding the accused pair. 'He tied her up,' Flynn told the court, referring to Stratford. 'We couldn't get them [the garments] round her mouth – she kept pulling them off ...' She claimed that the sheet (along with a duster) which they had tied round her mouth were loose, and that they had expected that the police would eventually arrive and release her. No mention was made of the savage beating that had been inflicted upon Ada Fortescue.

The defence counsel tried to take advantage of the pair's garrulousness at the time of their arrests (they were apprehended separately), claiming that they had been questioned before being formally properly charged. The police denied that this was how things had unfolded, stressing that they had gone out of their way to act according to normal procedure, and had done their best to explain the process to both Stratford and Flynn, who had been too agitated to be able to listen or comply.

Despite their statements at the police station, both pleaded not guilty in court.

The stills taken from the moving footage did play a part at trial, and at least two witnesses picked out both of the accused from photographs shown to them. Flynn repeated her claim that the tying of materials round the head was to keep the victim quiet and that they did not believe that she would die. Stratford, like Vickers, had injuries from the war, and had spent a lot of time in and out of military hospitals ever since. He had actually been awarded the DCM gallantry medal for saving a gun and limber, and at one point during the trial he rolled up a sleeve, revealing 'what remained of his left arm, enclosed in a steel and leather gauntlet'. He also said that he and Flynn were starving and penniless at the time. Despite the evidence of the crime, he also tried to play down the extent to which Mrs Fortescue's face was covered and the effect it was having on her ability to breathe. He told the court that she was alive and moving when he and Flynn left the building, and he expected that she would soon free herself.

Stratford did his best to exonerate Mary Ann Flynn, saying that she had tried to pull him out of the room during the course of the encounter. Mrs Fortescue had surprised them by returning while they were looking for the money, and Stratford said he had grabbed her and initially tied a handkerchief over her mouth. Flynn, he said, 'never put a hand on her [Mrs Fortescue] in any way. She herself told the court that she had attempted to commit suicide so that Stratford would be 'relieved of the burden' that she felt herself to be to him because of their financial plight before the robbery.

A spanner was thrown into the works when a witness, Marshall Payne, was called; he had seen a man coming out of Mrs Fortescue's house on the day of the crime looking 'agitated'. Somehow, the defence had got hold of that man – who wasn't Stratford, but someone called Price – and brought him into court where Payne confirmed it was the person he had seen. Inspector Rawlings, one of the lead detectives on the case, was called to confirm that Price had a criminal record, though no convictions for violence. The defence clutched at this confusion and suggested that Price entered the property after Stratford and Flynn had left, and finished her off. 'It might be a coincidence, but coincidences did happen.'

Coincidences do indeed happen, but this was a rather desperate strategy, and the Crown quite rightly asked why this man should come and finish Mrs Fortescue off when Stratford and Flynn had already left with all of her money.

The jury found Flynn not guilty of murder but guilty of manslaughter, and she received an eight-year sentence. Stratford was guilty of murder, with a recommendation to mercy. The judge told Stratford that the evidence did not 'permit any doubt of your guilt', but that he would forward the jury's recommendation to the Home Secretary. A petition against the death sentence hanging over Stratford, who had no previous convictions, was raised in Bethnal Green where he had been living. In December 1936, the Home Secretary commuted the death sentence to one of life imprisonment. Ironically, and without anyone knowing it, it was Mary Ann Flynn who had a death sentence hanging over her.

It wasn't revealed during the trial, but at the time she must have been three or four months pregnant with Stratford's child. She gave birth in Holloway prison in May 1937, and died of complications a day later.

After his retirement, Hambrook featured in an article in *John Bull* magazine, written by a journalist who knew him personally. It called him the last of the Big Five, the original detective chief inspectors at Scotland Yard 'held in reserve to tackle the most complex crimes and murder mysteries, no matter where'. The department had been expanded and reorganised since then, in part a measure of its success, but also because of the rapidly rising London population and crime rates.

Stanley Bishop, writing of Hambrook, said that you would never imagine him to be a policeman. He was quiet and slow speaking – and might even give the impression of being 'slow thinking' – but his reserve and apparent hesitancy 'just cloak the activity of his mind'. He had a penetrating mind, along with a powerfully intuitive one when it came to solving crimes and identifying criminals. Shortly after the Elvira Barney murder case, he was chosen to head an inquiry into a mutiny at Dartmoor prison which led to twenty-one prisoners being convicted and handed down heavy sentences. But, said Bishop, his investigation was so fairly conducted that when the judge praised his efforts, the prisoners joined in the congratulations.

Hambrook told Bishop what it was like when he joined the police – a 'stiff medical followed by three weeks' drill at Wellington Barracks'. He and his other novices were issued with a small instruction book, uniform, helmet, whistle and truncheon, 'and there I was, a raw country lad from the hamlet of Betteshanger in Kent, a constable in the Metropolitan Police, with all the thousand and one responsibilities such a position involves'. A few years after appearing in the *John Bull* articles, he went one step further and wrote a book about his life and career: *Hambrook of the Yard*.

His career had come a long way since he had been a young constable living in what he described in the autobiography as a 'wretched barn-like section house', where he slept and ate with numerous other officers in the hostel-type arrangement then common for young, single policemen.

Promotion to detective sergeant, along with his marriage on Trafalgar Day 1905, were his means of escape and a chance to establish a more normal, private lifestyle. But he had only been married for three months when he got a taste of what it must have felt like for future Flannelfoot victims.

One evening, wife Mary decided to leave their Kensal Green house to meet her new husband at the police station and walk home with him. They arrived at about 10.15 but as Hambrook put his key in the lock, he heard sounds from inside – panicked footsteps in the hallway, followed by the back door slamming. He hurried round the side of the house to the rear, but the intruder had gone – and so had most of the wedding presents they had been given.

The burglar had got away, but he had picked on the wrong man. Thanks to his profession, Hambrook already had a shrewd idea of who the culprit might be: not so much a specific individual, but he guessed it would prove to be one of a known local gang of house-breakers. He was travelling to work on a horse-drawn tram one day soon afterwards when he spotted one of the gang members outside a pawn shop. Hambrook's investigations at that and other such shops led to the man he had spotted receiving a three-year sentence and the detective getting his belongings back (though he refunded the shops half of the money they had lost because of the case).

Just to show once again in this story what a small world it can be, in retirement Hambrook was living on West Lodge Avenue, Acton with his wife Mary. This was a ten-minute walk from one of the burglaries that led to Vickers' first arrest, and close to several other of his night-time exploits over the years.

In his memoir, Hambrook looked back on Flannelfoot as a 'mean and despicable burglar who ought never to have been allowed his liberty, as he was often the cause of poor families whom he robbed having to go without their Sunday dinner'. Surprisingly, he makes no mention in his book of his crucial tip-off regarding linking the anonymous Flannelfoot with the burglar called Williams/Vickers whose incarceration in 1911 he had played a leading role in.

In 1956 Hambrook found himself on the wrong side of the law for perhaps the first and only time in his life. He was in a car accident involving a motorbike being ridden by a tax inspector called Raymond Byrning. Byrning was injured,

Hambrook admitted liability and paid damages, presumably through his insurance company, and no doubt imagined that the unfortunate incident was all done and dusted. He must, therefore, have got a shock when a letter came through the post informing him that he was being sued over the accident – not by Byrning, but by the Crown itself. Byrning had spent quite some time off work as a result of his injuries, and, in what was a test case, the Crown was after Hambrook for lost earnings during that period. What I'm sure was meant by this was that Byrning's employers had paid him while he was absent recuperating and probably also paid someone else to do his work, and now they wanted to get that money back.

Fortunately for Hambrook, the Crown lost the case.

By now, he was living on Albany Road, West Ealing – again, right in the heart of what had been Flannelfoot territory. And he had remarried – at the age of 76. His first wife Mary had died in 1940 after thirty-five years of marriage, and thirteen years later he was betrothed to 70-year-old Gertrude Booth. He outlived his second wife by two years, dying in Surrey in 1966, aged 89.

The Ada Fortescue case proved to be Hambrook's last as serving officer – but the seed he had planted in the race to identify and locate Flannelfoot had been nurtured by Tommie Thompson, and was getting close to blooming.

Chapter 21

Thompson and the Norfolk Connection

It's inconceivable that Vickers didn't come across the story of Elsie and the Patient Number 27 saga, which featured prominently in both the national and local press. He could have got to Elsie much quicker than his wife Alice did – who first had to write, then wait for a reply before getting the train to London. (At this time it was uncommon for working-class people to have their own phone. She could obviously have found a call box, but I suspect that the very concept of finding numbers and telephoning people was alien to her.) We know that there were conflicting accounts regarding the relationship between Vickers and Elsie, but whatever the situation was he surely must have been tempted to see her at Highgate Hospital. He would have had to balance that urge against the fact that the world now knew that Elsie's father was Flannelfoot. Instead, he soon returned to his burgling ways, and let Alice go to Elsie, unaware that Chief Inspector Tommy Thompson was working hard on his capture, and getting ever closer.

In early May 1936, the police again sent the former Tufnell Park Road neighbour of Vickers, Miss Stockhardt, to Reading to try to coax more information out of Elsie – and this time she had more luck. Stockhardt discovered that the 'Norfolk woman's' relatives worked on the Elveden Estate of Lord Iveagh, a few miles from Thetford in Norfolk. Learning that Lord Iveagh's accountants were based in St James's Square, a short walk from Scotland Yard, Thompson paid them a visit. They were able to give him contact details for the steward of the estate. Thompson then conveyed this information and the whole Flannelfoot story to Inspector Dye of the Thetford police, who was happy to collaborate on the case. They would make enquiries at their end to try to identify the family of Vickers' mystery woman, and report back to Scotland Yard.

Another lead came out of Miss Stockhardt's talk with Elsie and her family. She was told about a niece of the woman called Phyllis Handslip, who was currently domestic servant at Barkway House, Royston in Hertfordshire. (The first name was wrong, and the correct spelling of the surname would prove to be 'Hanslip'.) Thompson was on his travels again, and the owner of Barkway House, a Mrs Chapman, went so far as to allow him to 'discreetly examine Handslip's belongings'. They found nothing that would help them to identify their target, but Thompson told his boss that, 'Enquiries in that direction' were being continued.

Soon afterwards, there was another conference at Scotland Yard headed by Chief Constable Horwell, attended by Thompson and all other senior officers who had any involvement with the case. Horwell bemoaned the fact that the 'best type of officer' was not available for the discreet surveillance operations they were trying to carry out in search of Flannelfoot. To make up the numbers, there was a rota of uniformed officers who were given a plain clothes role for the night, 'whether suitable or not'. Furthermore, there was a knock-on effect on ordinary policing caused by the withdrawal of uniformed men from their normal duties. Superintendents in the affected areas were seeing a rise in crime, and putting pressure on Horwell to end this practice after such a long operation without any results. But he illustrated how difficult his task was by pointing out that in one area where observation had been withdrawn, Flannelfoot struck the very next night. (It was almost as if he knew – which is unlikely, but, given how sharp and shrewd he clearly was, it's not impossible that he worked it out for himself.) All Horwell could offer the superintendents was the carrot that hopes were high of something arising out of the continuing Norfolk enquiries: if Vickers' female partner could be identified and located, there was every possibility that it would lead them to Flannelfoot.

One thing that came out of the meeting was that they were spreading their resources too thinly. It was estimated that it would take around 2,000 men to completely cover all 'vulnerable points', so ways of allocating smaller resources more effectively were needed, such as focusing on locations where Flannelfoot had struck previously and swamping the area with plain clothes men. Also, some hand-picked men would be provided with a photograph of Vickers and attend race meetings.

By July, with neither the Norfolk nor Suffolk police turning anything up, Tommy Thompson paid another visit. His investigations led him to a Miss Drew, a schoolmistress who knew of the Hanslips. She had a vague memory of a female of that family running away with a married man, but, frustratingly, no other details. Thompson updated Horwell, requesting permission to stay on in Norfolk to pursue this line of enquiry: 'I feel that we ought to be able to find out a great deal more about this woman, as except for an "accidental" arrest of Vickers, this is the most promising of the few slender clues we have to work on.'

Thompson was granted his wish. While he was still in Norfolk a new lead turned up by officers making enquiries at Vickers' former addresses in London would prove to fit in neatly with the work he was doing nearly 100 miles away.

Fulham Palace Road was one of the locations where Vickers was known to have stayed, and there officers found a little stash of letters which had arrived after his departure. On the face of it there was no connection with Vickers himself: they were addressed to an 'A. Norden'. The contents of the letters were of no relevance to the case – but the address from which most were sent *was* of interest: Thetford, the very place where Thompson was carrying out his enquiries right at that moment. The name 'A. Norden' was added to the file. Was Norden another of Vickers' pseudonyms? Could the 'A' be his wife Alice? Thompson would find out within days.

On 15 July, Horwell received an update. Tommy Thompson had called in at the Newmarket police station, where he had been offered the services of one Sergeant Mills, a man with extensive local knowledge. Acting as a team, Thompson and Mills zoomed in on one particular woman who was known to have left her husband some years back and gone off with another man.

Her maiden name was Hanslip, and she had married Abraham Adolph Norden. Her Christian name was Alice.

Finally, Thompson had identified his woman.

He and Mills next travelled to Ely, where they visited a young woman called Mona Coleman, the niece of Alice Norden, née Hanslip.[1] He was able to borrow from her a photograph of Hanslip (photographs were not then the cheap, ubiquitous, easily copyable items they have since become), and he also gained an interesting little insight about the real Vickers. Mona had gone down to Brighton to stay with Vickers and her aunt while they were living there in 1933 – but hurried back home after 'Vickers made improper advances to her'.

Mona didn't know where her aunt was living now; she did sometimes get letters from her, but Hanslip never added an address to them. She promised to let police know if she found out anything else.

Thompson left Norfolk for the time being and headed to Somerset House in London, then the repository for birth, death and marriage records. There he discovered that Alice Hanslip was born in the Lakenheath district in 1898, making her ten years Vickers' junior, and had married Abraham Adolph Norden in Wandsworth in 1920. Thompson knew from his Norfolk contacts that the couple separated only around six years later, meaning that she would have been living as a single woman for some years before Vickers left his wife for her. (But, of course, it is quite possible that he had been conducting

---

1. Since she had the same first name as Vickers' wife, I shall henceforth mainly refer to her as 'Hanslip', the name predominantly used in the police records despite her married name.

an affair for quite some time while still living with his wife: his midweek disappearances might not all have been down to racing and burgling.)

Despite the best efforts of Thompson and others, there were those who were sceptical about the 'myth' of Flannelfoot and its connection with the Henry Williams/Harry Vickers who had been caught and dealt with all those many years ago. Superintendent H. Battley wrote a lengthy memo virtually demanding a rethink of the whole investigation, pointing out that 'Williams' had only had one conviction all those many years ago, 'and to my mind it is not definitely known at the moment whether [he] is dead or alive – in this connection, is it definitely known that the picture in the Secret Confidential Notices is that of Williams?' He suggested that officers in areas where Flannelfoot was being sought should spend less time looking for 'Williams' and widen their scope to other criminals (especially juveniles, who he believed were imitating Flannelfoot) who may escape being stopped and questioned because they didn't match Williams' description.

But it sounds very much as if Battley, although a very senior Yard officer, had little genuine knowledge of the investigation, and was unaware of the steady progress being made by Tommy Thompson and others. For example, Battley claimed that for many years, the criminal in question had been labelled 'Gimlet Joe' and had only recently acquired the nickname 'Flannelfoot'. Chief Constable Horwell, it turned out, was in a better position to rebut this than anyone else. He wrote a strongly worded memo to the commissioner to point out that Battley's claims were 'at variance with the facts'. For one thing, he knew Battley was wrong about Gimlet Joe – since he, Horwell, had arrested that particular man himself some years ago. Gimlet Joe's real name was Joseph Blackwell, and officers on the Flannelfoot case were able to confirm that Blackwell was at home when Flannelfoot was known to be burgling houses. Battley's suggestion appeared to be based on what Horwell described as unsubstantiated 'idle boasts' made at the back of the police court while Blackwell was waiting for his case to be heard, the man wanting to appear 'a clever crook before his fellow prisoners'.

Based on the intelligence they had accumulated, said Horwell, any police officer should be satisfied that Vickers/Williams/Flannelfoot was alive and well and still preying on the residents of London. He and 'all the officers who are engaged in this work' disagreed with Battley's assertion that the crimes attributed to Flannelfoot (in London) could not have been committed by one person. There were many stories of Flannelfoot burglaries in the press which could be dismissed, and even ones by regular police officers, but these were fairly easily filtered out by the actual Scotland Yard team which had been working on the case all this time, and they were very confident in the pins on their map.

'The officers in my secret squad,' added Horwell, 'have reason to believe that Vickers might be back in his old district somewhere near Highbury,' and arrangements had been made for early morning observations in various places in that locality. Vickers moved around so often that it's not clear whether Horwell's information was up to date or not at this point. We know from Elsie that their last address had been Tufnell Park Road, which is quite close to Highbury in North London, but it's likely that Vickers would have expected the police to have got an address out of Elsie and moved on. His final address would be quite some distance outside this area, but we don't know when he moved there.

John Horwell put forward some suggestions for future progress. One was for a kind of prototype Neighbourhood Watch scheme. He recommended enlisting a few 'bright inhabitants' to keep a special eye out, particularly on Friday and Sunday nights, in areas of the kind which attracted Flannelfoot, i.e. streets with houses valued at around £550–£750 – but especially those that backed onto 'fields, open spaces, farms, cemeteries, athletic grounds and railway embankments' – and call the police if they saw anything suspicious. (Which in those days, for most people, entailed 'rushing out to the nearest phone'.) Whether this plan was ever put into effect is not recorded.

In October 1936, a few months after Elsie had temporarily stolen the headlines from him, Flannelfoot struck again. And as if to make up for the fact that he had been eclipsed by his daughter's adventure, the *Western Daily Press* described him as the 'Modern Raffles'. He has been described in such terms elsewhere over the years, and while it's easy to see why and it has a nice ring to it, the idea of the actual Raffles breaking into gas meters in Ponders End doesn't quite hold up.

Lincoln's Lane, Ponders End, to be specific, was on the receiving end of his attentions this time, and we are told that Scotland Yard alerted all stations in the Metropolitan area that Flannelfoot was back at work. We do know that by this time, the Yard was putting more resources into catching their man. They had the map dedicated just to his activities, with pins marking the places where he had struck.[2] They allocated officers to 'wander round' those areas, driving

---

2. Another area where Horwell's memoir is surprisingly at variance with known facts. He describes a single huge map of the Metropolitan area upon which different coloured flags to mark all crimes were stuck, and that Flannelfoot had his own flag but not his own map. But the actual Scotland Yard file, in which documents written by Horwell feature prominently, makes it clear that a map was devoted solely to Flannelfoot.

what was then a recent innovation (one which, as we have seen, Hambrook played a key part in implementing) of 'radio cars'. This was the first time that mobile police officers had had a means of communicating with headquarters in real time, and transformed the way they, and eventually all police, worked. Officers were even given special incentives: there would be an extra fourteen days' leave for the person who arrested Flannelfoot, together with a reward of '£10 or so'.

But it didn't do any good – at least not yet. In fact, Flannelfoot was perhaps becoming bolder. On 30 May 1936, Scotland Yard received a message from the Winchmore Hill police station near Enfield in North London, saying that they had received a phone call from a man purporting to be Flannelfoot. His message was that the police wouldn't be troubled by him for two weeks, as he was going to Brighton for a holiday and would oblige them by informing them of his return.

Was this really Vickers? The call was traced to a phone box on Green Lane, Palmer's Green and officers were there in just two to three minutes, but there was no sign of the caller. Chief Constable Horwell alerted the Brighton police, but was open to the possibility that it had simply been a hoax call. Palmers Green is in North London, an area Vickers was known to have lived in and close to some of the places he had burgled, such as Ponders End itself; but then again he had lived and burgled all over London, so that is a tenuous link. Two things in favour of the call having actually been made by Vickers is that there seem to have been no reports of Flannelfoot-style burglaries for a good few months from the time it was made; and, as we have seen, Vickers had lived in Brighton for a time so clearly had an affinity for the area.

In December of that year he was believed to have been behind three break-ins in one weekend: one in Stanmore, which is as far north as Winchmore but over in Flannelfoot's favoured western part of the capital, and the other two on Middleton Avenue in Greenford, a district he had hit before on more than one occasion – once literally just round the corner from his latest job. It was his usual haul of small items of no great value – and the inevitable bicycle, which in many ways was as much of a Flannelfoot trademark as the actual 'flannel' he made use of. It was said that the police took the hiatus between June and December to indicate that the Winchmore Hill phone call really had been Flannelfoot – even though he had not kept his promise of letting them know of his return. But then, you can't have everything.

As if making up for lost time he was soon in action again, allegedly, this time in Orpington, Kent. This is a long way from the places Flannelfoot is associated with, at least 15 miles to the south-east even as the crow flies, so there has to be a big question mark over the attribution of the crimes committed there to him.

But it's easy to see why they were. Four houses were burgled on the same night without any of the occupants having been aware of the intruder's presence till they woke the following morning, and some of the homes even had dogs. Only small amounts of cash were taken, and the burglar made his getaway on a bike.

Some in the Metropolitan Police began to wonder whether Flannelfoot had, like some sort of twentieth-century Fagin, trained younger men in his methods. This was partly because they were beginning to find it hard to believe that one man could carry out so many burglaries. It was also obvious that since they knew he had been active since around 1911, when he was in his early twenties (a witness back then had seen an 'athletic-looking' man of about that age escaping on a bicycle from the scene of one crime) he must now be approaching or well into middle-age, and surely not so nimble.

More than that, though, because of the eagerness of the press to ascribe any stealthy burglary to Flannelfoot, there were times when he would have had to be in two places at almost the same time in order to have committed both crimes, hence the theory that other burglaries demonstrated a similar modus operandi because the perpetrators had been taught by him. On one day at this time, in December 1936, there had been a 'Flannelfoot' burglary in Enfield and another in Tooting within thirty-eight minutes of each other. The two places are north and south of the Thames respectively, at least 15 miles apart, and even today it would take over an hour to travel between them by public transport. Not even an avid cyclist like Flannelfoot could have made the journey in such a short space of time on one of his stolen machines.

As we shall see later, the police knew that Flannelfoot had also been at work in Totteridge, near Barnet, sometime during 1936 or 1937. It has been hard to pin down any specific crimes associated with him there, but there are a couple of strong candidates from 1936. In March, there were a number of break-ins in Totteridge and neighbouring Whetstone. The culprit chose houses that backed onto each other, and took only small amounts in cash and articles.

More interesting was that there were two raids in four days on a Totteridge house in September *even though the police had been keeping a special watch on the premises because the owners were abroad*. The second burglary was on a Friday, entry was through a rear window and items valued at £15 were taken. What makes this stand out, should it have been committed by Vickers, is that the absent owners were Lord and Lady Hewart – and Lord Hewart was the Lord Chief Justice of England.

On 5 December 1936, there was a rare occasion when Flannelfoot was observed while at work. He was burgling a house in Staines (about 20 miles to the west of central London and again some way beyond his normal area of operations).

The description given by the witness was that the offender was aged between 37 and 40, 5 feet 9 inches tall, wearing a fawn raincoat, dark trilby and dark shoes. Horwell noted that Vickers was 'of the type who might look younger than his years', and in fact he was then aged 48. The estimate of his height also tallied more with that of Vickers' family than the official record. Vickers did also wear a trilby, but so did many other men at that time. I have been unable to find any further details of this crime, but bearing in mind Vickers' predilection for betting on the horses, he might have been tickled to put a few shillings on a runner at Kempton Park that day – it was called 'Burglar' …

On 18 December, *The Daily Mirror* ran a story stating that 'One of the widest "drag nets" was thrown round London last night in an attempt to catch Flannel-Foot, the will-o'-the-wisp housebreaker', and that detectives disguised as railwaymen and tramps had been deployed. But this may well be a piece of fanciful journalism, as there is no mention of such measures in the Yard's own paperwork. The article also says that the dragnet consisted of 'picked men', but we know from the internal complaints that there simply weren't enough specialist detectives to do such a thing, and that men who had no experience of covert surveillance were having to be taken out of uniform and thrown into the role.

It wouldn't be long before the 'multiple Flannelfoot' theory was abandoned, but as we move into 1937, Vickers' last year at large, a new burst of energy on his part must have made sceptics of this idea wonder.

The year 1937 represented Flannelfoot's final fling, his last months of freedom. (There is a certain amount of irony in the fact that this was the year in which 999 calls were first introduced, starting in London.) In February, a quantity of silver was stolen during a raid on a house on Denham, not far from Uxbridge, so this was on Flannelfoot's patch. But the house and immediate area were not typical targets of his. For one thing, they were more upmarket than his usual haunts of rows of lower-middle class detached and semi-detached suburban properties. Red Hill was (and still is, despite being next to the busy A40) a much more rural area; the houses were bigger and grander, and further away from a handy tube or railway station for a quick escape.

The burgled house was called The Chilterns – a typical name for the kind of 1930s houses that so annoyed people like Greene and Betjeman ('The Cedars' was just down the road). The owners, the Robinsons, were asleep in the house when the intruder gained silent entry through the kitchen window. When the Robinsons' maid arrived for work in the morning, she was puzzled to find that she couldn't get into the kitchen from the hall because the internal door had been locked from the other side. The back door and kitchen windows were wide open.

A large cupboard had also been left open. This was where the Robinsons kept their family silver – and there had been quite a lot of it. Tea sets, tankards, plate and other ornaments, most of which were family heirlooms, all gone, along with a gold watch.

Was this Flannelfoot? There are signs that he may have varied his methods somewhat towards the end, so it can't be ruled out. Apart from the points already raised, it was not like him to steal lots of valuable silver, for which a fence or shady pawnbroker would be needed in order for him to capitalise on it – but then, perhaps he was getting greedy. But, as we know, more Scotland Yard officers had been assigned to the manhunt, and some had been detailed to 'wander round' the areas where he was known to operate with detailed descriptions and probably photographs, so perhaps it was another burglar.

Recently built housing areas attracted Flannelfoot like a moth to a light, and in early March he decided to explore the new Harlington estate in Hayes, West London, built by Wimpey – and he must have liked what he saw because he visited another nearby Wimpey estate the following weekend. On 1 March he burgled five houses, all on Monmouth Road, Hayes. He appears to have started work at the home of Mr and Mrs Sweeney, using one of his tools to get at the catch of a rear window and let himself in. He swiftly relieved Mr Sweeney of a wristwatch, which had been left on the sideboard, and left Minnie Sweeney's handbag, 12 shillings lighter. Flannelfoot then slipped out as quietly as he had entered and climbed the fence into the garden of No. 25 next door. Perhaps the security was better here because he was unable to get inside – but he did treat the garden rather like a hardware store before moving on. He cut a long portion of the radio aerial wire, tying one end to the back gate and securing the other to a drainpipe. One can only assume that this prevented the gate from being opened from the other side, making it less likely for him to be taken by surprise from that direction. Using his knife again, he cut off a section of the washing line, which he carried with him to his next address.

He hopped over to No. 23 and this time was successful in finding a way in. Here he grabbed 15 shillings, and took the time to help himself to supper before continuing his night's work. It's a sign of Vickers' nerve and experience that, having already burgled two adjoining houses, he felt relaxed enough to sit munching his way through food while the owners slumbered upstairs.

Next came No. 21 Monmouth Road. A purse provided easy pickings, but finding only a disappointing 4 shillings inside it he turned to the electricity meter, which coughed up between 20 and 30 shillings like a one-armed bandit at the seaside.

His final act of the night took place at No. 19, but this was the second disappointment of his night's work. He couldn't gain entry, and contented himself with getting into the garden shed and making his escape on the bicycle he found in there. He left what remained of the washing line in the garden, and while none of the reports stated what he used it for, he may have been able to slip it through the holes drilled into the window frames in order to loop it over the latch.

Unusually for Flannelfoot, he left physical evidence behind that could have proved his undoing had he been caught. When the police arrived the following day, fingerprints were lifted from the rear windows of No. 21, as well as the meter boxes.

The second raid in the area, a week later, almost led to his downfall, and his daring escape earned him yet another nickname: the not particularly original 'Spring-Heel Jack'. This time he was a little further east in Ealing, on Colebrook Avenue.

A resident of that road had been out for a spin in his car on the evening of 6 March, returning home at about 7.30. When he pulled up, he noticed that the back door of No. 37, two doors from his own house, was open, and this immediately rang an alarm bell because the witness knew that the occupants, the Lloyds, couldn't have been at home: Mrs Lloyd was in hospital, and Mr Lloyd was out for the evening. Cautiously approaching the house to investigate, the neighbour suddenly caught sight of a man, probably alerted to his arrival, climbing out of one of the Lloyds' bedroom windows and swung himself up onto the roof. The intrepid neighbour found himself a big stick from his own garden, but just as he was climbing the fence between the two properties, according to reports, the cat-like burglar lowered himself down from the roof and dropped into the Lloyds' garden. The neighbour ran to intercept, swinging his stick and catching the intruder a glancing blow on the head – but it wasn't enough to bring the man down and he was able to make his escape.

It was later discovered that Flannelfoot had grabbed a gold watch and a wallet containing £2 and 10 shillings. Further investigations revealed that before entering the Lloyds' home, he had already burgled the neighbours on the other side. Here he had taken three gold bracelets, 3 shillings and sixpence in cash lying around, and a further 2 shillings and sixpence each from two children's money boxes. Both the electric and gas meters had also been prized open and emptied.

The gallant occupant of No. 35, whose house, despite being sandwiched between the two burgled premises, had for some reason been left untouched, described the man he had almost caught as being of medium height, wearing a dark overcoat and, once again, a brown trilby hat. Vickers was certainly of medium height, but, as with the hat, it was again hardly a decisive piece of evidence. Nevertheless, this was almost certainly his handiwork.

What was described as an 'epidemic' of Flannelfoot burglaries took place in October 1937. On one night alone, four houses on Allenby Road, Southall, were broken into, with £5 in cash being taken, along with the inevitable bicycle.

On 12 October, Flannelfoot broke into 6 Bargate Close in New Malden, where he had struck in the past. The occupant, Alfred Beadle, came down in the morning at about 7 to find the dining room in 'disorder'. The French windows had been broken open, and keys, gold rings and other items had been taken, as well as 8 shillings from a savings box. When Detective Sergeant Edward Chilcott of New Malden Station was sent to survey the scene of the crime, he saw that entry had been made by forcing a thin instrument through the jamb of the French doors, allowing the 'tongue of the lock' to be pushed open.

On 15 October, Flannelfoot turned his attention to Lynton Mead, Totteridge. There was nothing unusual to wake the owner, Herman Chambers, during the night, but the next day he found that the window had been opened by Flannelfoot's usual method and drawers in the dining room were all open. A gold watch chain had been stolen, but, oddly, not the watch to which it was attached.

It was business as usual for Flannelfoot – but though he didn't know it, this proved to be his final fling. The extra efforts and resources the police were throwing at catching the notorious criminal were finally paying off.

On 16 October, Tommy Thompson told Horwell that his efforts to locate Vickers were progressing, and he had learned that their man had sent Elsie some money not long after she had been reunited with her mother. Thompson suspected, although they both denied it, that Vickers was regularly writing to them, and he proposed that a request be made to the Home Secretary to sanction the interception of their mail. Such steps were not taken lightly, but this idea, which might finally allow the Yard to pin Vickers down to a current address, was backed by all senior officers to whom the memo was circulated. After some initial reluctance, the Home Secretary, Sir John Simon, did sign a warrant to that effect about a week later, but the Yard was warned that 'He has done so, however, with some hesitation and his intention is that the warrant should be withdrawn if the exam has produced no results at the end of the month'. This letter was dated 26 October so it must be assumed that he was referring to November, since if he meant the current month, he really must have had his doubts if he was allowing the police only four days of 'mail tapping'!

But all of this very soon proved academic.

Just two days after he had given the go-ahead, Sir John Simon was informed that there would be no need to enforce the warrant. There had been a major development.

Chapter 22

The End of the Road

In October 1937, Chief Inspector Tommy Thompson's year-long dogged determination in pursuing the Norfolk connection with the help of the doughty Sergeant Mills of Newmarket finally paid off. After pursuing what Thompson described as 'One hundred and one lines of enquiry which brought us no result', Mills was able to provide him with the news he had been waiting for. He had heard on the grapevine that the woman who had been born Alice Hanslip, and who was strongly suspected of being the person with whom Vickers was cohabiting, was due to visit relatives who were employed on Lord Iveagh's Elveden Estate. Mills himself had moved on to another posting, so Thompson hurried to Norfolk to make himself known to his replacement, Sergeant Adams, ready to prepare for their next move.

He was accompanied on this trip by a female officer, WPC Walker. They had no definite date for Alice Hanslip's arrival, so the plan was for Thompson to return to London after everything was put in place, while Walker stayed on incognito to await the arrival of Hanslip. When her visit was over, Walker would follow her on the return journey – hopefully leading straight to Vickers.

They did know that Hanslip would travel back to London by bus, so Thompson's strategy was that once they had word that their target was on the move, numerous officers would take up various positions at the London end and lie in wait. Thompson himself, accompanied by Inspector Duncan, would take a car and follow the bus at a distance from a point on the outskirts of London. This was to cover the possibility that Hanslip might realise she was being followed and leave the bus before its final destination, to avoid leading the police to her lover.

As things turned out, Walker was good at her undercover work and this latter precaution, though wise, proved unnecessary. She discreetly followed Alice Hanslip to the bus stop in Thetford, rang Scotland Yard to give them their estimated time of arrival, then boarded the bus behind Hanslip and settled in for the ride. At the London end, the bus station officials allowed Detective Sergeant Orson, Woman Police Sergeant Jean Stratton, and PC Percy Woolway, to take up positions in their offices, out of sight but with a view of where the bus would pull up and disgorge its passengers.

Time ticked slowly by for the waiting officers, but finally the Thetford bus trundled into sight and pulled in, with the car containing Thompson and Duncan not far behind it and taking up a position at a safe distance.

Alice Hanslip was picked out from among those alighting, with WPC Walker slipping off seconds later and hanging back, waiting to see where in London she might lead them. But within seconds the situation changed dramatically. A man emerged suddenly from the throng to meet Alice Hanslip, and for the first time in his life, Tommy Thompson was able to set eyes on the man he had been after for so long: Harry Edward Vickers – *Flannelfoot*.

It was a vindication for Thompson's cautious plan – if his team had been any less cautious in their surveillance, Vickers would certainly have spotted the unusual activity and melted away before they even knew he was there. Even so, and despite almost certainly being unaware that Alice Hanslip had been followed, Vickers took his habitual extreme counter-surveillance measures as he left the bus station with his dark-haired companion – 'extraordinary precautions', as Thompson described them.

Of course, the Scotland Yard detectives could easily have pounced there and then: Vickers was at their mercy. But that was the last thing they wanted. They were in no doubt that Vickers was Flannelfoot, but they had no solid evidence. To avoid the risk of watching him walk out of court a free man, they *must* be patient and catch him red-handed.

The journey Vickers and Hanslip embarked upon should have taken them no more than five or ten minutes, yet Vickers led the woman on such a circuitous route, randomly turning this way and that, suddenly stopping and retracing their steps, that an hour passed before they reached what proved to be their first stopping point in Victoria. Here, disaster threatened to strike – the pair unexpectedly parted company.

There can be no doubt that they were still oblivious to their covert police tail, yet, without warning, Hanslip leapt aboard a passing bus while it was still rolling along. The scattered officers watching them had to act quickly and decisively: some attempted to follow the bus as it nudged its way slowly through the busy streets, while others stuck with Vickers.

Hanslip remained on the bus for nearly a mile, slipping off and vanishing, as Thompson later described it, 'somewhere in the turmoil of traffic at Hyde Park Corner'. They had lost her.

The officers who had latched onto Vickers were led to a tea shop in Leicester Square. Hovering as far away as they dared, they waited till Vickers finally emerged, refreshed, and ambled to Lilley and Skinners' boot shop on Tottenham Court Road. Here, he bought a pair of galoshes – an essential component of his burgling outfit. Next it was a twenty-minute walk to the hardware shop of Buck and Ryan on Euston Road to further add to the tools of his trade, in this case an auger. Finally, after two hours of tramping around London, the police team found themselves in a quieter residential area. Flannelfoot had finished his shopping – he was leading them home.

After the busy thoroughfare of Holland Park Avenue, it would have been much harder to follow him when he turned into quiet, leafy Royal Crescent without their surveillance looking too obvious. I suspect that one person, or a male and female acting as a couple, took the lead with the rest hanging back, perhaps only with eyes now on their colleagues and Vickers out of sight. A sensible precaution, given their man's sophisticated tactics for avoiding capture, would have been for some officers to continue along Holland Park Avenue to the other end of the crescent, in case he simply walked along its length and emerged on the main road again. But if so, the measure would prove unnecessary.

Observers watched Harry Vickers approach one of the many elegant, white stuccoed, four-storeyed houses which, at that time were divided into apartments. He took out a set of keys, and let himself into No. 20. They had Flannelfoot's lair.

Thompson was taking no chances. 'We decided that it would be unsafe to leave the man for a single moment,' he reported. From now on, the lodging house where he had a room would be under observation all day and all night, for as long as it took.

The team of watchers could be rotated to keep everyone fresh, but they obviously couldn't hang around in the street all day and night, so Thompson acted quickly to secure the renting of an adjacent flat whose windows gave a view of No. 20. They also brought in a police car disguised as a taxi cab. It would not look out of place idling by the side of any road, and would be much less likely to look suspicious following a bus or other vehicle. Thompson requisitioned it for the duration of the operation, and it was always available night and day. They also borrowed one of the Flying Squad's 'wireless cars', to be used by Tommy Thompson himself and Inspector Duncan. Thompson alerted the Information Room – what might now be called a dispatch or operations centre – to be ready to send any other available mobile officers who could identify Vickers by sight should the alarm be given.

The surveillance operation began on Monday, 25 October 1937, the day they followed him home. Vickers did leave the house from time to time, but never at night and only on innocent, mundane trips. From everything they knew about him, they felt that a Friday night would be their best bet. And despite the fact that, as we have seen, he did vary his habits more than most people realised, their hunch was to prove right.

On the evening of Friday 29th, Thompson and Duncan wended their wireless car through the London streets in the direction of Holland Park at just after 8 pm. They were in no hurry, since if Flannelfoot did decide to go to work that night, he wasn't expected to set out for another two or three hours. In fact, when they arrived at Royal Crescent at slightly before 8.30, they were only just in time to see him emerge from the house.

At last, Flannelfoot was going to work.

The team swung into action, following a plan they had had plenty of time to devise. They simply couldn't afford to spook him now, so a four-person team hung back as far as possible, following Vickers on foot: WPS Stratton, WPCs Walker and Burnett, and PC Woolway. They probably split up, with one pair on the other side of the road, and it may well be that Woolway and one of the female officers played the part of a couple.

Sergeants Mead and Orson, along with DC Massey, started the police 'taxi' – or at least they tried to. As Vickers threatened to disappear into the autumnal gloom, to their horror they discovered that after repeated attempts the engine wouldn't fire up. Thompson and Duncan heard their urgent call on the radio, and Thompson made a quick decision: the taxi crew had been watching Vickers for four days and were more familiar with him than either him or his colleague. He raced up to the taxi, and both men jumped out and beckoned the men in the stricken car to take their places.

Luckily, Vickers didn't go far on foot: he was seen to board the No. 17 Ealing bus, the officers following him on foot getting on at the same time. Knowing the route the bus would take, Mead, Orson and Massey put on a burst of speed and settled in front of it, keeping watch in the mirror. 'Following' the bus by this method, once Vickers did get off they wouldn't have to drive past him and risk being seen by the ever-alert criminal.

When Vickers alighted, he made straight for the Ealing Underground station. While the foot officers followed, the wireless car men gave Vickers a moment, then one rushed inside to ascertain from the staff where he was heading. Soon, the unmarked police car was speeding north-west for Eastcote, arriving three minutes ahead of the train after a hair-raising seven-mile dash. They parked at a discreet distance from the station, waited and watched.

It wasn't long before a figure wearing a trilby and dark coat emerged from the station. He turned into Field End Road,[3] and set off at a brisk, confident pace,

---

3. Referred to as Field End Lane in the Yard accounts, but according to contemporary maps it was called 'road', not 'lane', even then.

making the officers watching him feel sure that he had already familiarised himself with the district. They were right. In February of the previous year, he had burgled a house a few streets away from where he was currently heading.

On every occasion when they had seen him during the course of their surveillance, Vickers had been bare-handed – as he had been on leaving his home. Now, despite it being a mild night, he pulled out a pair of gloves and put them on.

So he knew where he was going, and he was getting ready for action.

The surveillance team had by this time split up into smaller groups again, with DC Herbert Massey maintaining the closest contact with Vickers. But the operation now hit its first problem, and it seemed as if it might be a fatal one.

Today, Field End Road, Eastcote, is a typical London suburb thoroughfare: the station is next to a busy junction where two shop-lined streets meet, and retail premises and flats line the road for as far as the eye can see. In 1937, things were very different. Much of the area beyond the station in one direction was barely developed, and Vickers headed off down an unlit street. It was just after 9.40 on a late October night, and with the watchers not daring to get too close, they could only look on as Vickers was swallowed by the total darkness. Again, had they simply wanted to catch him, Massey and the others nearby could have put on a burst of pace and grabbed him. But the whole plan relied on catching him in the act of burgling. They decided to hang back, still well spread out, and bank on him returning by the same road.

It wasn't long before their patience paid off. A distant, shadowy figure appeared to cross Field End Road and walk in the direction of some houses. Ten or fifteen minutes later, emerging out of the gloom came the trilby-hatted figure who was, at that moment, the centre of their world, and now it was time to act.

DC Herbert Massey was joined by PC Woolway as they hurried their pace, all thought of subterfuge forgotten, and moved in to intercept the infamous Flannelfoot. They had no idea how he would react, but knew that at least one internal memo warned that he might put up a fight. Sergeants Orson and Mead were closing in from a different direction, and now they confronted Flannelfoot.

'We are police officers,' said Orson, 'and I have just seen you come from the direction of the front garden of a house in this road.'

'I don't think so,' came Vickers' insouciant reply. 'It must have been somebody else.'

Needless to say, this didn't impress the cordon of policemen which had formed around him. 'I have reason to believe you are in possession of housebreaking implements, and we are going to search you,' Orson insisted.

To their relief, Vickers, though unhappy, remained calm and made no effort to resist. When he had first set eyes on a couple of men heading his way, he might have hoped they were merely passengers just come from the tube station: when he saw two more converging, he must have sensed there was a synchronicity to what was happening, and with a feeling of dread in the pit of his stomach, he would have realised long before anything was said that it was the end for him.

Checking his mackintosh pockets, they pulled out a brown paper parcel which was unwrapped to reveal a pair of galoshes – quite possibly the ones they had seen him buy from Lilley and Skinners' on Tottenham Court Road just a few days previously. From his waistcoat pocket a small leather pouch was produced, and in it were found a large number of keys. More rummaging brought to light an array of other items – basically, a complete burglary tool kit.

When told he was under arrest, Vickers maintained a stony silence but agreed to accompany the officers to the nearby police car, and from there to the nearest station, which was Ruislip.

The Flannelfoot squad had no inkling of the direction their man would take at the start of the evening, so the officers at Ruislip station would equally have had no idea that an operation to catch possibly the most famous criminal of the day had spilled into their territory. News that Flannelfoot himself was being processed on their patch must have caused a minor sensation, even among the most senior men there. A full search under the lights of the station revealed the full range of burgling equipment which Vickers presumably always took with him on a typical night's expedition. Laid out on the table that night were:

- two table knives
- a screwdriver
- a piece of bent wire
- two torches (with spare batteries)
- a pair of pliers
- a metal grip
- a piece of woollen sock with two safety pins attached
- a pair of galoshes wrapped in brown paper
- forty-seven keys in three bunches
- a pocket knife
- a pair of gloves.

It was noted from an examination of the gloves that they showed marked signs of wear in the palms, right in the place where pressure would be applied to boring tools. It was thought that the safety pins were used to fasten whatever material he used to cover his shoes once inside burgled premises.

He was duly charged and cautioned in the standard manner. For now, the charge was one of 'possessing housebreaking equipment at night', to which Vickers responded, 'I'll not dispute that. These things were found on me.' Otherwise, he was still generally uncommunicative. One of the few things they got out of him as they attempted to question him into the early hours of the morning was a grudging, 'You have not wasted your time.' Clearly still unaware that he had been under observation for days and followed from his house, he even refused to tell officers his flat number – until, however, he was informed that they already knew which house it was and could easily be discovered by a process of elimination. Then, Thompson was able to report, 'we were able to induce Williams to give his address'.

It was vital to strike quickly, and at 3.30 am on the night of the arrest, Thompson left Vickers to stew in his cell and took some colleagues over to the house on Royal Crescent which had been the centre of their attentions for so long. Alice Hanslip did her best to refuse the Yard men entry, but this was futile and a search was soon under way to the sound of Hanslip's protests and claims of the pair's innocence.

It was all bluster, of course, but for a time the searchers feared that any incriminating evidence must have been moved out of the flat before their arrival. The breakthrough came when they delved beneath the divan bed.

There, they found a suitcase. It was locked, but Thompson had come armed with the keys found on Vickers, and sure enough one of them opened it. Inside was a kit bag, also locked but also soon opened. Inside were eleven wristwatches and numerous other articles. Another item of interest, albeit incriminating only in a circumstantial way, was a diary containing a list of names of the London suburbs where he plied his trade, featuring tram times and fares in each case.

What was the mood like back at Scotland Yard, in police stations all over London, once the news broke that *the* Flannelfoot had been caught? Word must have spread very rapidly on the police grapevine. From the most senior Scotland Yard detectives to the humble beat bobby, and in the face of press report after press report that Flannelfoot had struck again while the police were no nearer to catching him, there must have been a mixture of relief and euphoria. He had been caught, and he had been caught by proper, boots-on-the-ground detective work.

And what of Vickers himself? His unblemished criminal career had lasted far, far longer than anyone in his line of work could reasonably expect it to.

Prolific criminals weren't and aren't unusual, but their histories are almost invariably dotted with sentences of varying lengths. Many spend a good portion of their adult life in prison.

Vickers had gone out night after night, year after year since at least the early 1920s but probably during the decade before that, often to the same areas again and again. There is nothing admirable about breaking into people's houses and taking their property, but for him to have not even come close to getting caught (other than his Batman-like escape out of a bedroom window and onto a roof only a few months earlier) is a kind of testament to his felonious proficiency.

He was clever, he was cunning. He often hit several neighbouring or almost neighbouring properties in one evening, which sounds reckless – but I would actually say it was, in a sense, a prudent approach. He only pressed on to the next house and the next when he knew it was safe to do so, when he was sure he hadn't made any noise and hadn't been observed. In that sense, the fourth or fifth house was no riskier than the first and involved less prowling around the streets.

In the middle of the night or early hours, in the kind of areas he preferred, the silence would have been so profound that as long as he himself worked silently, he would be highly likely to hear the movement of any suspicious householder who might be coming to investigate, giving him plenty of time to slip out quietly without the need for panic and noise.

He gained entry skilfully and, again, quietly – no smashing windows or kicking in doors. And once inside, he didn't vandalise places for no reason, again creating unnecessary noise.

For the most part, he knew his territory – the quickest ways in and out, where the nearest public transport was, the best escape routes. I strongly suspect he carried out daytime reconnaissance work.

Last of all, he wasn't greedy. In one of his final burglaries he did bag a haul of silver, but mostly he came away with amounts which to us today seem paltry, barely worth the trouble. It goes without saying, though, that just a few pounds went a long way in the 1930s, and he is likely to have made at least as much as he would have done working as a butcher, and probably more. He forsook the lure of riches, of big, wealthy homes full of valuable but easily recognisable items of jewellery, artwork and the like. Satisfying himself with enough to keep him in beer and trips to the racecourses and greyhound tracks meant that he avoided getting his name and face known by fences, pawnbrokers and blokes in the pub who would pay you for dodgy gear but who might also be police informants on the side. Chief Constable John Horwell in *Horwell of the Yard* goes further, saying that Vickers always avoided taking silver and gold cigarette cases (though he did take the cigarettes from inside them) because he knew they were easily identifiable – especially those that were engraved – but although this may have been generally true, as we have seen, there were some exceptions to this rule. Vickers also didn't use gangs or accomplices, who might one day get caught and give him away because they weren't as careful as he was.

These, I believe, were the qualities which kept Harry Vickers out of prison for so long. Except, the man arrested at Ruislip police station was *still* not officially Harry Vickers, but Henry Williams. It puzzled me for a long time that the police frequently referred to Vickers as 'Williams' long after they knew the truth of his identity. It was only when I was wading through the thick files on the case at The National Archives that the probable answer came to me: bureaucracy. When a man was convicted, he was allocated a number, one which, rather like the National Insurance numbers of today, stayed with a criminal and was used throughout his 'career' every time he was arrested subsequently. When Vickers had been sent to prison in 1911 under the name he had given the authorities, he became Henry Williams, C.R.O. No. S/140810. And that's how things stayed. Even shortly before his arrest, in an internal 'wanted' notice bearing his picture and description, he was 'Henry Williams alias Vickers', rather than the other way round.

In a sense, it didn't matter whether the man in custody was Henry Williams or Harry Vickers – the one thing for sure was that he *was* Flannelfoot.

Chapter 23

Reckoning

A couple of days after the arrest, Thompson provided Horwell with a longer summary of the momentous event. Williams, as he persisted in calling him, had been found 'in possession of a complete outfit for effecting entries by methods of which hitherto he has been suspected only'. Thompson's account of the capture of Flannelfoot was passed on to other senior officers, one of whom annotated it thus: 'A highly satisfactory result of the good work of the Squad, to which special attention will be called in due course.'

Thompson was full of pride over how his select team had worked so hard and so well in the final days of the operation. 'This most difficult observation,' he wrote in a memo to his superiors, 'I suggest, merits really special praise. It was as difficult as could possibly be.'

He praised Detective Sergeants Mead and Orson, WPS Stratton, and WPCs Walker and Burnett. 'Their excellent work, of which I cannot speak too highly, was really of vital importance.' He had a special additional mention for the unsung heroes and heroines – the officers who worked behind the scenes in the map room: JSI [Junior Station Inspector] Harvey, and PCs Woolner and Harrison. 'I have benefited by their help in this enquiry and feel that they deserve commendation for the extremely meticulous recording of the details of these burglaries over such a long period.'

Arresting Vickers was by no means the end of the job for the officers involved: there was work to be done if a cast-iron case against Flannelfoot was to be presented in court. One thing which proved fruitful was a cloakroom ticket Vickers had on him when arrested. This led detectives to Ludgate Hill Station, and a large box containing several small items later linked to burglaries in the police records.

When they returned and reported their finds to Vickers, who was by now well aware that a stiff sentence was inevitable and perhaps hoping that being cooperative might help reduce it somewhat, relented and admitted that they were the proceeds of his burglaries he had committed, and also admitted to 'other cases committed on the same excursions in the same localities'. When asked about an Albert watch chain, he said, 'I'll tell you about that. I got it at

Motspur Park about two years ago.' A couple of days later Vickers was actually shown the item, prompting him to say, 'That's the one I told you about. If you can get any of the other things identified I'll tell you about them as far as I can remember.'

Thompson ended up with a list of thirty-nine crimes that Vickers had confessed to. It was a satisfying number, but the Detective Inspector reported to senior officers that there could be 'no doubt' that there were at least 135 others *during 1937 alone*, based on the modus operandi involved. He recommended that they be listed as 'solved' in the crime records.

Thompson also questioned Vickers about the chances of recovering some of the still-missing forty out of the 154 bikes he was known to have stolen. 'Not the slightest surprise was expressed,' Thompson noted, 'and he made no demur at the figure.' However, Vickers insisted that if some of the machines had not been recovered, 'it must be due to dishonest finders, as without exception he had abandoned every one when it had served its purpose'. This was probably true – but Vickers was not known for stealing bicycles for fun, and surely the fact that he readily admitted to stealing 154 of them – *bearing in mind that he rarely, if ever, burgled only one house in an evening* – must be seen as a tacit admission to his having committed many more than 154 crimes? Very many more, in fact, considering that he by no means stole a bicycle on every burgling expedition. We shall look at how many crimes he might have committed throughout his time as Flannelfoot in due course.

Thompson and his team now set to circulating descriptions of the recovered stolen property to all stations and forces in areas where it was believed that Flannelfoot had struck, as well as a request for details of any unsolved burglaries which fitted his modus operandi.

Detectives in Hove laid claim to a 9ct gold bracelet from a break-in recorded in December 1935, a gold tie pin from a January 1937 job, and gold cufflinks and other items from September of the same year. Unfortunately for Inspector Thompson, leading the post-arrest investigations just as he had the operation to catch Vickers in the first place, when the owners were traced by the Hove police and invited to London to see the recovered property themselves, none was able to make a positive identification of the jewellery. Vickers had lived in Brighton for a time, but this was at the end of 1932 and into the following year. The gold bracelet was stolen in December 1935, and it's clear from Scotland Yard's own list of his crimes that he was very active in London throughout that month.

Victims of known Flannelfoot crimes were contacted to see whether they could identify any of the items found. Kenneth Guerrier, the teacher whose house in Motspur Park had been raided, now lived in Goole, Yorkshire. He was tracked down and confirmed that the gold Albert watch chain in the haul was his. Thomas Pounder of Oakwood Hill in Loughton was invited to Scotland Yard and shown a watch; even though the face had been altered, he was able to identify it as his from the number inside the case. Alfred Beadle of Bargate Close recognised a ring that had been taken from his house in May of the previous year. Minnie Sweeney laid claim to her son's watch which Flannelfoot had taken from her house on Monmouth Road in Hayes.

Once all the groundwork had been done, the Yard decided to focus on just a handful of solid charges mostly relating to the more recent crimes, which they were confident would stand up in court. The charges were as follows:

- Feloniously breaking and entering 6 Bargate Close, Motspur Park, 11 October 1937, stealing one gold ring, two door keys, and 9 shillings & sevenpence.
- Ditto 5 Bargate, 19 May 1937, stealing one Albert watch chain with fob.
- Ditto 41 Oakwood Hill, Loughton, Essex, 18 December 1936, stealing 19 shillings in cash, one gold wrist watch, one Post Office savings book – all told £4 and 19 shillings.
- Ditto 93 Lynton Mead, Totteridge, Herts, 15 October 1937, stealing one double Albert watch with half sovereign attached, value £5, property of Herman Chambers.
- Ditto 27 Monmouth Road, Hayes, 2 March 1937, stealing 14 shillings cash and one wristlet watch, valued together at 17 shillings and 9 pence, property of Minnie Sweeney.
- Feloniously receiving a gold Albert watch chain knowing it to have been stolen or unlawfully obtained.
- Ditto one gold ring value 35 shillings, parish of Kensington.

Meanwhile, more replies from forces around the country were coming in.

Staffordshire police asked Scotland Yard to question Vickers about a break-in in December 1935 at the offices of an engineering company in Burton-upon-Trent.

Cambridge police 'strongly suspected' Flannelfoot had been behind no fewer than thirteen burglaries, including a Co-op in Waterbeach near Cambridge, where a bike was stolen and found abandoned at Ely railway station. A grand total of eleven houses were broken into in just one night – 8 June 1937 – by the simple expedient of entering through open fanlights on the hot summer's evening. Not only did the small amounts of money and minor items of jewellery taken fit in with Flannelfoot's methods, but a man who matched his now widely circulated description was seen leaving the area at 4.30 am heading in the direction of Cambridge. Vickers was busy in London in 1937, though there does seem to have been a hiatus in the summer of that year, including June when this burgling extravaganza took place.

Worcestershire police offered up several cases, but none had any very convincing Flannelfoot connections, with the possible exception of one in Kidderminster which did at least feature the use of a getaway bike. East Sussex police had a list of unsolved break-ins from the same year, all in newly built Bexhill residential areas of the kind that so attracted the infamous burglar. Berkshire police felt it 'very probable' that Flannelfoot was behind an office break-in in 1935, and he was also suspected of operating in places as far afield as Ilkeston, Nuneaton, Northampton, Coventry, Evesham and Wendover.

All of these cases were put to Vickers during lengthy and 'strenuous' interrogation, and he must have experienced a growing sense of alarm and dismay as it perhaps began to look as if the police were determined to pin on him just about every burglary that had been committed in Britain over the past five years (including one which resulted in a murder). Vickers vehemently denied responsibility not only for the thefts in the Brighton and Hove district, but for *any* of those outside the Metropolitan area.

To be fair to him, the avalanche of claims and accusations risked turning Vickers into some kind of super-criminal capable of popping up anywhere in the country at will, and although it was better to cover all eventualities and they were grateful for information received, Thompson and his team were experienced detectives, perfectly realistic, and had no intention of fitting their man up for crimes he couldn't have committed. When the chief constable of Glamorgan tossed one of his own recent unsolved crimes into the ring, it was pointed out that 'Henry Williams' had been under constant observation in London at the time. The Lancashire police thought he may have been involved in not only burglaries but a murder in the Manchester area – but this was at a time when Vickers was, by his own admission, sneaking into houses in Orpington, some 240 miles away.

Such was Flannelfoot's reputation and the heightened state of alert regarding him, even in London there seems to have been something of an over-eagerness to attribute break-ins to him. The Yard's own fingerprint department complained to senior officers that articles were being sent to them for checking on an almost daily basis 'invariably stated to be those of Flannelfoot, but ... not identical with any of the finger impressions of Williams alias Vickers'. One superintendent pointed out that crimes were being put down to Flannelfoot in the force's Weekly Survey of Crime 'which could not possibly have been committed by one person'.

Having said that, although it may well be true that the vast majority of burglaries attributed to him outside London may have been down to either coincidence of method or copycat criminals (of which there were certainly a few), there is at least some reason to suspect that he did operate in Brighton, a place he not only visited regularly for the races, but, as we have seen, where he lived for around a year in the early 1930s shortly after whisking Elsie away from her mother.

Just over a year before Vickers' arrest, but already knowing of his Brighton links, Horwell had written to Captain Hutchinson, his opposite number there, describing Flannelfoot as 'the craftiest night thief that I know … He has troubled us at night time for a few years, mainly between the flat racing seasons.' Horwell told Hutchinson about Vickers' sojourn in Brighton and asked if he could make enquiries. Hutchinson was quick to reply, and was able to provide some very interesting information.

In January 1933, a man known as 'W Dean' rented a flat in Hove. He fitted Vickers' description, and had with him a dark-haired woman of between 35 and 40, and a girl of about 13. The icing on the cake was the address: 28 Brunswick Road – the same address remembered by Elsie when questioned by Tommy Thompson.

Another tenant had been questioned, and said that 'Dean' and the two females didn't speak to other tenants and even seemed to go out of their way to avoid being seen. But their habits were noted. They never went out at the weekend, but 'Dean', although he didn't appear to have a job, often left the flat at around 9 am and returned at 6 pm. The girl did not go to the local school. In May, 'Dean' applied for the tenancy of a bungalow called Downlands on Warren Road, Woodingdean, Brighton. This just happens to be a twenty-minute walk from the racecourse, and Hutchinson's intelligence revealed that when 'Dean' was asked about his occupation, his cryptic reply was 'Ponies'! Here, he seemed to replicate the life he had once led with his wife, in that he was away from home during the week and only returned at weekends. The woman and child with him rarely ventured out at all.

This was all good in positively tying Flannelfoot to Brighton at that time, but whether he burgled houses there must remain a mystery. Hutchinson said that the unsolved burglaries of that period involved methods unlike those used by him, but at the same time it's hard to imagine Flannelfoot living in a place for a whole year and not committing any crimes.

On 30 October 1937, Vickers, still doggedly assigned the name Henry Williams by the authorities, made a very short appearance at Uxbridge Police

Court. The kind of status this essentially small-time burglar had attained, and how important his arrest was viewed, becomes clear when we learn that this was a special sitting on a Saturday, and that thirty-five detectives from stations all over London were present, as were Chief Constable Horwell and the assistant commissioner of the Metropolitan Police, all no doubt fascinated to get their first glimpse of the elusive figure they had been after for over a decade but had only read about and seen in photographs.

The prisoner was described as being smartly dressed, wearing a dark grey suit and a striped shirt. Detective Sergeant Rasin Orson outlined the circumstances of the arrest in Eastcote. The magistrate asked 'Williams' if he wanted legal aid, to which he replied, 'I think I had better. I don't feel qualified to cross-examine a witness.' (In fact, there were to be no witnesses and no real cross-examination, merely statements given by the officers who had cornered him.)

The initial hearing only related to the possession of housebreaking implements when Vickers was arrested, but the case was adjourned to give the police more time to establish a case and was reconvened a few days later, when five cases of housebreaking were presented. These were the result of Thompson's visit to Vickers' Royal Crescent address and the subsequent identification of stolen goods by their owners.

The magistrate remanded Vickers for trial, and he was led out of court with a coat over his head.

There was again a large police presence at the trial, but this was not a security measure. Vickers would doubtless be in prison for a few years, but before he was back out on the streets Thompson wanted as many officers as possible, especially younger ones, to know what Flannelfoot looked like. To that end, three junior CID officers from each division were sent to witness his court appearance. Thompson also recommended that uniformed officers should at some point also be provided with the chance to see their man in the flesh.

The trial took place at the Middlesex Sessions on 2 December. Astonishingly, Vickers was actually tried as 'Henry Williams', despite Chief Inspector Thompson stating that his correct name was Harry Edward Vickers. Quite why even the courts were prepared to continue with this charade even now is beyond comprehension. It's tempting to think that Vickers was somewhat amused that a name he had invented nearly thirty years previously and probably never used again, perhaps even forgotten about, was still being bandied about by these great legal minds.

And yet another nickname came to light when 'Footpad Jack' was added to the mix, although this is as inappropriate as some of the others, since footpads robbed people outdoors, on roads, and weren't burglars. But, of course, the most important name by far was 'Flannelfoot', which had become so notorious in the public imagination that Vickers' counsel was, as we shall see, eager to disassociate his client from that character.

Vickers was smartly dressed when he entered the court, sporting a neatly trimmed moustache. Observers said that he smiled when offering his plea of guilty.

The *Daily Herald*, reporting on the trial, described 'Williams (whose real name is Harry Edward Vickers)' as having perpetrated crimes of a 'petty character', adding that all his victims were working-class men and women. In fact, they were mostly middle-class – lower-middle, perhaps, but still middle-class. (Later in the trial, the prosecution would describe the kind of house he targeted as the 'small villa type'.)

The court was told of how jewellery and other items found by Thompson and his men at Vickers' flat had been identified by victims of the burglaries in which they were taken, and that this had helped to tie him to the five specific charges against him. Vickers, who replied to questions in a 'soft-spoken' voice with a gentle manner, asked for thirty-four others to be taken into account (albeit the thirty-four were picked by him from a far longer list compiled by the police). There was also the additional charge of being in possession of house-breaking implements.

The prosecution was led by Christmas Humphreys. As we have seen, his father Travers Humphreys was the judge at Hambrook's Elvira Barney murder case. Christmas Humphreys himself was an interesting character. At the time of the trial he was only 36, a young, up-and-coming barrister who would eventually become a judge himself. In the decades to follow he would play a leading role in popularising Buddhism in Britain, both as an author and as founder of the British Buddhist Society.[1]

Humphreys recounted how Vickers had been followed by Scotland Yard detectives from his home in Holland Park to Ealing Common and then Eastcote. One of the key pieces of physical evidence against him was that footprints taken in the gardens of some of the houses he burgled matched the galoshes he was carrying with him on the night of his arrest. For all the precautions he took when *inside* a house, there was very little he could do to cover his tracks outside. Humphreys described how the gloves that were found on Vickers when he was apprehended were 'worn thin at the palms through constant use as burglary tools'. He brought to the jury's attention the fact that Vickers carried out his raids on Friday or Saturday nights, 'when the bulk

---

1. This author, being of that faith, owes a debt of gratitude to him and his organisation for their work at a time when Buddhism was far more obscure than it is today.

of the householder's weekly earnings were in the house'.[2] 'You could almost make a map of his tours around London,' Humphries wryly remarked (which, of course, Thompson's team literally had done).

Chief Inspector Thompson gave some background information on Vickers – despite still calling him Williams – including his Reading origins and the fact that he was the son of a butcher, a trade he had initially taken up himself. Thompson spoke of his abandoning his wife and taking their daughter with him, and of how he was living with another woman at the time of his arrest. He also told the court of his one and only earlier arrest twenty-six years earlier, in 1911.

One other interesting piece of information that Thompson brought to light was that Vickers had at one time run a small publishing company in the Strand for a year. Horwell's memoir claims that Vickers 'had not done an honest day's work while burgling', but Thompson presented his biographical information as a statement of fact, so it gives us pause for thought. It invites us to reconsider, at least to some extent, our image of this small-time petty crook. He was a trained butcher and there were many other things he could have tried his hand at if he wanted to do an honest day's work. Not only does this revelation make him sound as if he had more of an intellectual bent than one would have imagined, but the claim that he didn't just work in but *ran* the business, on a prestigious London street, takes us a world away from the shady character skulking around the midnight streets in search of a fiver from a purse here and a few shillings from a gas meter there. (His job title was given as 'clerk' in court, but Inspector Thompson later stated that he knew of no other occupation than the publishing business during the time they had been investigating him.)

It would be fascinating to know more about his business, short-lived though it was if it even existed, but I have been unable to find any trace of it. We can only speculate that it was either unsuccessful, or that the profits were eaten up by Vickers' gambling habit.

Vickers' counsel, Mr E.J.P. Cussen, seemed to accept that there was no hope of fighting the charges. His client pleaded guilty, and the defence candidly admitted that 'he knows he has got to be severely punished. If he can, while in prison, he wants to learn a trade, such as boot-making'.

On the subject of boots, something Christmas Humphreys said about the ones Vickers had been caught with in a brown paper parcel also put a rather different slant on the whole 'Flannelfoot' legend. It was – and still is – assumed that the 'flannels' he stole were wrapped around his footwear in

---

2. At this time almost all workers were paid in cash, usually weekly.

order to deaden his footstep, as well as ensuring that no footprints were left behind. Humphreys, however, stated that the pants, towels and whatever else he used, were for wiping his galoshes clean 'so that he might not be seen wearing muddy shoes that might give him away'.

With all due respect to m'learned friend, this doesn't seem to be a likely explanation. For one thing, there is nothing inherently suspicious or incriminating in walking around in muddy shoes. Yes, the mud was acquired in back gardens, but not only could mud also come from grass verges and the like, but it's clear from the circumstances of Vickers' arrest that he wore ordinary shoes when travelling to and from the scene of a crime, only changing into the boots when entering someone's garden. The boots were then hidden in a brown paper parcel, making the wiping away of the mud with 'flannel' pointless. Yes, when caught he would be found in possession of muddy boots, but by then it would be too late anyway since the pattern on the sole, not the mud, would be the incriminating thing – not to mention his extensive burglary kit. Furthermore, not one single report of his crimes refers to the cloths or other items found at the scene being muddy or dirty. (And as far as we know, he always left them behind.) Finally, as we have already seen, the police believed that the safety pins found in Vickers' possession on the night he was arrested were used to keep in place the cloths he wrapped around his footwear when inside homes. I rest my case.

Chief Inspector Thompson told the court that he could positively identify the work of the accused from any other burglaries 'owing to the number of peculiarities in the work'. Humphreys explained that Vickers entered houses via French windows where possible, that he did so without breaking the glass, 'by methods which he (Humphreys) had better not explain too openly in court'. But as we know now (and most of the public did then, thanks to press reports) he used a knife or a gimlet, a thin boring tool, which he either used to bore through the wooden frame to access the latch, or to force through a gap to do the same. One of John Horwell's melodramatic flourishes in his memoir was that Flannelfoot used a 'stiletto' to break in, but that sounds far too exotic for Flannelfoot, and Horwell is the only person to ever make such a claim. (Vickers had about him two table knives and a pocket knife, much more mundane implements and hardly to be confused with a stiletto.)

Another allegation about Vickers' methods made during the trial, said to be one of several practices peculiar to Flannelfoot, was that upon entering a house he took out the bulb from the hall at the bottom of the stairs. The reasoning provided was that if, as was common, there was a two-way switch, it would prevent a householder from turning the hall light on from the landing upstairs.

On the face of it, this sounds like a clever and sensible precaution; however, this is another alleged practice that never crops up in any of the reports of his break-ins over the years, and the value of doing so is open to question. It might be said that someone upstairs turning the light on in the hall downstairs was actually a *useful* thing for a burglar, since rather than the occupant being able to creep up on him, turning on the light gave him early warning and additional time to escape.

Similar caution must be given to a claim that when Vickers helped himself to a meal, if he had tea or coffee with it he always heated the water in a saucepan – never a kettle in case it was one that whistled when the water boiled. I suspect this to be another Flannelfoot myth. Once again, although we know he without doubt ate cold food while burgling, no resident ever reported that he had made a hot drink. Heating water on a gas stove to boiling point, or almost boiling point, takes a good number of minutes (far longer than a modern electric kettle), and would have unnecessarily extended his stay inside a property, as well as creating steam and heat.

Towards the end of the trial, to his credit it was Humphreys for the prosecution rather than Vickers' own defence counsel, who stressed that the accused should not be regarded as a dangerous man: 'He had never used violence, he has never caused undue damage; has never so much as frightened a single individual; he had never had on him anything in the nature of a lethal or dangerous weapon.'

Cussen, for the defence, warned the jury not to assume that his client was the legendary figure he was being portrayed as 'Flannel Foot', since 'whoever he may be, [he] is not indicted here, and has not had anything at all to say to you in this court. It would be dangerous for anyone to assume on what we have heard in this court that the person known to the public as "Flannel Foot" is appearing here today.' His disingenuous pleas fell on deaf ears, certainly as far as the press went. Almost all newspapers featured 'Flannelfoot' in their headlines, and it's unlikely that anyone in court was deceived either. It probably didn't make any difference to the sentence in any case; Vickers had a previous conviction and had freely admitted to numerous offences.

We get a tantalising glimpse into Vickers' life during the last few years before he was caught because of something Chief Inspector Thompson mentioned. He alleged that Vickers 'kept his own daughter almost as a prisoner while he was robbing houses in every part of London'. As the trial neared its end, the chairman, St John Gore Micklethwaite, KC, asked Vickers if he had anything to say, and it was this slight on his qualities as a father which was on his mind, rather than any plea for leniency for his crimes.

'I would just like to say that the statement by Inspector Thompson about the child is entirely untrue. We were inseparable. She was never a prisoner – she went walks by herself.'

There is a ring of plausibility to this, though I suspect that the truth lies somewhere in the middle. Vickers may not have kept Elsie literally locked up, but her own claims of not being allowed out tally with those of neighbours in the various places where they lived – the girl never seemed to leave the house. And even if she was allowed some liberty, it still doesn't mean that she enjoyed either being taken away from her mother and her friends, nor that she preferred the cloistered lifestyle she was now forced to lead. The very fact that she was found wandering the streets, distressed and suffering from amnesia, point to some level of stress and unhappiness, to say the least.

Vickers also still showed a surprising amount of concern that he was being seen as a bike thief, and again attempted to put the record straight relating to his getaway machines. He might be a self-confessed career burglar, but it was clearly of some importance to him to stress that he never 'stole' the bikes; rather, he always left them where they might be found and recovered. At the height of the investigation against him, in late 1936, someone at Scotland Yard did some totting up regarding the bike situation. In two months alone – April and May – he was believed to have taken no less than forty-nine bicycles, of which thirty-six had not been recovered. (And, the memo being written in November, there must have been little or no chance they ever would.) Vickers was no doubt sincere in his statement about the bikes, but he left them lying around and he wasn't the only man in London who took things which didn't belong to him!

The chairman of the court described the case as an unusual one, and announced that the Bench would retire to consider its decision.

When they returned, the chairman addressed 'Henry Williams' thus:

'The class of people you have been robbing must be protected, and I have no doubt that you have been getting your living this way for a very long period; most certainly so for the past two years. You must go to penal servitude for five years.'

The chairman then recalled Chief Inspector Thompson, commending the work of the police: 'They are to be congratulated in capturing a man who was a dangerous criminal, and the thanks of the community are due to you, and the officers under you.' In his commendation, he specifically named Chief Inspector Thompson, Detective Sergeants Mead and Orson, and Constable Woolway.

Back at the Yard and with his man behind bars, Chief Inspector Thompson, clearly a man who was quick to praise colleagues and slow to blow his own trumpet, emphasised the value of those whose work had led to the capture of the notorious Flannelfoot, especially the smaller 'elite' unit of twelve which had hunted him down at the end. He asserted that 'No discrimination in merit be made between them ... All worked with me personally for a long time, and like myself have grown used to simply doing their best and saying nothing about it. They acted as I expected – perfectly.' Inspectors Thompson and Duncan, Detective Sergeants Mead and Orson, and PC Woolway, were recommended for rewards, and Thompson himself was 'highly commended' by the Metropolitan Police commissioner. (However, in a separate note he turned down Thompson's suggestion that 135 crimes that had 'no doubt' been committed by Vickers should now be marked as closed. It was important to 'only take credit for cases specifically admitted by the individual concerned ...', but in the annual report of crime figures, a note might be added that 'beyond any reasonable doubt ... this man was responsible for at least 100 cases of housebreaking during the year.'

After the trial, reporters headed to Reading to get Alice Vickers' reaction. In an intriguing article, the *Daily Mirror* described her as having 'lived as a widow' for five years after her husband left her, and spoke of her struggle to provide for herself and Elsie during that time her daughter was with her. Most interesting of all, it claimed that she 'still protects' the man who deserted her and left her penniless: 'I know a great deal about Flannelfoot, but I will never tell it. I cannot.'

According to the *Daily Mirror* (probably going on what they had learned when they had covered the story of Patient Number 27), Elsie was much less inclined to protect her father's reputation. She allegedly spoke of his regular night-time absences, saying that 'He used to come in and pour money all over my bed.' The paper went on to claim that she was so unhappy with this lifestyle that she ran away from Vickers and got a job in a bakery somewhere in London. There is no mention in the story of why she didn't try to go back home to Reading, or even get in touch with her mother. Within a few days she quit the job too, unable to honestly answer some of her employer's probings into her background. It was after this episode that the police constable came across her, leading to her admission to hospital.

In the words of *Daily Mirror* journalist John Drummond, '[And] London homes will be safer because a girl lost her memory.'

Certain elements of the local press were underwhelmed by the conviction of Flannelfoot, which is surprising considering that he had plagued their readers for years. In a decidedly churlish article, the *West Middlesex Gazette* calculated that the lengthy search for the burglar had cost ratepayers £20,000. This not uncommon way of looking at police operations almost seems to assume that if the officers involved hadn't been looking for Vickers, they wouldn't have been paid, whereas, of course, the £20,000 (even assuming the figure is accurate) would simply have been paid to them for doing other police work, which may or may not have been of more benefit. 'Where has the money gone?' the *Gazette* demanded to know, complaining of the 'transport charges' involved in trying to catch him, such as bus and tube fares, along with the use of police vehicles – even the cost of phone calls was brought into their analysis! The *Gazette* had been one of the papers complaining of the catalogue of home break-ins in its area and demanding that the police do something about it. Now, clearly unaware of just how difficult a job it had been, they chose to carp about the time it had taken and the costs involved.

Chapter 24

Flannelfoot's St Helena

Early one morning in July 1815, the warship HMS *Bellerophon*, veteran of Trafalgar, arrived unexpectedly off Brixham harbour. Local boats went out hoping to sell food and other supplies, but, unusually, they were warned away by officers and marines on board. The small boats reluctantly turned back to shore – but not before a sailor threw a bottle out of a gun port which was retrieved by a schoolboy. Inside was a note, which read: *We have got Bonaparte on board*. Word soon got round, and the *Bellerophon*'s arrival quickly became a local sensation. Vickers may not have been in Napoleon's league, but it's not fanciful to think that his arrival at his allocated prison led to an animated buzz and the passing of messages from prisoner to prisoner and wing to wing. In prisons, thieves and robbers were ten a penny; it wasn't every day that a Flannelfoot arrived to serve his sentence.

Harry Vickers was sent a long way from London to do his time. He was led from court on 2 December 1937, and probably arrived at his allocated prison, Parkhurst on the Isle of Wight, within days to begin his five-year sentence.

HMP Parkhurst, near the town of Newport, had a long history, having been established as a prison for adults in 1863. Prior to that, the island location proved a handy interim holding place for juvenile prisoners, some as young as 12, who had been sentenced to transportation to Australia and New Zealand. Before Vickers' spell there it had a reputation for harsh conditions, but judging from the accounts of men who served their sentence there at or just before his time, it was considered one of the better places to be sent. There were trees, lawns and flowers in the grounds, and Parkhurst Forest was right on the prison's doorstep. One ex-con said that Parkhurst Prison was 'to the world of crime what the Riviera is to the other world'. Most of the workshops were outside the main wall, 'surrounded by only a "half-hearted" wooden fence, with a gate leading to the prison farm'. This farm was also enclosed by only a low wooden fence. 'Gentleman George' Smithson, a self-proclaimed Raffles-like criminal who was sent to Parkhurst in 1917 (and who we shall hear more of later), said it was 'a convicts' home from home … better than any other convict prison in England'.[1]

---

1. Ben Bethell, *The 'Star Class' in English Convict Prisons, 1863–1914* (2020).

There are also some signs that things may have become somewhat lax, and possibly even corrupt, by the time Vickers walked through its gates. Harry Young (who, like Vickers, appears to have served his sentence under a pseudonym, even though his real name – Day – was known *and* his two brothers, indisputably called Day, had appeared in court with him on the same charge!) was arrested for owning a mould for making counterfeit coins. At his trial, he said he was taught the art by fellow prisoners while working in the tinsmith's shop at Parkhurst Prison. More sensationally, he further alleged that the coins the prisoners made were given to warders in return for tobacco.

While Vickers was actually serving his sentence, a fellow inmate called Stone was sent for trial after being found with 'photographic paper' in his cell bearing images of various banknotes. Despite the fact that he was in Parkhurst for making counterfeit currency, he was cleared, partly because of what the judge called 'the grave irregularities in this prison'. His lordship said that the photographic items found 'must have been introduced into your cell with the connivance and complicity of other people who ought to have been protecting you.' There can be little doubt that he was referring to prison staff.

All prisons have their escape attempts, and in the years running up to Vickers' incarceration the matter was even raised in Parliament in relation to Parkhurst. The Home Secretary was questioned about the number of escapes, and the alarm they caused to the law-abiding citizens of the island. The questioner wanted to know whether warders could be re-armed – at Dartmoor prison there were still what were called Civil Guards, who, unlike ordinary warders, were armed with rifles loaded with buckshot. (In true politician's fashion, the Home Secretary promised to hold an inquiry.)

In what we would now call an 'Alcatraz'-style plan, Cecil Davidson created a dummy out of rolled-up bedding to fool warders that he was still asleep in bed. He got away in the dead of night by picking two locks and climbing over the wall with a ladder created from bedsheets. To some, though, the daring escape seemed almost too good to be true, and a few days later prison officer William Bartholomew was charged with helping Davidson to escape. When it came to court, however, the prosecution decided to offer no evidence against the officer, but proposed to take out a summons against him on a different charge. Not long afterwards, Bartholomew pleaded guilty to passing a letter from a different convict, a jockey, and forwarding it to a 'professional backer of horses' in London. The prison officer was fined £10 plus costs, and just to rub salt into the wounds, the horse the jockey was so keen to place a bet on failed to win.

Parkhurst might not have exactly been Alcatraz, but it was an island prison and would-be absconders faced the dual problem of first escaping from the building and compound, then the island itself. A few prisoners managed to get away over the years, but none had ever avoided recapture by the time Vickers was sent there. One of the more determined escape artists was Arthur Conmy. He absconded in May 1922 and managed to remain at large for nearly two weeks – in doing so, setting what was a record at that time. Conmy slept during the day in empty houses (of which there appear to have been numerous) in the coastal town of Ryde, 8 miles from Parkhurst, and hid out in woods during the night, from where he launched raids on various homes, helping himself to food and drink and accumulating a motley assortment of clothing to wear. But when the police began searching empty properties, Conmy was found lying in an attic, dirty and dishevelled, with a bottle of lemonade and a pile of stolen food. He came quietly, but he hadn't finished yet.

Seven months later, Conmy was on the run again. After his first escape he had been put in chains and made to wear 'distinctive dress' (probably dark prison clothing with yellow stripes). This was not an uncommon treatment for escapees, but it was hated by prisoners and, it seems, the public too. The outcry which followed, mainly to do with the chains, led to the decision being reversed. Then, one gloomy December morning, a warder overseeing convicts carrying hay into the stables to feed the prison's prize shorthorn cows, saw a door open at the far end of the dimly lit building and a shadowy figure slipping through it. It was Conmy, but this time he didn't break any records.

A labourer working on a nearby farm saw a man crawling under a hedge and raised the alarm. The escapee soon found himself being chased by a posse of farm hands and their wives, and in his panic to outrun them he fell into a deep ditch. The hunt was over, and instead of two weeks he had lasted just two hours. 'I shall have another try,' he ruefully warned the warders who came to take him away.

One example of why locals were so concerned about Parkhurst escapees comes in the form of the Wheeler family of Cowes. After enjoying an evening out, they returned to find their house had been ransacked. A large number of valuables and clothes had been taken, and a sodden prison uniform left behind. The former wearer had been William Miller, who had escaped the day before and who was found lording it in a Cowes hotel with a bagful of the Wheelers' possessions in his room.

When farmer Percy Holbrook challenged two men asleep in the straw of his cowshed, they claimed to be fishermen from Yarmouth, sheltering from the heavy rain that had fallen during the night. Mr Holbrook gave them some breakfast, but in the meantime sent someone to inform the police. A constable caught up with them on the road to Cowes, where they meekly surrendered to him, grumbling that they were 'fed up'. The idea of being free from the confines of a prison and its stifling regime was an attractive one, but a miserable, apprehensive existence was usually the reality.

Not all such shenanigans caused alarm to the communities in the vicinity of the prison. In 1921, an Indian prisoner took it upon himself to scuttle up a 50-foot elm tree during exercise time in the prison yard, much to the amusement of local passers-by and soldiers at neighbouring Parkhurst Barracks. He hopped from branch to branch 'with monkey-like ease', even among the thinner uppermost branches which swayed alarmingly under his weight. This wasn't an escape attempt, however. He was quite happy to sit up the tree entertaining the soldiers and a crowd of children which had gathered outside, singing and calling to them, while the prison authorities were equally happy to let him stay there till cold and hunger forced him down.

If Vickers had served his first sentence in 1911 at Parkhurst rather than Wandsworth, he might have been a subject in a strange study into the characteristics of criminals and what, if anything, set them apart from everyone else. Dr Goring, one of the medical officers at Parkhurst, had back then carried out his own survey which disproved the rather bizarre theories of Italian criminologist Lombroso. Late in the previous century, Lombroso had reached the conclusion that a tendency to criminality was hereditary, and could be observed through various physical characteristics or deformities, similar to the discredited 'science' of phrenology, but in this case not just confined to the head.

Dr Goring's own experience of observing Parkhurst inmates ruled out what *The Times* referred to as 'the ear which goes with homicide, the fingers or misshapen toes which are an index of a disposition to larceny, the shape of skull which dooms a man to a life of crime ...' Goring's more mundane explanation of what made a criminal was based on character not physical appearance: 'a constitutional incapacity ... weakness of will' resulting in an inability to adhere to normal social standards led to a man becoming a criminal. We do not know whether Vickers had misshapen toes or a constitutional incapacity. Perhaps he was just lazy and greedy, but he would have to change his ways in Parkhurst, and he seems to have been willing to do so.

In those days, prisoners were allocated to jobs and 'went to work' every day, almost in the same way that a civilian would in the outside world. There was manual work like concrete block making, but also skilled trades too, and a man could work as a baker or a tailor. Then there was the outdoor labour, which as we have seen provided the best opportunities for escape, such as working in the prison gardens and on nearby farms. For leisure, there would probably have been a library, and from time to time there were lectures on various subjects, illustrated travel talks and the like. In 1925, the BBC 'radiated' a concert to the prison from Bournemouth.

But it wasn't all a bed of roses. Having been given a hard labour element of his sentence when imprisoned as a young man, this time it was 'penal servitude' – the successor to transportation.[2] This meant that for the first nine months of his sentence, Vickers would have been segregated from other inmates – virtually in solitary confinement, although he would have been allowed to exercise, but not with other prisoners. The only time he would have been in the company of his fellow inmates was when attending chapel, and even then he was not allowed to speak to anyone nor they to him. The only people he would have had the opportunity of conversing with during those first nine months were the chaplain and the governor.

Perhaps it will come as no surprise by now to learn that even by the time Vickers got to Parkhurst, he was still being called 'Henry Williams' and was entered into the books under that name.

Vickers got his wish, as expressed at his trial, to work as a surgical boot maker. He certainly wasn't an escaper – in fact, he was said to have been a model prisoner. Because of this, he would have been released 'on licence' when three-quarters of the allotted sentence had been served (unlike today, when prisoners routinely serve only half their nominal sentence). That would have been approximately August 1941. He had led such a hedonistic, carefree life, responsible to no one, that the thought of a return to the outside world once again perhaps meant more to him than the average prisoner. He would initially have had to report to a police station on a regular basis, and may have been eligible for charitable assistance to help him get back on his feet.

I even have a gut feeling that he intended to go straight after his release – but, perhaps without yet realising it, Harry Vickers was not a well man.

Napoleon didn't survive his stay on St Helena, and while Flannelfoot lived long enough to sail from the island of his own captivity, his remaining time as a free man would prove to be shorter than his prison sentence.

Harry Edward Vickers suddenly fell ill towards the end of 1942 and was rushed to the Emergency Hospital, Burntwood, Staffordshire. He died from heart and respiratory problems on 9 December 1942. He was 54 years old.

---

2. Rupert Cross, *Punishment, Prison and the Public* (1971).

Chapter 25

Fallen Angel

One of the key figures in the surveillance and final arrest of Vickers was Detective Jean Stratton. It may come as something of a surprise that in the 1930s there were female police officers at all, let alone among the ranks of Scotland Yard's CID. Women had famously been given the vote in 1918, but that Act only enfranchised a minority: by the time Vickers was arrested, it had only been ten years since all women over 21 had been entitled to vote. Yet there were not only three female officers in the hand-picked Flannelfoot team but one of them, Stratton, was a sergeant, thus senior to some of her male colleagues.

At least part of the reason behind the employment of female police officers must surely stem back to the First World War, when women not only filled jobs previously only performed by men, but had demonstrated that there really was no need to even doubt that they couldn't continue to do so in peacetime. The Met had first recruited women straight after the war, but only those within a limited age range and only with the powers to arrest other women, or children. As time progressed, the status between male and female officers began to level up, but not when it came to marital status. If Jean Stratton had been married at the time she wanted to join the force, it would not have been a barrier to enrolment. Yet, somewhat paradoxically, if, as a serving officer, she had got married at any time up until the mid-1940s, she would have had to resign.

As it was, Jean never did marry. She was one of several Scots on the Flannelfoot case, and her career after taking part in Flannelfoot's capture contains elements of both mystery and personal tragedy.

Like Vickers, Stratton did military service during the war, although quite what she did is a little hard to work out, for reasons we shall soon discover. She entered the Metropolitan Police in 1924, joining the CID after eight years, with promotion to sergeant coming in 1934. She would have been 44 when involved in the Flannelfoot case. She was known for her undercover work and use of disguises, which included wigs of various colours, different ways of applying make-up, and no doubt a variety of clothing styles.

She donned more than one of these disguises while tracking a woman called Winifred Simner, an elderly and otherwise upstanding citizen, but one whom the police had reason to suspect was behind a series of poison pen letters being sent to local council officers. Stratton's surveillance of Simner's movements enabled her to identify the post office in Wimbledon as being the one where she bought her postage stamps, and a ploy was devised (probably by her boss Tommy Thompson) to make a positive link between Simner and the inflammatory and libellous letters. Using invisible ink, Thompson initialled a set of stamps, and Stratton took the two postmistresses into her confidence to ensure that when Simner next came in to buy stamps, it would be these which she would be sold.

The plan worked perfectly. Simner's next series of nasty letters bore the stamps marked by Thompson, and she was duly arrested. Because of her age and previous exemplary conduct, Miss Simner was spared a prison sentence but bound over for three years.

In the 1930s and 1940s the police seemed to have a strange antipathy towards mediums and spiritualists, employing the ostensibly bizarre tactic of prosecuting them under the 1824 Vagrancy Act. The legislation was designed to tackle – surprise, surprise – vagrancy, but for some reason also referred to 'every person pretending or professing to tell fortunes, or using any subtle craft, means, or device, by palmistry or otherwise, to deceive and impose on any of his Majesty's subjects ...', perhaps because at that time they plied their trade in the streets. It declared that any such person 'shall be deemed a rogue and vagabond'. The phrase 'deceive and impose upon' would seem to rule out any situation where both medium and client were happy with their interaction, especially when it took place within the home of the person providing the service – but that doesn't seem to have prevented the police from acting nor the courts from finding such people guilty.

Perhaps because it was considered that women were more likely to visit such people, Stratton was given the task of investigating a number of them. In May 1942, she, accompanied by Detective Constable Margaretta Low, visited the home of a woman called Stella Hughes in order to gather evidence that she was acting as a medium. Jean Stratton, who was single, donned a wedding ring – perhaps in the hope that Hughes would 'psychically' provide information about her husband, late or otherwise, and so expose herself as a fraud. Stratton and Low told Hughes that they had been recommended by a 'friend', and were granted an audience with the medium, leading to her arrest, conviction and a fine of £10, five guineas. However, this would prove to be the last case Stratton and Low, who often worked together, would ever undertake as police officers.

Britain had, of course, gone to war again after Stratton had helped put Flannelfoot behind bars. London had been heavily bombed during the blitz of the year previous to Stratton's last fraudulent medium case, and even though the intensity of that period no longer endured, bombs were still regularly falling on the capital. Many families had to vacate their bomb-shattered homes, often leaving some possessions still inside. In Pimlico, those who had been lucky enough to avoid the devastation and remain behind began to notice that damaged and unoccupied houses were being entered and items taken – mostly minor things, since most home-owners had taken valuables with them – but it was still an unsatisfactory situation, and the police were informed.

One day in April 1942, eight months before Vickers' death, locals may have noticed a man apparently idling in the vicinity of Elizabeth Street, Pimlico. He was, in fact, Detective McVernon of Scotland Yard, keeping a discreet watch for whoever might be stealing property from empty houses.

After a long and boring vigil, he spotted a woman enter No. 85. She was empty-handed upon her arrival, but carrying a parcel when she left. McVernon intercepted her. To his surprise, the woman identified herself as another plain clothes police officer. She said the parcel contained rubber stair treads which she had bought from a street seller in Putney. This didn't really make sense since she wasn't carrying the package before entering the house, but perhaps the sight of her warrant card threw McVernon off balance because he allowed her to carry on her way. The woman in question was Detective Sergeant Jean Stratton.

This is where the story gets even stranger. Knowing that the street was under police observation, Stratton returned to 85 Elizabeth Street later that same day. This time, she arrived with the same parcel but left carrying a different, smaller one. It emerged that, because she'd been seen taking away the rubber treads (which did indeed belong to the house) she had returned them – yet still, for some inexplicable reason, and knowing she was almost certainly being watched, she attempted to leave with a jumper. This time, she was arrested as she tried to walk away.

This was an officer who had been commended by the Commissioner of the Metropolitan Police no fewer than thirty-three times, one of which, of course, was for her work on the Flannelfoot case. She had been a pioneer, one of the first female detectives. Now, the woman who had caught the most notorious house-breaker of the day had become a burglar herself.

Regardless of her morals, it's almost incredible that an experienced and capable officer like Jean Stratton, one who specialised in covert surveillance, should not simply have decided to cut her losses, or even moved her operations elsewhere. Returning the treads was risky in itself, but to attempt to walk away with a jumper in full view of onlooking police officers she knew may well be around beggars belief. It can only be imagined that because she had provided an explanation which had proved satisfactory before, *and* that she was known to be a CID sergeant, it would be assumed that she was working and would be left alone. If so, this was wishful thinking boarding on naivety. Jean Stratton had appeared in court many times to provide evidence in support of a prosecution; now she would be the one in the dock.

Information gained after her arrest led to the apprehension of her police colleague, Detective Constable Margaretta Low, and it was Low, the younger woman, who proved the most talkative of the two. She admitted that they had been systematically stealing property in such a manner for quite some time; her only rather pathetic plea of mitigation was that they never broke in but only entered houses whose doors weren't locked.

Stratton herself said little, other than 'I'm glad the suspense is over. This terrible affair has been going on for two years.' What's even more astonishing is that, like Flannelfoot, she and Low took things of little value, and clearly weren't stealing to make money on the black market (they never sold anything they had stolen, in fact). They only pilfered items for their own personal use – the vast majority of which Stratton, on her sergeant's wage, could surely have easily afforded herself. The haul included egg cups, towels, linen and light bulbs.

Detective Sergeant Jean Stafford and Detective Constable Margaretta Low appeared at the West London Police Court on 4 May 1942, with both pleading guilty. Stratton's exemplary career was put before the court, but if she was expecting mercy she was mistaken. 'You have betrayed your oath,' said the magistrate. 'No police officer who betrays a trust as you have can expect leniency.'

When he announced that both women would be sent to prison for twelve months, Low, a university graduate whose father was said to have been a police superintendent, collapsed and had to be carried from the court.

Jean Stratton was 53, not long from retirement, and would have been entitled to a 'substantial pension' according to a senior Yard officer in court. Quite why she turned to stealing egg cups and light bulbs is a bigger mystery than any of the crime cases featured in this book.

Another, more trivial, mystery is that the age ascribed to her seems to be out by a few years, and that 'Jean' doesn't appear to have been her real name.

'Jean Stratton', based on the dates and other information about her put before the court, proved very elusive in all official records. It was stated that she had been born in Dundee, was 53 years old (making her birth date 1890), had served during the First World War, and before joining the police had had to take care of her siblings after the early death of her mother. No such Jean

Stratton matched these details in government records – but one Margaret Langland Stratton did fit the bill.

In 1939, a 'register' was taken in England and Wales; it was similar to a census but less detailed, requiring people to provide little more than name, age, address and occupation. This lists a Jean Stratton living in Camberwell at around this time, a 'Woman Police Officer', born in 1890. (Margaretta Low is shown as occupying a flat in the same building, which also accords with what was revealed at their trial.) So far, so good. However, the 1939 Register entries were amended during ensuing years as new information or changes to personal circumstances came to light, such as marriages. 'Jean' Stratton's first name was subsequently crossed through and two alternative names were inked in by different officials at different times. One was 'Annie R', the other 'Margaret L'. This second version leads to a positive identification, since we can say with certainty that Margaret Langland Stratton was born in Dundee, and all other details, such as losing her mother and moving to Camberwell (where she was baptised), do match her story.

Margaret L. Stratton was born in 1886, which would mean that 'Jean' knocked four years off her age for whatever reason. It's not impossible that it was to enable her to serve during the war, since there may have been an upper age limit for female applicants. What she actually did in the war is also open to conjecture. Her senior officer told the court at her trial that she served in France, and we have no reason to doubt that. A Jean Stratton was a truck driver for the Women's Royal Air Force and her demobilisation record describes her as five feet four inches tall, of medium build, with dark brown hair and light brown eyes, and her performance as having been 'very satisfactory indeed'. She enrolled in May 1918 and ended her service in August 1919. Her age on the form was initially written as 27 but was amended to 26. Depending on which age we take and whether it applies to her age at enrolment or demobilisation, which isn't clear, it is not too far from tying in with her stated age when convicted.

But we can feel sure that Margaret Langlands [*sic*] Stratton who served in Queen Mary's Army Auxiliary Corps is our woman. This was a three-month stint from the end of June to the beginning of October 1917, which means that she could have served under her real name first, then again as Jean Stratton the following year. Almost everyone else on the page on which her name appears served for much longer than her, mostly a year or more – was there some reason for her abrupt discharge and possible re-enlistment under a different name? The answer could lie in the fact that upon the formation of the Women's Royal Air Force, thousands of women were transferred to that body from the Auxiliary Corps – though why she should have used a different first name upon transferring, if such was the case, is harder to explain. Whether or not Jean was the same person as Margaret in this instance, we do know that Margaret received the Victory Medal and the British War Medal for her services.

Chapter 26

Flannelfoot Strikes from Beyond the Grave

Neither prison nor even death could keep Flannelfoot down.

On 6 November 1936, a maid in the employment of Samuel Highley, a mill owner who lived in Harrogate, Yorkshire, came down in the morning to find that the house had been burgled. The intruder had got away with cash, silver and clothing, amounting to a haul worth just over £200. He had also helped himself to some dates and some meat from the fridge. But he had left something behind – a note in the hall, written in capital letters, which read:

MY MOST SINCERE THANKS. WITH KINDEST
REGARDS, FLANNELFOOT.

PS FLANNELFOOT MOVES NORTH.

There were several reasons for believing that Flannelfoot had not moved north, not least of which was the fact that he was currently incarcerated and awaiting trial in London. There are, though, an almost bizarre number of parallels between the activities of the two criminals, as we shall see later.

It may be that the burglar panicked during the course of his (non-bicycle) getaway. Some of the coats were later found discarded, which is perhaps understandable, but in addition four silver plates and a few other things were also tracked down.

The police, probably having been tipped off, paid a late-night visit to a house on Cheltenham Parade, Harrogate, around three weeks after Mr Highley had been burgled. Overhearing the officers being admitted, the man they wanted to question slipped upstairs to his room. After listening intently as several sets of footsteps came up the stairs, he cautiously opened the door a crack. As soon as he saw the four-man reception committee, he suddenly pushed the door open with all of his might, sending one policeman flying and stunning him. It may be that another officer barged the door back with equal violence because the wanted man staggered backwards momentarily, before somehow managing to fly past the officers, scrambling helter-skelter down four flights of stairs with the policemen hot on his heels.

The bobbies were more than a match when it came to a sprint, and the absconder was taken to the police station and charged. The man in question was one Karl Wolstenholme, an out-of-work waiter of no fixed abode. At the trial his story began to emerge, and this is where the coincidences begin.

Wolstenholme was 29, born in the year that Vickers served his first prison sentence. He had served in the army (albeit a dragoon regiment, from which he had deserted). The burglary he was arrested for took place on the day that Vickers appeared for his preliminary hearing at the Uxbridge Police Court. Wolstenholme had only been released from a previous burglary sentence in May, from where he had travelled to Nottingham, and then London – meaning that at that time there were actually two Flannelfoots (or perhaps Flannelfeet?) in the capital in 1936. Not only that, but he admitted to various other offences, including ones in Flannelfoot's very own territory of Ruislip and Loughton, and also Reading, where Flannelfoot's wife lived. (It is not beyond the realms of possibility that he could have burgled Flannelfoot's former home!) When arrested, Wolstenholme had thirty-three keys on his person – not quite matching Flannelfoot's forty-seven, but still a decent collection. His method was slightly cruder than Vickers', in that he had cut a whole pane of glass out of a back door in order to open a catch and get into Mr Highley's house.

In fact, for all his 'Flannelfoot' bravado, Wolstenholme cut a very sad figure when he appeared in court for his pre-trial hearing. He related how he had been determined to go straight after his previous release. He spoke of how he was 'determined to die of starvation' rather than continue his life of crime – 'moreover, I found the only person in the world I had ever cared for – one who is my whole life. We were to be married at Christmas'. Sadly, he fell in with people who he thought were trying to help him, but who turned out to be a bad lot, and things went downhill from there.

When asked whether he intended to plead guilty or not guilty, he replied, 'Guilty, very much to my regret.' When the chairman informed him that he would be committed for trial, he pleaded to be given bail in the meantime. 'I'm a changed man now. I won't let you down.' When his request was refused, he broke down in tears.

On 10 January 1938, as Vickers began to adjust to life in Parkhurst, Wolstenholme passed through the granite archway of Dartmoor prison in Devon to begin a three-year sentence.

Stepping into the breach came Flannelfoot 2. He was also known by the slightly more original names of 'Towelfoot' and 'The Night Man' when he came onto the scene in 1938. His first crime was reported in February, almost before the clang of Vickers' Parkhurst cell door being slammed shut for the first time had stopped ringing in his ears. Several robberies ascribed to Flannelfoot 2 occurred on the Becontree Estate in Ilford, Essex, even though the area was supposedly saturated with police as the number of similar crimes in the area began to mount.

This new Flannelfoot had almost certainly taken his lead from the original, operating on Friday nights, wrapping any handy material round his shoes, and even stealing bicycles for his escape. But this man was considered to be small and slightly built, since he got into one house through a window whose dimensions were 14 inches by 10, and needed a chair to get to the gas meters he raided. It perhaps wouldn't have been surprising if he had made his getaways on a child's trike.

It could be that the police attention made the area too hot for him because he next popped up in the Upminster district, and he was believed to have amassed close to £1,000 in cash and valuables during a six-month spree – probably a considerably better return than Vickers' average during any similar period of time.

By September of that year, the police resorted to distributing leaflets to householders in the areas considered to be most at risk, advising them to make sure to lock all doors and windows at night (though these were precautions which had never deterred the real Flannelfoot!).

Some 'Flannelfoots' didn't use the name, but did borrow the methods. In May 1937, a cook originally from Blackburn called Cecil Mercer was caught trying to break into a shop in Wigan – and was found to be wearing rubber surgical gloves on his hands and woollen socks over his shoes.

Long after Flannelfoot was known to be no longer of this world, his spirit lived on. Four years after Vickers' death, nine houses were burgled by a 'flannel-foot thief' in Newham, Essex, and it's easy to see why they were so labelled. In some of the houses, the offender took items from bedrooms while people were asleep in bed, and the burglar was able to force windows with metal frames which residents are said to have believed burglar-proof. Three months later, what was thought to be the same person was operating in Chelmsford. In one home a 76-year-old partially sighted woman was sleeping downstairs in her daughter's house when a noise alerted her to a presence in the room. She switched the light on, but whoever it was fled, knocking a table over in his panic to get out. 'I wish I could have caught him,' lamented the plucky woman. 'But, you see, I cannot see very well.'

In 1951 and 1952, the spirit of Harry Vickers roamed the country. In Portsmouth, what was described as a 'local Flannelfoot' burgled six houses in a single Friday night, managing to deftly release the catches of rear windows to let himself in. Licensees in the West Midlands towns of Brierley Hill and Dudley were reported to be reinforcing the locks on their doors and windows 'to keep out "Flannelfoot"'. Hundreds of pounds had been taken in several pub raids by a man who 'came and went unheard'. By the following year he had migrated north to Leicester: 'Flannelfoot Robs Old People', cried the *Leicester Evening Mail* in 1952. Poor Harry Vickers simply wasn't being allowed to rest in peace. He had apparently robbed two elderly people of their 'rations' (rationing was being wound down but still in force, even so long after the end of the war). Entering three houses by forcing kitchen windows, he stole rations and cash from two houses, but in his haste somehow missed £40 in another.

The ghost of Flannelfoot had still not been exorcised by the 1960s. He was alleged to have broken into no fewer than forty-one houses in one month in 1960, including eight in a single night. He continued his northward progress and by 1966 materialised in Scotland, where the police of three counties were looking for him. At least thirteen houses had been burgled in Fife and Perthshire, with the culprit letting himself in through insecure windows – again leading to the Flannelfoot nickname.

In the early hours of an October morning, a beat constable saw a man running along a street, and at the same time noticed a light on in a nearby house. The constable gave chase, and the suspected thief lightened his load as he ran by throwing away a pair of gloves and a torch. It wasn't enough to keep the distance between the two from rapidly closing, and when arrested he was found to be wearing a watch from a recently burgled Lanarkshire house.

The man in custody turned out to be the habitual criminal Edward Dymond, alias Edward Dymond Jones, alias Edward Jones. It emerged that the 38-year-old had so many variations of his name not because of his criminal career, but because, having had a troubled and unsettled background, he genuinely didn't know his real surname. It was only when he joined the army and needed to obtain evidence of his identity that he discovered his real surname was Dymond.

Like Karl Wolstenholme, Dymond's mitigating personal circumstances did appear to be genuine. After being fostered at the age of 2, he was now a married man with five children living in a house that only had two rooms – and one of those was uninhabitable. He eventually secured a council house, but because he owned no furniture to go in it, he had to spend £200 to make it habitable, and the only way he could do that was by hire purchase. Being unemployed, he predictably got into difficulties and turned to crime as a way of paying off his debts. He now found himself paying off an additional debt to society – two years in Perth Prison.

Then, just for good measure, we have the Sons of Flannelfoot. Parts of Greater Manchester experienced a spate of burglaries early in 1937, in particular the Moston and Blackley districts of the north-east. Things had got so bad – thirty-nine properties had been broken into, including shops – that the police had had to cancel all leave in order to deal with it. These raids involved damage as well as theft, and in one of the homes affected a note was left behind saying 'Wishing you a happy New Year, Flannelfoot'.

In fact, the culprit was a gang rather than one person: six schoolboys, three of whom were on the run from a remand home. They had drunk cocktails, and even fired off a gun they had found in one property. The extra policing paid off, and the boys were hit with a range of sentences. The 'Flannelfoot' note-writer was 11.

For all the Flannelfoot copycats, in many ways the heir to his throne was a burglar who had his own style and nickname. He had probably been at work for much of the 1930s and possibly before, but, as if taking up the baton from Vickers, he seems to have commenced his career in earnest under an equally catchy nickname just after Vickers' incarceration. From early 1938 he became known as the Thin Man.

Where Flannelfoot tended to operate mostly to the west of London, the Thin Man favoured the east: places like Romford and Ilford. Like Flannelfoot, though, his crimes came to the attention not just of local police, but Scotland Yard too – one newspaper, comparing the Thin Man to Flannelfoot, said that the former had 'revived their nightmare'.

But his Thin Man spree was to be far shorter than that of his more famous contemporary. Over a span of around fifteen months he is believed to have broken into approximately 116 homes: in the towns mentioned above, and also Hornchurch, Barking, Goodmayes and Seven Kings. These places are all reasonably close to each other north of the Thames, making his patch much more compact than Vickers'. This, in turn, probably increased his chances of being caught.

The Thin Man, like Flannelfoot, gained entry through rear windows where possible, but tended to force them open rather than employ Flannelfoot's neater and quieter method. It soon became clear that he could fit through extremely small gaps, and police speculated that it might be an adult burglar employing children to slide in through the crevices of partially opened windows. However, fleeting glimpses of him in action proved that the robberies were all his own work, leading to the 'Thin Man' moniker, a title which in turn came from a crime film of that name which had been in the cinemas four years previously.

Like Vickers, he helped himself to snacks while on the job, and the smell of cigarette smoke was often detected at the scene of the crime. He employed a simpler version of the 'flannelfooted' approach by removing his shoes (which he left outside on the lawn if the weather was dry) and moving around in stockinged feet.

The number of uniformed police and detectives in the area was boosted, but for a long time the Thin Man continued to slip through the net to strike again. On one occasion the police received reports that he was active in a specific street and hurried to the scene, but arrived moments too late. What led to his downfall was, of all things, a love of animals.

The first example of this trait came from a robbery in Goodmayes, very close to Becontree, where Flannelfoot 2 struck. (To the best of my knowledge, Flannelfoot 2 was never identified, and it may even be that he and the Thin Man were one and the same.) His entry into the Goodmayes house came to the attention of the family's puppy, which began to yap at him. Rather than flee, the Thin Man poured some milk into a bowl, picked the dog up, and took it outside to enjoy its drink before resuming his work.

One morning in August 1939, Francis Rutland of Glanville Drive, Hornchurch, got out of bed and pulled back the curtains to see what the day's weather was like. He quickly forgot about the weather when his eye was drawn to activity in a garden opposite, at the rear of a house on the intriguingly-named Wingleteye Lane. A man was ushering a kitten out of the back door, and although there was nothing unusual in someone letting a cat out early in the morning, Mr Rutland happened to know that the person doing it didn't live in that house. It wasn't common for people to own phones in 1939, but Mr Rutland was one of those lucky ones who did. The police sped to the scene, and the Thin Man's burgling spree came to an end. They caught him sitting on the sofa, rifling through a handbag, and had about his person items known to have been stolen during other break-ins the previous night. The Thin Man, after leaving his shoes in the garden and putting on gloves, had taken pity on the kitten's mewing to be let out.

The Thin Man's real name was Alfred Simmons. 'Tall and slender', he was 31, and originally from Belfast. The prosecution at his trial described him as 'rather an artist in the burglary line'. He had three previous convictions, one of which led to an eight-month sentence in 1935, and asked for 115 other offences to be taken into account. He made a surprising burglar in many ways. He was neither poor nor out of work, being a printer who had even lectured on the subject in a technical college.

Just as with Vickers, it was emphasised that Simmons never used violence, and had cooperated with police after his arrest. In view of his track record, he was given a relatively short sentence of twenty months' imprisonment, with hard labour.

Chapter 27

Thompson and the Epileptic Killer

Very soon after arriving at Parkhurst, Vickers got some new neighbours thanks to Chief Inspector Tommy Thompson.

The detective's career went from strength to strength following his leading role in the capture of Flannelfoot. The following year, working as a member of Special Branch, he was on a case which was a world away from Vickers and his small-time housebreaking. During the interwar years, what would become the KGB (then called the NKVD) was successfully recruiting British people with strong communist leanings to act as agents and pass on sensitive information. One of these, Percy Glading, worked as an engineer at the Woolwich Arsenal. But he was also a founding member of the British Communist Party, and after being recruited by the Russians he eventually became part of a network at Woolwich leaking secret classified information and documents. MI5, despite being woefully under-resourced at this time, had managed to get their own people inside the Communist Party of Great Britain. They were watching Glading and building up a case against him and others in his circle.

Thanks to the stressful and brave work of Olga Grey, an MI5 undercover agent who befriended Glading, sufficient evidence was gathered to allow the authorities to act. Because MI5 did not have the power to make arrests under British law, Special Branch was called in – specifically, Tommy Thompson.

On 21 January 1938, Olga Grey learned that Glading would be meeting a contact at Charing Cross station where secret documents would be handed over. Thompson was in position to observe from a distance, and when he saw a brown envelope changing hands he quickly moved in and apprehended Glading. Blueprints were found in the envelope, and weapons and plans for a naval gun and an anti-submarine bomb fuse were later found at the 'safe house' Glading had been using. More incriminating evidence was discovered when Thompson arrested another member of the spy ring, and a case under the Official Secrets Act was brought. Glading and several others were tried in camera at the Old Bailey, and the background Thompson gave on Glading made it clear that the intelligence services had a very clear picture of his activities going back several years.

Glading and his co-accused all pleaded guilty, and Glading received a sentence of six years with hard labour. He was sent to Maidstone Gaol, but two of the other men involved ended up in Parkhurst to join Vickers.

Tommy Thompson rounded off 1938 with a harrowing case in Hove, Sussex. At 11 am on 21 November, 4-year-old Patricia Owens was out playing with her friend, 5-year-old Ray Thompson. A man came along on a bike and said to Patricia, 'Come along and play with my little boy. He's a nice little boy.' Patricia went with the man, and was last seen alive when they visited a sweet shop further along the road.

When she hadn't come home for lunch at midday and a search by her worried mother proved fruitless, the police were contacted. A large-scale search turned up her beret about a quarter of a mile from where she was last seen, and it was found near an abandoned bicycle. The following day, with Patricia still missing, Scotland Yard was called in and Tommy Thompson hurried to Hove.

Meanwhile, police from three forces, as well as numerous civilians, were out in force combing the area, and two bloodhounds were brought in. One man, searching scrubland near a local golf course, heard a rustling sound coming from a thicket. He quickly crawled in, and came upon a newspaper bearing the previous day's date which looked as if someone had been lying on it. He heard retreating footsteps on the other side of the thicket, and raised the alarm. A chase ensued, but whoever it was had too much of a head-start. The police weren't at all certain that this was their man, however, and there was a suspicion that the fleeing figure may have been nothing more sinister than a startled tramp. A number of soldiers were later drafted in to boost the search.

On Wednesday, 23 November, the third day after the disappearance, and after searchers had been working through the night, there was a breakthrough. Joseph Dell, a local man, had been detained. He initially told police he hadn't seen Patricia Owens, but after a lengthy interrogation he directed them to an allotment site just over a mile north of the girl's home. There, Chief Inspector Thompson and colleague Detective Sergeant Bray, both of whom had had very little sleep, along with local police, came upon the lifeless body of Patricia Owens. She was under a bench fronting onto an allotment hut, her fair hair cut in a fashionable bob, a white ribbon still in place. She was fully clothed, and had been covered with some discarded venetian blinds.

The lack of sleep was perhaps catching up with Thompson because the police car he and Bray were driving was involved in a collision with a lorry on the way to Hove Police Station. Thompson had a minor injury to one arm, but was able to continue with the investigation.

Later that evening, Dell was charged with the murder of Patricia Owens. He was married and had an adopted son of his own – whom, it later emerged, used to play with Patricia. At the preliminary hearing he was heard to mumble tearfully that he didn't know why he did it, until he was silenced while the magistrate spoke. By the time the case came to trial, however, he was pleading not guilty.

The trial took place in mid-December, where the court learned from Sir Bernard Spilsbury that Patricia had been strangled with a ligature wrapped around her neck; there was no indication of any sexual element to the crime. Dell's heel-prints were found beside the body.

The trial took an unexpected twist when the subject of Dell's mental history was raised. The court was told that he was an epileptic, and Dell himself said that he had given Patricia a ride on his bicycle but that 'a blackness came over my eyes with terrible pain. I remember nothing more until I came to, sitting on the seat with my head in my hands.' It was then that he saw Patricia's body under the seat in the allotment on which he was sitting.

A 'mental expert' testified that Dell had killed the girl while in a state of 'epileptic mania'. It must have been done, he said, 'independently of Dell's knowledge and will. He acted as an automaton'. The judge himself referred to cases he had come across when researching the subject where 'innocent' people had murdered someone without knowing what they were doing. This was the accepted view of possible effects of epilepsy at the time, and the jury took just seven minutes to find Dell 'guilty but insane'. The judge ordered him to be 'detained at the king's pleasure'.

My own research indicates that the medical profession no longer accepts that epilepsy can lead to such behaviour (it seems that sleep-walking has become the new 'epileptic mania' when it comes to psychological defences in murder and rape cases) and even if it had been the reason, the story still doesn't necessarily add up.

Dell's action in taking Patricia away – which, by his own admission, happened *before* the 'blackness' came over him – is classic child-abduction behaviour. What innocent person would approach two children playing together and take one of them away from their game? He took her to a sweet shop – the common bribe in such cases – having told her that he was taking her to play with his little boy. He did indeed have an (adopted) son, but he proceeded to take her straight to the allotment. He also admitted in court that he *remembered* taking her there, yet was at that time supposed to be in his 'blackout' stage of doing things without being aware. My own experience of people with 'waking' epilepsy, which includes an encounter with a woman in such a state behaving in a worrying manner on the roof of a multi-storey car park, is that they have no memory of the whole episode afterwards. It may well be that epilepsy can be so severe and persistent in a person's life that it can lead to a change of character and behavioural problems, but that isn't what was being suggested in Dell's case.

Chapter 28

Flannelfoot in the Media

The Thin Man burglar was named after a film, but Flannelfoot had a film named after *him*. In 1953, a British film of that name, starring Ronald Howard, Mary Germaine and Jack Watling, appeared in cinemas. The cinema website IMDb explains that it is about a 'notorious jewel thief and murderer', and the promotional picture, taken from the cover of the modern DVD, shows Flannelfoot holding a man up at gunpoint.

Now, as a writer whose work has been adapted for television I know that some liberties pretty much *have* to be taken when adapting stories for the screen. Nevertheless, the logic behind some such decisions has always struck me as odd. If film-makers wanted to make a film about a gun-wielding, murdering jewel thief, there must be plenty of such examples to choose from. If the true story of Flannelfoot is interesting enough to turn into a screen drama (which, without doubt, it is), why not actually make *that* film rather than abandoning what makes it (and him) distinctive from other crime stories? But I digress.

The silver screen version of Flannelfoot features a detective inspector who lost his memory after a wall fell on his head, and a crime journalist-cum-sleuth. After bumping several people off with his trusty pistol, Flannelfoot is not arrested near Eastcote Tube Station, but plummets to his death after a desperate struggle on the edge of a roof with the film's version of Chief Inspector Thompson.

The story, all names, characters, and incidents portrayed in this production are fictitious. No identification with actual persons (living or deceased) … is intended or should be inferred, as they say.

The year after the feature film was released, Flannelfoot was on our screens again, television this time in an episode of the still surprisingly good TV series *Scotland Yard*, introduced by Edgar Lustgarten, at that time a very well-known broadcaster and author. The programme was shown in the late 1950s and early 1960s, with each episode featuring a dramatised retelling of real-life crime stories from the casebooks of Scotland Yard. Unusually for the series, Flannelfoot didn't get a whole episode to himself. In an episode entitled *Blondie*, he took second billing to a longer story about the pseudonymous female burglar who, in fact, turned out to be a man in drag.

Flannelfoot features in numerous true crime anthologies, including the already mentioned *Great Cases of Scotland Yard* with its frustrating mix of fact and fiction.

The only book exclusively devoted to Vickers' reign, as far as I'm aware, is a crime novel called *Flannel-Foot* by Doug Dovey, published in 2000. It seems to be impossible to get hold of now, but the blurb tells us that its protagonist was abandoned by parents he never knew, and as an adult embarked on a life of crime: 'Set in England, Spain, five-star hotels, country mansions …'. Again, this is clearly Flannelfoot in name only!

As we have seen, Walter Hambrook and Chief Constable John Horwell both published memoirs, imaginatively titled *Hambrook of the Yard* and *Horwell of the Yard*.

Horwell's book gave Vickers yet another nickname to add to the already long list: The Phantom Burglar. It was written ten years after Flannelfoot's arrest and it was one of the many cases, both serious and not so serious, that he was involved in. Additionally, as a chief constable his role was more that of a supervisor or manager than a hands-on investigator. It's understandable, therefore, that it isn't entirely accurate in some respects. However, these mitigating circumstances aren't quite enough to excuse some of the glaring inaccuracies contained in his 'inside story' of the quest to capture Flannelfoot. In fact, there are so many problems with his version of the story as to make one question just which bits of it one *can* believe.

The issues range from the minor – such as whether Scotland Yard had a map specifically dedicated to Flannelfoot and his crimes, as most accounts say, or whether there were simply Flannelfoot pins or flags on a London map showing the locations of all ongoing crime investigations, as Horwell says – to the crucial details, such as how, specifically, Vickers came to be arrested on the night of 29 October 1937.

Horwell makes much of the fact that he arranged for the team under Thompson tracking Flannelfoot to have high-performance unmarked cars, and that on the night of the arrest officers in one of those cars second-guessed Flannelfoot, headed to Ruislip and lay in wait inside their car till he arrived from the tube station. From their car, they watched him enter a garden, gave him a few minutes, then left their car, crept round the back of the house and caught him literally in the act, 'stiletto' in window frame in an attempt to force the catch.

Every single report of what happened, including the reported testimony of the officers involved themselves, says that detectives watching his lodgings followed him by bus and tube to Eastcote. (To be fair, Eastcote is in the parish of Ruislip, but they are two different tube stations). They trailed him on foot but out of necessity at a great distance and lost him because of the lack of street-lighting, then encountered him in the street as he returned from having burgled a house, as opposed to catching him in the act.

Far be it for me to contradict the chief constable overseeing the whole Flannelfoot hunt, but there is absolutely no doubt in my mind that the less glamorous but more plausible testimonies of the officers on the ground are the ones we must believe.

It may be that Horwell was simply spinning exciting-sounding yarns to fill gaps in his memory, but the possibility also has to be considered that his memoir was ghost-written, that the writer – perhaps under pressure from the publisher – 'enhanced' the dry facts, and Horwell, happy to be the author of an entertaining and hopefully popular book, felt it prudent to sign off on it.

One clue which makes me think that this might be the case is Horwell's description of Vickers' trial. In his book, he says that Flannelfoot pleaded guilty to 'about 500' break-ins, but was not charged with them all. Chief Constable Horwell, of all people, would know that you can't plead guilty to something you haven't been charged with! It's possible that the phrase 'pleaded guilty' was only meant in the loosest sense of having admitted to other burglaries – which was a very common thing and which he did in fact do. But 'pleading guilty' is a term which has a very specific legal connotation, and I find it impossible to accept that Horwell would have made such a mistake – whereas a ghost-writer may well have.

A ghost-writer may also have made the following error – a glaring one to anyone who has made a study of Flannelfoot's crimes, let alone one who has been in charge of investigating them: 'Flannel Foot never at any time ascended upstairs. *Ground-floor work was his speciality, and he stuck to it.*' (author's italics). This is a strange claim to make, since creeping silently around bedrooms while the occupants were asleep is one of Flannelfoot's hallmarks, and one of the proofs of his cool nerve.

The Horwell version of the arrest is the culmination of a bigger picture he painted about the strategy he put in place when he took over as chief constable. He tells us he eventually realised that Flannelfoot was too good at evasion, too canny not to know when he was being followed, for the usual method of trailing a suspect to work. His master plan was to issue an edict that Flannelfoot was no longer to be followed, but that once his hideout was discovered, a watch was to be kept on it and when he left the premises at night, officers in cars were to 'precede' him, i.e. predict where he might go and get there before him, waiting to pounce.

With the greatest of respect to the memory of John Horwell, this sounds like something from a *Boys' Own* story, and, frankly, nonsense. Given the size of not only Greater London but also the Home Counties where Vickers also strayed, the idea that it would be considered an effective use of limited resources to almost psychically decide where he might go on any one night and head off there before he did beggars belief. It's true that he regularly revisited general districts, but most were still sizeable geographical areas containing warrens of streets and side-streets. No matter how good Flannelfoot was at shaking off a tail, *surely* it would be better to persevere with clever and discreet surveillance work – which is what all the evidence says actually happened. Besides which, nothing in the Yard files indicate that Vickers was ever followed before the night of his arrest, while there are several assertions that they had no idea where he was and hadn't for years – so how could they have followed him?

Hambrook's memoir goes almost to the opposite extreme, giving the Flannelfoot case only a brief mention, and saying nothing at all about his encounter with the barrister which jogged his memory of Vickers' first arrest.

Tommy Thompson doesn't appear to have followed his colleagues into the literary world, which is a great shame given his intimate knowledge of the case, his personal involvement in Vickers' arrest and subsequent questioning.

Flannelfoot lingered in the public imagination for a couple of decades after his death, and even though few people today will have heard of him, the legend does just about live on. Every now and then the nickname and the stories of Vickers' crimes will pop up in an article or a book on historical crime cases.

Chapter 29

No Robin Hood

The term 'Robin Hood' is sometimes used when referring to Harry Vickers and (as we shall see below) others like him. But of course, this is romantic nonsense.

Vickers was certainly a 'character' and did not represent a physical threat to anyone. I'm sure he would have been a fascinating person to chat to, someone with lots of stories to tell, probably recounted with a twinkle in the eye. But none of that makes him a Robin Hood, even in using the label in its loosest sense.

As we know, he almost always stole small amounts, and I'm sure that in most cases his victims were affected more psychologically than financially – although it would be surprising if some of them didn't dine out for years to come on having been paid a visit by the famous Flannelfoot. But the thing about breaking into other people's homes and taking what belongs to them is that it is a random act, and the perpetrator can never know what collateral damage his raid might do.

In one of his Isleworth burglaries, he took the whole monthly salary of a shorthand typist. This would have been a low-paid job and we don't know if she had much in the way of savings. How did the woman cope with the challenge of feeding herself and paying the bills for the next four weeks, thanks to Flannelfoot? On the same evening he came across a wedding breakfast which had been laid out for the following morning. He must have realised what it was and he didn't have to touch it. If he was starving, which is highly unlikely, he could have found food in the kitchen in that house or any of the others he hit on the same night. Instead, he ate as much of the wedding breakfast as he could manage before moving on to his next victim, and quite possibly ruined someone's big day.

Similarly, in Southall he took the £10 that Mrs Cleverly had earmarked to pay her rates bill. It may not sound much, but this was 1929 and she was a book-keeper so it could have amounted to almost a month's pay for her. How understanding might the council have been when she told them she couldn't pay her bill because 'Flannelfoot stole my money'?

Then there was the occasion when, in Harrow, he stole the life-savings – apparently all the money she had in the world – of a widow who had already lost her home in a fire.

For reasons known only to himself, when he took the shorthand typist's wages and ruined the wedding breakfast, Vickers chose not to break into a child's money box he came across during this particular night's work. On another occasion, in Hounslow, it was clear that he had examined another box, belonging to a little boy who lived in the house, but didn't take the contents. These two apparent acts of restraint might give us a glimmer of hope as regards his character, but, unfortunately, they were anomalies, and he emptied more children's money boxes than he left untouched.

In Northolt, he broke open a money box in order to get at the threepenny pieces which a child had no doubt been carefully putting aside for weeks or months, perhaps with a view to buying a particular toy they had set their heart on.

In Norwood Green, Vickers stole coins from another money box, and in another Northolt job he came across two children's money boxes each containing 5 shillings, and helped himself to all of it.

Harry Vickers was a father. Did an image never cross his mind of what Elsie's face might have looked like had she come downstairs one morning to find her money box smashed or broken, her savings taken by a mysterious stranger in the night?

Just what kind of a father (and come to that, husband) Vickers was is another area for speculation. On the one hand, the fact that he took Elsie with him when he left Alice might be seen as a good sign. He certainly didn't have to, and, given his lifestyle, having a young girl in tow could only have made things more awkward for him. Yet it's very hard to imagine that he thought he was 'saving' Elsie from her mother because from everything we know, mother and daughter had a loving relationship.

A more cynical way of looking at it is that he took Alice's daughter away from her out of spite. People do commit such acts when relationships turn sour, but if so in this case, Vickers was taking a massive and long-term responsibility on himself just to score a point.

Whatever the truth in all this, it surely wasn't much of a life for a child of 11, snatched away from her mother, home and everything she knew, and finding herself friendless in the Big City.

The examples provided earlier put paid to another Flannelfoot myth – that he only stole from the wealthy. In fact, as John Horwood put it, 'it was only the small people he robbed, people who had managed to secure a sufficient salary to enable them to live in comfort in those modern houses which were springing up in outer London ...' Horwell said he often thought of the housewives who woke up to find that their housekeeping money had vanished in the night.

Why a man of Vickers' evident criminal skill and abilities didn't aim higher, though, is one of the mysteries. Horwell calculated that he made an average of £10–20 a week – probably a pretty good wage for a working-class man then – but with the added risk and stress that came with being a burglar. Perhaps he just preferred the easy, familiar target. He was either already very familiar with, or soon became very familiar with, the suburbs on the western side of London, and felt safe there, less likely to get caught, get trapped.

The homes of the wealthy were more likely to have better security, and to have staff on the premises who might be up and about at unpredictable times. In the 1920s and 1930s, the live-in staff of the Victorian era had all but gone except for the very wealthy, but, as any reader of Richmal Crompton's *William* books will know, even reasonably off middle-class families like the Browns still often employed cooks and maids. The larger the house, the greater the number of rooms, which meant it was that bit harder to tell whether a light might be on somewhere indicating that someone might be up and about. A wealthy family wouldn't necessarily have that much more cash around than a middle-class one; the value was likely to be in things like paintings, ornaments and especially jewellery. But that kind of burglary, jewellery aside, meant more bulk to carry, and virtually all items of that kind had to be sold on, bringing into the equation outsiders who may or may not be trusted in the long-term.

Conversely, there was more on offer per burglary, which in turn would have reduced the number of jobs necessary to provide a decent income. One really good job might easily bring in the amount it would have taken Flannelfoot a year or more to 'earn'. And there were men to whom this idea was attractive.

As I mentioned earlier, the two decades of the 1920s and 1930s were the golden age of 'cosy crime' fiction – the likes of Agatha Christie, Dorothy L. Sayers, G.K. Chesterton. The idea of crime, detectives and criminals as entertainment, as an intriguing puzzle to be solved, took hold during this period.

It is somehow fitting, then, that this was also the heyday of the 'cat burglar' – in fact, it's when the then relatively recently coined term was popularised. The image of the glamorous, agile, stealthy, sometimes even (as in the case of Raffles) gentlemanly thief caught the popular imagination – a mood which helped to further Flannelfoot's notoriety.

One example of the kind of burglar Harry Vickers *might* have been (and the sort that many people assume he *was*, thanks to some fanciful versions of his life) can be seen in the person of Robert Delaney. He isn't as well remembered as Vickers, perhaps not least because he never seems to have acquired a catchy nickname like him. But his exploits were just as well known, and even marvelled at, during the period that Flannelfoot was making the news.

As well as operating at the same time as Flannelfoot, Delaney was virtually a West London neighbour, at least based on the addresses of both when they were arrested. Delaney's Shaftesbury Avenue home in 1934 was 4 miles from the Shepherd's Bush residence where Vickers was living when he was apprehended just three years later. Delaney was 39 years old, just seven years younger than Vickers, and was described as an 'engineer'.

An example of the different league that Delaney was in soon becomes apparent when we learn that he was arrested for a single burglary in which he took jewellery worth £1,100. This was the property of Mrs M. Gluckstein, who had a flat in the Royal Palace Hotel in Kensington. He was further charged with a burglary in Bexhill-on-Sea, taking jewellery and other items (including a revolver) to a value of £250.

The other big difference between Flannelfoot and Delaney was that Delaney didn't work alone. There had been rumours at one time that Flannelfoot was training an apprentice who could aid him and perhaps follow in his footsteps. This was untrue, but Delaney actually did recruit a 16-year-old boy. The youth subsequently gave evidence on behalf of the prosecution, presumably to save his own skin, leading to a further charge of inciting a boy to commit a felony.

Furthermore, a woman who had sold the stolen gems to a jeweller in Houndsditch was arrested soon after Delaney's apprehension, gave her name as Olive Delaney and was supposedly Delaney's wife. But when Delaney had married Olive, he had overlooked the small matter of a previous and still living wife, and he was now looking at charges of bigamy.

Vickers may well have read all this and felt a little smug that he preferred to work alone. He may even have felt somewhat justified in only stealing relatively paltry sums, since Olive only got £250 for the jewels when she sold them – less than a quarter of their value – though still an amount that would have taken Vickers many weeks to rake in.

The cat burgling side of Delaney's exploits emerged when he admitted to having climbed up a drainpipe to enter the hotel in Kensington – a common tactic for such criminals. When arrested, he ruefully admitted that it had been 'a tough climb'. But although Delaney undoubtedly was a cat burglar as we understand the term, statements made at his trial cast doubt on his story about this particular crime. Delaney had a track record of lying, cheating and stealing, but this trial revealed that he did possess at least some small concept of honour because he was attempting to shoulder all of the blame, and all of the punishment. As well as emphasising that Olive had nothing at all to do with any of the crimes – patently untrue – according to the youth's own testimony, it was *he* who had clambered into the Royal Palace Hotel, not Delaney, who was in fact waiting for him nearby with Olive.

But the teenager revealed that it was Delaney who had put him up to the attempted robbery in which he had been caught, and the allegation was that the purpose had been to raise funds for a defence barrister for when he was tried for another offence. But Delaney's apprentice was perhaps not quite ready for the big league. On the night in question, a night watchman in Kensington Palace Garden spotted the youth balanced precariously against the building, one foot on a window sill, the other on a rung of the ladder. The man didn't hesitate to pull the ladder away, leaving the young crook hanging on while he went to find a policeman. At the youth's home were found items taken during a burglary in Bexhill-on-Sea, including a fur coat worth £1,000. This arrest led to that of Delaney.

When police arrived at Delaney's flat, they found an extendable ladder with grappling hooks on the end for attaching to window sills, along with other incriminating items.

The charges of inciting a youth to commit crime and bigamy were ultimately dropped, although when the case came to trial Olive was described as his 'bigamous wife'. She received a three-year sentence for receiving stolen goods, while Delaney, in view of his previous record, was handed down a stiff nine years. The prosecuting counsel described him as 'notorious and extremely dangerous', and said he had criminal connections with both the South African and Australian underworld.

Flannelfoot may have been no Robin Hood, but Delaney was a positively unattractive character. As well as getting boys to do his dirty work and carrying a gun, he thought nothing of cheating those close to him.

Having lived near Flannelfoot, Delaney's final years also followed a not too dissimilar path. His final incarceration saw him, like Vickers, in Parkhurst Prison on the Isle of Wight, and the two were almost certainly there at the same time at least for a period. They both departed this life at the same relatively young age, being 52 or thereabouts. In Delaney's case, he died in 1948 while still serving his sentence.

Delaney would probably have passed himself off as a wealthy toff regardless of whether he had played the role of 'gentleman cat burglar', but in the latter regard he may well have been influenced by the enormously popular *Raffles* novels. The first book in this series by E.W. Hornung (Sir Arthur Conan Doyle's brother-in-law) was published when Delaney was at an impressionably young age, and the character began to appear in film adaptations when he was embarking on his criminal career.

Delaney's way of dressing and fake persona had lots of parallels with that of Raffles, the difference being that Hornung's debonair jewel thief was (like

Flannelfoot for most of his career) too good at his work to get caught – and he really was wealthy.

Raffles may have been based on one or more real people, but they weren't gentlemen cat burglars. Other real-life examples did exist at around the same time, however. 'Gentleman George' Smithson was one such, although, like Delaney, comparisons with Raffles owed a lot to his own talent for self-promotion: in 1930 he published a memoir entitled *Raffles in Real Life: The Confessions of George Smithson Alias 'Gentleman George'*.

The list of Smithson's victims sounds like something copied and pasted from Debrett's (The Earl of Jersey, Lady Constance Russel, Lord Henry Neville) and the locations from a National Trust handbook (Eaton Hall, Eridge Castle, Laverstoke Park). He had an eye for a painting, and his haul included Gainsboroughs and other valuable pieces. Smithson had a flat in Kensington, where Delaney sometimes lurked, and roamed much further afield than Flannelfoot, striking in the south-west and south-east of England, and travelling as far north as Berwick and Edinburgh.

Like Flannelfoot, Smithson wasn't afraid to creep around the bedroom of a sleeping occupant in search of loot. On one such occasion in Thoby Priory, Essex, he woke Lord Arran, eliciting a cry in the darkness of 'Who's there?' Smithson employed a Flannelfoot trick in such circumstances – he locked his lordship in his own bedroom and made good his escape.

But, like a lot of these 'celebrity' burglars, including Delaney, Smithson kept getting caught and being bundled off to prison, and this is the biggest and most significant difference between Vickers and all his contemporaries.

Chapter 30

The Man Behind Flannelfoot

Neither Vickers nor Alice Hanslip was ever very forthcoming about their lives. One story that emerged from the questioning of neighbours and acquaintances was that the man at No. 20 Royal Crescent had told the woman he was living with that he was a successful gambler who went out at nights to bet on the dogs and take part in card games that sometimes went on till the early hours. This woman would always prepare him some sandwiches to take out with him. All this may be true, but I suspect it's more likely to be something Vickers and his Norfolk woman concocted between them as a cover story. Alice Hanslip had been Vickers' constant companion for at least four years and probably more, and it's almost inconceivable, even if she didn't realise that her partner was Flannelfoot, that she was unaware of his nocturnal life of crime.

The exact number of burglaries Vickers committed will never be known for sure. Estimates of the number of break-ins range from the low hundreds to over 1,000. Horwell claims that at the time he became chief constable, the number was already into four figures, and that the ultimate total could have been 'a few thousand'. If Vickers really did go out on a nightly basis, pretending to his mistress that he was working a night shift (perfectly true, in its own way!), then this seemingly enormous number starts to sound not impossible despite Horwell's claims needing to be treated with caution. Thompson's team were no fools nor prone to exaggeration, and readily dismissed unlikely stories of his exploits. Writing after Vickers' arrest, Chief Inspector Thompson mentioned '600 or so' burglaries attributed to him, which might sound more reasonable – but is it? If we take a fairly conservative estimate of the length of Vickers' career and call it fifteen years, we arrive at just forty burglaries a year. Even if he was only active for ten years, 600 hundred burglaries still amounts to only 60 per year, or put another way, five per month – a suspiciously low figure for Flannelfoot.

We'll never know how many crimes Vickers committed before he was caught on that first occasion in 1910, but it's a reasonable bet that a fair few undetected crimes lurk behind almost every 'first offence'. It's true that he was only 22 when he was convicted, but that's more than old enough to allow for an earlier stint of several years.

There is little strong evidence that he was burgling during the ten years after his first conviction. First, there was the relatively short sentence of nine months to be served, then Vickers, a newlywed, fathered two children (not including Elsie, who didn't come along until the new decade), and in the middle of it all was his two years of army service and his injured leg, following which there may have been a period of recuperation.

The Flannelfoot name and reports really take off from around 1920. Elsie was born in 1921, in Reading (as Jack and Vera had been), so it appears that Vickers must have been commuting to London in order to carry out his raids at this time. He may even have had a spell of employment in the capital. The 1921 census, which would have been taken in June, shows him and Alice living in Reading in his parents' home. This indicates that he and Alice may have been struggling financially, and this is reinforced by Vickers being listed as a canvasser of electric lamps (which presumably means he was a salesman) – to which 'out of work' is added. The London connection comes from his erstwhile employer's workplace: Kentish Town. Perhaps this lack of money and a home for his family helped to push him deeper into his life of crime.

Vickers was certainly very busy in the early years of the 1920s especially, but managed to keep the pace up throughout the decade. It really is astonishing that he was able to commit so many crimes, night after night, week after week, month after month, mostly within a relatively small geographical area, without even really coming close to being spotted (apart from one instance), let along captured. He was to petty theft what Jack the Ripper was to murder.

He didn't let up into the 1930s, despite the apparent turmoil in his private life. If during some of this time he was still journeying between Reading and London, it may have been one of the strains which led to the marital split. We have no idea whether he travelled to the capital and back all during the course of a single night, or whether he stayed overnight in lodging houses, or with friends, or the London relative we know he had. Could he have afforded to run two homes – one with each of the Alices in his life?

Anyhow, neither the split from Alice, nor Elsie running away from him, nor the sensational headlines accompanying Alice's identification of her, did anything to cramp his style, and he continued burgling at his usual rate right up till his arrest.

He was a clever criminal, but perhaps the biggest criticism one could make of him in that context was that in the final years before his capture, he *must* have known that the police were closing in, yet, no matter how many precautions he took, he didn't seem to think fit to make any changes to his modus operandi. There is some evidence that he occasionally avoided his usual haunts, perhaps prompted by observing pairs of men in dark overcoats standing on street corners. But by and large, he persisted in travelling to the western districts of London. Not long before his arrest he targeted Southall, a place he had struck at least three times previously, and on the night he was taken, he initially led his tailing detectives to Ealing, which was not only another place he had hit several times but was the location of one of the burglaries for which he had been convicted in 1910.

Criminals not unnaturally feel more comfortable on territory they are familiar with, but after 1936, when the police announced in the press that they *knew* Flannelfoot was Harry Edward Vickers, *knew* he went under the alias Henry Williams, *and* had a full description and probably at least one photograph, it's surprising that he never seemed to think of doing things differently. The police couldn't swamp the whole of London for one burglar, so just a shift of territory ought to have thrown them off the scent at least for a time. He could have stopped wrapping materials round his feet, devised a new method of breaking in. He could even have moved away from his usual minor cash and valuables thefts and risk going out with a bang – a spree targeting the homes of the very wealthy, making himself some real money, perhaps enough to enable him to give up burgling while the going was good.

Or is it possible that the strain of having been a notorious wanted man for so many years was beginning to tell on him? Did he realise that his luck must be close to running out, leading to a certain level of recklessness, a kind of 'death wish'? This is more or less what John Horwell implies in his memoirs.

Horwell said Vickers admitted to Inspector Thompson that he lived in constant expectation of being caught, and because of that his life had been one long purgatory. 'He seldom had a day's peace of mind,' if Horwell is to be believed. 'Since his arrest he had plenty of time for reflection and had come to the conclusion that the game had not been worth the candle. If he lived through his sentence, he would not touch crime again. Well, I'm glad to say … he did live through his sentence, and he kept his word.' This may technically be true, though again Horwell seems to be betraying his ignorance, given the fact that Vickers died very soon after his release – something which he would surely have mentioned had he known of it.

Many of Vickers' burglaries must have gone unreported, or at least were briefly mentioned but with a Flannelfoot connection not being made. In the early 1960s, a reader wrote in to the *Daily Mirror* after reading a retrospective article on Vickers which had appeared in the paper. He reported that one night in the 1930s, three of his neighbours were broken into by Flannelfoot, and he believed his house was spared because his family had deliberately left a light on in a bedroom. He doesn't give a date, but this seems to be one of what must be quite a number of Flannelfoot crimes which are absent from popular accounts, and weren't covered by the press of the day.

Vickers' limp is mentioned a lot, but mostly in a second-hand way by people who had never met him, and it's not clear to what extent his mobility really was affected by his war wound. It doesn't necessarily follow that a person with an old injury must have a permanent limp, and even if they do it doesn't necessarily mean that their mobility is greatly impaired.

John Horwell, in *Horwell of the Yard*, goes to town in his description of Vickers' physical prowess: he was an 'expert athlete' who made off 'at miraculous speed' if he thought he was in danger of being seen or caught; he vaulted garden fences 'like an expert hurdle jumper – fences even six feet high held no terror for him. He jumped them like a greyhound and disappeared quietly as a shadow'. I'm comfortable in saying that every word of this can be ascribed to literary licence, but the overall impression is of a man who remained fit and physically capable well into middle age, limp or no limp. Now it's time to take a last look at some of the other characters in this story.

In 1939, with Harry into the second year of his sentence, Alice Maud Vickers was living with her daughters Vera and Elsie. Alice, who seems to have been known as 'Lally' according to family sources, didn't remarry after Harry's death (which occurred when she was 58) but returned to Reading and worked as a seamstress.

Most genealogists have Alice Vickers down as dying in 1967, but this death occurred in Wokingham (listed as Alice M. Vickers), and although this is only 30 miles from Reading, there is an Alice Maud Vickers in the National Probate Calendar who died in the Woodlands Old People's Home, Reading Road, Woodley, Reading on 22 March 1968. That establishment was less than 4 miles from her last known address (in 1965, the electoral roll shows her as living with her brother William on Brigham Road, Reading). Woodley does appear to have come under the Wokingham registration district for deaths at that time, but that still wouldn't explain the discrepancy regarding the different death dates. If the Alice who died in the old people's home is ours, it would make her 83 at the time of her death, and she left an estate of £943, not a small amount for a woman in her position.

Elsie, who had found herself a job as a clerk in a laundry, married Ronald Bryant, a GPO engineer. She was described as a pretty girl in the newspaper reports of her disappearance and discovery, and she did indeed grow into an attractive woman. She also stayed in the Reading area and had at least two children. She was 81 when she died in 2002.

Alice Norden, née Hanslip, was born in Lakenheath, Suffolk, and married Abraham Norden in Wandsworth in 1920, but it seems that they may not have stayed together for very long at all. As early as 1924, electoral register entries show that Alice was living in Wandsworth under her maiden name with Frederick J. Hanslip (presumably her brother or other relative), while Abraham Norden was in Whitechapel with his sister Esther. With Vickers in prison in 1938, she is back with Frederick, now in Camberwell. (Specifically, Camberwell Grove – the very street where detectives Jean Stratton and Margaretta Low were living at the same time. Jean Stratton lived at No. 50, Alice Hanslip at No. 158.) Alice and Abraham Norden probably divorced, since records indicate that he remarried, but Alice appears to have remained single.

Thomas Basil Thompson moved to Haslemere in Surrey, where he lived with his wife Marion. At around this time he was promoted to superintendent, and took up a post in the Criminal Record Office. In 1945 he was awarded the police's Distinguished Service Medal, having been a serving officer for approximately 34 years.

In the year of his retirement, 1947, he took a little of the media limelight that had once shone on his nemesis Flannelfoot. An old copy of the *Radio Times* lists Thompson as appearing in a weekly show called *It's Your Money They're After*, a kind of early crime awareness programme. It always featured a Scotland Yard officer providing advice and words of warning to the public, and Thompson appeared in at least two episodes: both of which had confidence tricksters as their theme.

Tommy Thompson was the longest living of any of our characters. He ended his days in Hill Head, a little coastal village in Hampshire. There he died in 1981, at the age of 92.

Of the other members of the Flannelfoot team about whom it has been possible to gather any information of note, Thompson's colleague on the night of the arrest, Inspector Duncan, proved equally hard to pin down with any certainty, owing to the fact that there seems to have been a plethora of 'Inspector Duncans' active during the Flannelfoot era.[1]

---

1. Chief Inspector Alec Duncan became head of the Flying Squad in 1936, the year before Flannelfoot was caught; Inspector George Duncan was also a Met officer in the 1920s and possibly into the 1930s; and there was a Chief Inspector James Duncan, based in Preston, whose cases made the national news several times.

He had joined the Metropolitan Police almost as soon as the war was over as a beat constable. Within two years he was a detective sergeant; his promotion to first-class inspector came about as part of a major reshuffle following the retirement of Walter Hambrook in 1936, and he was made chief inspector the year after the arrest of Vickers. 'His rise has been extremely rapid,' an article in the *People's Journal* said in 1939, adding that Duncan was known as 'The man with the card index memory' – no doubt, one reason why his next role was as head of the Yard's Criminal Record Office. 'Time and again his brilliant work has led to the capture and conviction of criminals.' He was only 64 when he died in Surrey in 1962.

The officer with the most unusual name, Detective Sergeant Rasin Nelson Orson, was one of the officers secretly watching when Alice Hanslip arrived in London and met Vickers. On the night of the arrest, he was one of the three officers whom Thompson handed his car over to when the police car disguised as a taxi, which they had been intending to follow Vickers in, broke down; and he was one of the arresting officers.

Orson was born in Essex and he joined the police force in 1924, aged approximately 23. He was 34, married and living in West Ham when he took part in the final operation to catch Vickers. He must have either joined the merchant navy before becoming a police officer, or have served on merchant ships as part of the war effort between 1914–18 because he was a recipient of the Mercantile Marine Medal. To qualify, Orson must have served at sea for at least six months during the war and have made at least one voyage through what was classed as a 'danger zone'. His Mercantile Marine Medal would have made him the automatic recipient of the British Medal.

Just a few months after obtaining the satisfaction of putting Flannelfoot behind bars, Orson was teamed up with Chief Inspector Bridger when the Norfolk police asked the Yard to investigate the suspicious death of Lewis Sandford in Downham Market. His death had originally been ascribed to natural causes, but the enquiries of Bridger and Orson led to the exhumation of his body. The post-mortem (not, for once, performed by Spilsbury) revealed strychnine in Sandford's stomach. Following a lengthy investigation, involving several trips between London and Norfolk, the dead man's pregnant widow was charged with his murder by poisoning, but was found not guilty when the case went to trial.

Then at the end of that year, Orson was involved in a harrowing murder case when Essex police called for the assistance of Scotland Yard after the body of a 9-year-old girl was found naked in a ditch in South Hornchurch. The child had been strangled, and Orson again accompanied Chief Inspector Bridger from London to join a large team of officers which had been assembled to search for evidence and clues to the identity of the culprit. The signs were that the girl, Pamela Coventry, had not been killed where she was found but had been brought from the murder location, probably by car, and dumped in the ditch. She had been found trussed with an electric cable and gagged. Sir Bernard Spilsbury was assigned to carry out the post-mortem, and he found that poor Pamela had been struck in the face before being manually strangled, and that her body bore signs of sexual activity.

Orson and the others in the team discovered from Pamela's friends that she had been seen talking to a man near to where she lived, and were provided with a vague description. There was an RAF base not far from where the body was found, and a number of airmen who had been on leave at the time of the murder were questioned. Bridger and Orson between them spoke to literally hundreds of men and women over the course of the next few days.

The investigation took a new twist at the end of January 1939 when Orson was dispatched to Bristol after he and Bridger learned that a man who had been living in the Hornchurch area had abruptly left for that city just after the murder. This lead came to nothing, but in another surprising turn of events following a meeting between Bridger and chief constable John Horwell, a local man, Leonard Richardson, a married father of two, was arrested by Bridger and another inspector as he left work. He was charged on what appears to have been the flimsiest of evidence. The case reached trial, however, where Richardson pleaded not guilty.

One of the few pieces of tangible evidence was a cigarette stub which fell from the wire flex with which Pamela Coventry's wrists had been tied when Sir Bernard Spilsbury untied it during his examination. The cigarette paper was supposed to have been similar to the hand-rolled ones found on Richardson. He had made one up and smoked it while giving his statement to police, and they had preserved his discarded cigarette end. But knowing about this evidence, Richardson's wife had been playing detective while her husband had been locked up on remand. What she uncovered using her own initiative showed that thousands of people used the same paper and the same sort of tobacco to make their roll-ups – there was nothing at all unique about what had been found on Pamela's body.

That left little more than the girl's wellingtons being found in a lane where Richardson had been seen on the day of the murder, and a few other small items belonging to her which were discovered on a route he used frequently, wrapped in a newspaper he had delivered to his house. But again, this was a national daily, so hardly a smoking gun from an evidential point of view.

That this would be slight evidence indeed with which to condemn a person to be hanged is reflected in the jury's rather unusual action in sending a note to the judge asking whether the trial could be halted prematurely.

'May I take it that you do not think there is enough evidence to justify you finding this man guilty?' the judge asked. The jury were of the unanimous opinion that this was so, and the judge (who presumably felt the same way) had no hesitation in putting a stop to the proceedings and allowing Leonard Richardson to walk free without a stain on his character.

Orson must have been promoted within two or three years of the Essex case because, in 1945, it was Detective Inspector Orson whose fraud investigation led to a London businessman being fined and jailed for a year.

Having lived in the London area most of his life, it looks like Rasin Orson retired to the coast after retiring from the police force, since he was living in Holland-on-Sea near Clacton when he died in 1973, aged 69.

PC Percival John Woolway was another of the hidden observers when Vickers rendezvoused with Alice Hanslip in London, and was one of a team of four who followed him on his meanderings that day. Woolway paired up with DC Massey to tail Vickers from his home in Shepherd's Bush to Eastcote, and they were among those who surrounded their man and effected his apprehension. He was one of the younger of the seasoned men and women who formed Thompson's team, being 31 years of age. Just a couple of years previously he had travelled to Avoch in Ross-shire to marry Mary Ann Patience in her home town. Woolway hailed from Knowle, Bristol, and was back in the West Country by the time of his death in 1996 at the age of 89.

Detective Constable Herbert Massey, who also followed Vickers in the radio car when the police taxi failed to start, was from Lincolnshire. He may have been promoted the year after helping catch the arch-criminal because, in September 1938, a Sergeant Massey was behind the conviction of a fraudster in West London, and the arrest of a thief of furs and jewellery from a hotel in Piccadilly in 1943. He died in Birmingham in 1989, aged 85.

Detective Sergeant Thomas William Mead appears to be the man of that name who was born in Grays, Essex in 1890 and, like Rasin Orson, earned the Mercantile Marine Medal. He is almost certainly the Thomas W. Mead serving on board the coastal sailing barge *Carina* of London, which happened to be in port at Great Yarmouth when the 1911 census was taken. He had been involved in the 'Brentford Torso' case in 1935, which had an unsatisfactory ending in as much as the dismembered and decapitated body in question was never identified and no murderer ever caught. The following year he arrested a fraudulent palm reader, Albert Waite, who was able to psychically ascertain that a young woman's late mother had left her money which was being withheld from her, money which he could track down if only the daughter would pay him in order to do so. What Waite didn't divulge was that he also saw himself pocketing this money and absconding. He perpetrated the same trick on other unsuspecting victims before being collared by Mead and sent to prison.

After later seeing Vickers put behind bars, Mead again teamed up with one of the two female officers on that case, Detective Sergeant Stratton, to catch the elderly poison-pen letter writer, Winifred Simner, whose story we have already heard.

Mead had joined the Metropolitan Police in 1923, and died young – in fact, predeceasing Vickers by passing away in 1941 at the age of 51.

We have already looked at the enigmatic Jean (aka Margaret, aka Anne) Stratton, Mead's invaluable right-hand woman in the Simner case. Despite her conviction and what can only be described as disgrace, it's still hard not to admire what she did achieve before it all went horribly wrong. She was one of the eldest in a large and probably not very well-off family, and when she was only 20 she probably made many sacrifices in order to act as a mother to her six younger brothers and sisters when they lost their real mother. She then went on to contribute to the war effort, followed by a successful career in the police at a time when female officers were still relatively rare, especially in the CID. Not only was she a major player in the hand-picked team working on one of the most high-profile cases of the decade, but, having gained promotion to sergeant, she was senior to at least a couple of her male colleagues in that elite team.

Margaret Stratton was born in Dundee but probably spoke with a London accent, since her carpenter father moved the family to Camberwell in London when she was still a baby. She was baptised there and died there, having reached her century in 1986. Even then her name was still causing confusion, since she has the rare distinction of having two separate entries in the death register. One is in the name of Anne Stratton, one of the variations noted on the 1939 Register and which she was presumably using in her later years. But there is a second death entry elsewhere, with the same reference details but in the name of Margaret Langland Stratton, meaning that what was almost certainly her real name was belatedly discovered upon her death – perhaps from papers in her effects, or from family members.

It would be fascinating to get hold of a time machine and meet any of the people who feature in this story. Obviously, Harry Edward Vickers would be at the top of the list. But Margaret/Jean/Ann Stratton would be a close second – not least to ask exasperatedly 'WHY?!'

The final Flannelfoot mystery brings us back to Vickers, and how he came to die in a Staffordshire hospital. He was a Reading man, a long-time resident of London where most of his connections must have been, and fresh from incarceration on the Isle of Wight. He had no known connections with the West Midlands.

On Vickers' death certificate he is described as a carpenter, which is perhaps a little surprising considering that he had learned, apparently at his own request, how to make surgical boots while in prison. His final address is recorded as 48 Hampton Road, Birmingham 6. This is in the Handsworth district, and the house itself, despite being on the corner of a street of regular semi-detached homes, is quite a substantial one and appears to comprise numerous rooms. It may have been a lodging house, but my guess is that it could have been used as a probation hostel, a sort of half-way house for released prisoners to help them to get back into normal life. Advancing that line of speculation a little further, I wonder whether Vickers' probation officer helped him find the carpenter's job, and that it just happened to be in the Birmingham area. This is pure guesswork, but in the absence of any other clues it would help to explain why he would end his days so far from home. The authorities may have felt that he was more likely to stay on the straight and narrow if he stayed away from his old haunts and associates.

The death certificate records that he suffered from aortitis, inflammation of the aorta, the main blood vessel leading from the heart. This led to chronic bronchitis, and finally cardiac failure. And there is one more interesting and poignant thing to be learned from that document.

When Harry died, Alice was by his side. Not Alice Hanslip, but Alice Vickers. We don't know whether they reunited as the first step in getting their marriage back on track, or if she rushed to be at his side on learning of his illness. That's not the most important thing. After everything that had happened, everything he had subjected her to, they were back together again in his last days.

Appendix

Crime Then and Now

If anyone ever tells you that you are looking at the past through rose-tinted spectacles when you tell them that crime has got worse over the years, here are a few statistics comparing the Flannelfoot era to today which you can add to your armoury.

- In 1900, the population of Britain was just over 30 million, and there were 3,812 recorded burglaries. By the year 2000, the population had grown to 59 million, and the number of burglaries was just over 1 million. In other words, whereas the population had almost doubled, burglaries had increased 250-fold. [Source: The National Archives]
- In 1900, there were 312 homicides in England and Wales ('homicide' includes manslaughter). In the year 2000, there were 859. Even taking into account a doubling of the population, this represents a one-third increase. [Source: UK Government]
- In 1900, the number of 'serious woundings or other acts endangering life' was 269. If this had doubled by 2000 in line with population growth, the figure would have risen to 538. The actual figure for the year 2000 was 15,662. [Source: UK Government]
- As for crimes in general rather than just burglaries, between 1900 and 1930 there were an average of 90,000 indictable offences each year. By the 1980s, this figure had reached 3.5 million. [Source: UK Parliament]
- In 1900, there were 1,908 cases of 'violence against the person' of various kinds. A doubling of that figure by the year 2000 would have resulted in a total of 3,816. In fact, there were 600,922 such crimes. [Source: UK Government]
- In 1900, there were 2,763 cases of Flannelfoot's forte: 'burglary in a dwelling'. By the year 2000, we see a figure of 399,927 – a rise of no less than 14374 percent! [Source: UK Government]

My own, anecdotal, non-scientific impression, from the countless hours I've spent trawling through historical crime records and newspaper reports, alongside an interest in modern crime stories, is that even a hardened criminal like Harry Vickers would be shocked at the world he witnessed if he had seen a glimpse into the future. I'm not making a political point by stating that modern police are under-staffed and over-stretched. If Flannelfoot were active today, many victims would be lucky to even receive a visit by the police, and the idea that modern police would spend a second worrying about the stolen bicycles which featured in many of Flannelfoot's raids is so far-fetched as to be almost funny (if it weren't so depressing). In fact, the very thought that senior Scotland Yard detectives would be involved, let alone investing so much time, effort and money in setting up a special task force to investigate a single prolific burglar, of whom there are now several in almost any urban district, is also now a notion of fantasy only.

Vickers (and Thompson and his team) might notice that the age of the average criminal profile has changed. Many burglars of Vickers' era and before seem to have been more mature men like him, whereas today my impression is that older men are more likely to be found at the 'heavier' end of the criminal spectrum, with burglaries being perpetrated by very young men and teenagers, often, so we are told, in order to facilitate a drug habit. This in turn is partly because so many children and youths are able to drop out of the school system or leave it illiterate (something virtually unheard of during my own childhood on an inner-city estate in the 1960s and early 1970s), and then as adults get lost in the benefits system without ever needing to get a job.

Then, when someone is caught, the weight of evidence/burden of proof needed to convict, I am absolutely certain, has shifted in favour of the criminal. When evidence from CCTV and other camera systems began to be introduced as evidence in trials, I recall predicting that there would come a day when hardly anyone would be convicted *without* such evidence against them, and I believe we are pretty close to that point now. But getting to trial at all is the first hurdle. Anyone who watches modern reality police programmes on TV will have seen criminals as good as caught in the act (such as a car chase followed by a foot chase and an arrest), then for the segment to end with the phrase 'released without charge/released due to lack of evidence'. This is not the fault of the police, but of the cumbersome and overwhelmed legal system.

Modern trials take place many months, sometimes years, after the offence, sit for shorter sessions, run on much longer and are very much more expensive than in Flannelfoot's day. And a mention must be made of the CPS, which stands for the Crown Prosecution Service but which I have heard an ex-police officer wryly refer to as the Criminal Protection Society. Their role is to decide whether there is enough evidence to send a case to trial, but there is a strong suspicion that the *cost* of a trial, as much as the need for justice, plays a big part in the decision-making process.

So now we've had the trial and the guilty verdict, and our career criminal, a man demonstrably with no means of support other than benefits and the proceeds of his crimes, probably for most of his adult life, awaits his sentence. Flannelfoot received a nine-month sentence for his first conviction, and five years for what, despite the number of crimes committed, was only his second conviction. I will leave the reader to decide whether such a criminal would even see the inside of a prison today.

Bibliography

Bell, Amy, *Murder Capital* (Manchester University Press, Manchester, 2015) [Google books]

Bethell, Ben, *The 'Star Class' in English Convict Prisons, 1863–1914* (Birkbeck University, London, 2020) [Google Books]

Cross, Rupert, *Punishment, Prison and the Public* (The Hamlyn Trust, Steven & Sons, London, 1971)

Hambrook, Walter, *Hambrook of the Yard* (Robert Hale, London, 1937)

Hensby, Jeanette, *The Rotherham Trunk Murder* (Createspace, 2016)

Horwell, John E., *Horwell of the Yard* (Andrew Melrose Ltd, London, 1947)

Robinson, Curtis B., *Caught Red Starred* (Xlibris Corp, 2011)

Various authors, *Thirties Housing: Routledge Library Editions* (Routledge, 2018)

Woodhall, Edwin T., *Secrets of Scotland Yard* (John Lane, The Bodley Head, London, 1936)

Principal Websites Used

9th Rifle Brigade War Diaries, WO 95/1901/4 (www.nationalarchives.gov.uk)

Ancestry (Ancestry.co.uk)

Britain from Above (www.britainfromabove.org.uk)

British Newspaper Archive (www.britishnewspaperarchive.co.uk)

Cocktails with Elvira blog (elvirabarney.wordpress.com)

FamilySearch (Familysearch.org)

Great War Forum (www.greatwarforum.org)

Herts Past Policing (www.hertspastpolicing.org.uk)

National Archives (www.nationalarchives.gov.uk)

'The Politics of the Rising Crime Statistics of England and Wales, 1914–1960', Howard Taylor, 1997. (https://journals.openedition.org/chs/989)

The Times Digital Archive (https://go.gale.com)

The Wartime Memories Project (wartimememoriesproject.com)

Index